SHERMAN'S BATTLE

FOR

ATLANTA

SHERMAN'S BATTLE

FOR

ATLANTA

BY

JACOB D. COX, LL.D.,

LATE MAJOR-GENERAL COMMANDING TWENTY-THIRD ARMY CORPS

WITH A NEW INTRODUCTION

BY

BROOKS D. SIMPSON

DA CAPO PRESS
NEW YORK

Library of Congress Cataloging in Publication Data

Cox, Jacob D. (Jacob Dolson), 1828—1900.
  [Atlanta]
  Sherman's battle for Atlanta / by Jacob D. Cox; new intro-
duction by Brooks D. Simpson.—1st Da Capo Press ed.
    p.   cm.
  "Original title: Atlanta"—CIP data sheet.
  Includes index.
  ISBN 0-306-80588-X
  1. Atlanta Campaign, 1864—Personal narratives. 2. Cox,
Jacob D. (Jacob Dolson), 1818–1900. I. Title.
E476.4.C69 1994   94-11264
973.7'378—dc20   CIP

First Da Capo Press edition 1994

This Da Capo Press paperback edition of *Sherman's Battle
for Atlanta* is an unabridged republication of the edition
published in New York in 1882 under the title *Atlanta*.
It is here supplemented with a new introduction by
Brooks D. Simpson.

Published by Da Capo Press, Inc.
A Subsidiary of Plenum Publishing Corporation
233 Spring Street, New York, N.Y. 10013

INTRODUCTION

Hardly had the guns fallen silent across the battlefields of the American Civil War when participants in the conflict renewed the struggle, with friend and foe alike, in volumes of memoirs, battle and campaign accounts, and biographies. While the war still raged, Horace Greeley began publishing his military chronicle, *The American Conflict*; a year after Appomattox, Richmond newspaper editor Edward Pollard responded with *The Lost Cause*. Newspaper correspondents, self-appointed military analysts, and others contributed to the growing stream of historical literature about the war. They were joined in the 1870s by the first of many memoirs by leading participants when Joseph E. Johnston offered his *Narrative of Military Operations* (1874), followed a year later by William T. Sherman's equally controversial *Memoirs* and in 1880 with John Bell Hood's posthumously-published *Advance and Retreat* (all three available from Da Capo Press). These accounts fueled controversy about the conduct of military operations. Several historians, most notably Thomas Connelly and William Garrett Piston, have traced how such debates shaped evaluations of the generalship of Robert E. Lee and his subordinates in the Army of Northern Virginia. Just as important, however, were exchanges about the performance of other generals in other places, with many of the participants having vested interests in shaping postwar narratives. Indeed, most present controversies about the conduct of military operations during the American Civil War first appeared in this literature.

The public's lust for such narratives and recollections seemed insatiable. Still to come in the 1880s were *Century* magazine's extensive collection of accounts, eventually repackaged with new material in *Battles and Leaders of the Civil War* (1887), and the most renowned memoir of them all, the two-volume account produced by a dying Ulysses S. Grant. But it was also quite clear that while these works provided much raw material for military historians, it was time to prepare accounts of military operations based upon the vast documentary record available to researchers. In 1880 the first volume of *The Official Record of the War of the Rebellion* appeared; it would be followed by 127 more, with separate series for naval operations and medical reports. The project would take over two decades; in the meantime there seemed to be a need for a type of narrative that would serve as a transition from the first generation of participant-prepared accounts to the subsequent work of scholars, military historians, popularizers, and buffs.

It was this need that a New York publishing house sought to meet. Charles Scribners' Sons of New York commenced its series, *The Campaigns of the Civil War*, by declaring that it intended to publish accounts "by a number of leading actors in and students of the great conflict of 1861-'65, with a view to bringing together, for the first time, a full and authoritative military history of the suppression of the Rebellion." Of the sixteen volumes that

eventually appeared, nearly all were prepared by participants in the conflict (all members of the Union forces); indeed, the civilian military historian John C. Ropes
remarked in the preface to *The Army Under Pope* (1881)
that "it may be presumptuous in a civilian to attempt a
history of a campaign." Some authors, most notably Abner
Doubleday, seized the opportunity to reopen old controversies; others, however, proved more restrained in setting
forth their own story. Among the latter may be classed Jacob D. Cox, the military book reviewer of *The Nation* and
author of two books in the series, *Atlanta* (1882) and *The
March to the Sea—Franklin and Nashville* (1882)—both
now available from Da Capo Press.

Cox saw service in several theaters during the Civil War.
Elevated to the rank of brigadier general of volunteers in
1861, his commission bore the date of May 17, as did those
of Ulysses S. Grant, William T. Sherman, Joseph Hooker,
and several other men who would make their mark during
the war. He saw action in western Virginia under George
B. McClellan in July 1861, and remained in the region for
a year. In August 1862 he was elevated to division command in John Pope's Army of Virginia, but he did not arrive in time to witness Pope's disaster at Second Bull Run
at month's end. Instead, Cox and his "Kanawha Division,"
so called because it had seen service along western Virginia's Kanawha River, were assigned to Ambrose Burnside's Ninth Corps of the Army of the Potomac. At South
Mountain on September 14 his command distinguished itself in cracking the Confederate position at Turner's Gap.
After the battle Cox took charge of the entire Ninth Corps
after Burnside was advanced to command one wing of the
army and Jesse Reno, Burnside's successor, was killed.

Three days later at Antietam, Cox, uncomfortable with his new and unfamiliar responsibilities, was in direct control of the assault on the Confederate right, and spent a good part of the battle forcing a crossing of Antietam Creek at what would become known as Burnside's Bridge.

In 1863 Cox returned to what was now West Virginia. He soon found himself in command of the District of Ohio and of the Third Division of the Twenty-third Corps. It was in this capacity that he served under Sherman during the Atlanta campaign; his division was among those left under the command of George H. Thomas to keep an eye on John Bell Hood's Army of Tennessee as Sherman commenced his March to the Sea. In 1865 Cox's division and the rest of the Twenty-third Corps were transferred to North Carolina to participate in Sherman's closing campaigns; Cox rose to command the entire corps by the end of the war.

After the war Cox entered politics. Elected governor of Ohio in 1865, four years later he joined Ulysses S. Grant's cabinet as secretary of the interior. A supporter of civil service reform and an opponent of so-called Radical Reconstruction measures, Cox became an irritant to the President, who once growled, "The trouble was that General Cox thought the Interior Department was the whole government, and that Cox was the Interior Department." Eventually Cox resigned; while he later served a single term in Congress as a representative, his political fortunes never quite recovered from his break with Grant, and he had to rest content with offering political advice to others while practicing law in Ohio.

During these years Cox developed an interest in the military history of the Civil War. As the military book critic of *The Nation*, he became embroiled in a debate over the accuracy and fairness of Sherman's *Memoirs*, as he chose to defend his old chief's account. Almost as notable, especially in light of his continuing criticism of Grant as president, was his dispassionate, insightful, and fair review of Grant's *Memoirs*. Obviously Cox possessed just the qualities that Scribners' sought—a participant who could prepare a comprehensive and concise history—when the publisher approached him to contribute to the series with a volume on the Atlanta campaign. It was a wise choice. Certainly Cox played a key role in the campaign against Atlanta. At Kenesaw Mountain in June his division seized a ridge opposite the Confederate left, allowing Sherman to flank the Confederates out of their prepared position; in late August, swinging to the southwest of Atlanta, it severed that city's rail link to Macon, eventually leading to Atlanta's evacuation by Hood's army on the night of September 1.

Cox realized the importance of preparing accounts of historical events in order to assure that his viewpoint would be preserved in the record. In this he was no different than many of his peers, North and South, who took up the pen to defend what they had done with bayonet and sword. In this battle of the books protagonists were just as likely to feud with former comrades as they were with their old enemies; Cox's volume shows traces of both types of conflict, as he attacks the veracity of several accounts by friend and foe alike. Most interesting is his effort to counter the tendency of Confederate writers to underestimate their numbers and exaggerate enemy strength—an argument characteristic of Lost Cause apologists.

Cox never quite successfully resolves the tension between offering a military history and presenting his personal version of events. He is at his best as a dispassionate observer in discussing maneuvers and battles that did not involve his own command. But when it came to writing about the activities of his own division, Cox's narrative is sometimes open to question, although in other cases he was able to correct the accounts of others based on his personal knowledge. One must also keep in mind that he wrote without the benefit of the *Official Record of the War of the Rebellion*. Instead, his account reflects a reliance on the memoirs of Sherman, Johnston, and Hood; most of his discussion of Confederate command options, in fact, reflect his assessments of the arguments advanced in the latter works.

In other ways, however, Cox composed a model narrative. One of his signal contributions is setting the Atlanta campaign in context. He reminded readers of the importance of the oft-overlooked Meridian campaign in February 1864 in crippling the ability of the Confederacy to supply a serious offensive to recapture West Tennessee, as well as of the difficulty of securing East Tennessee in the winter of 1864. It is among the more remarkable aspects of Civil War scholarship that the Atlanta campaign, despite its unquestioned importance in contributing to the eventual Union victory, has been relatively neglected by scholars. Indeed, Cox's account remained the standard one for over a century. Albert Castel's *Decision in the West* (1993) was the first original piece of published scholarship on the campaign that could be held up alongside Cox's account. To be sure, there have been other studies published about aspects of the campaign, including biographies of the army commanders. Lloyd Lewis's *Sherman: Fighting Prophet* (1932) has been supplanted by John F. Marszalek's *Sherman: A Soldier's Passion for Order* (1993); Craig L. Symonds has offered us *Joseph E. Johnston: A Civil War Biography* (1992); and Richard M. McMurry has composed *John Bell Hood and the War for Southern Independence* (1982).

William T. Sherman emerges as the primary hero of Cox's account. The campaign of 1864 was Sherman's first experience in independent command since an ill-fated stint in Kentucky in the fall of 1861, where his demands for more men and his dire predictions of Confederate success led some to believe that he had gone insane under the pressures of responsibility. In 1862 Sherman joined Ulysses S. Grant at Shiloh, and the two men soon formed a tremendous partnership based primarily upon trust, loyalty, and open communications. When Grant won elevation to command the Military Division of the Mississippi (stretching from the Appalachian Mountains to the Mississippi and points west), Sherman succeeded him as head of the Army of the Tennessee; when Grant assumed the position of general-in-chief, he named Sherman to his old spot. Years later, Sherman recalled that the two men met at the Burnet House in Cincinnati. "We finally settled on a plan," he remarked. "He was to go for Lee and I was to go for Joe Johnston." In the end, of course, Sherman settled for Atlanta.

From the commencement of the campaign in early May, Sherman chose to maneuver his opponent out of position after position, rarely considering pitched battle as an alternative. As a result, in contrast to Grant's struggle with Lee, Sherman's men suffered few casualties as they patiently made their way to Atlanta; even the losses at Kenesaw Mountain, where Sherman attempted a frontal assault on June 27, faded in comparison with Grant's losses at Cold Harbor. Still, Sherman erred at several points during the campaign. At Resaca he entrusted James B. McPherson with leading a critical flanking march through Snake Creek Gap; McPherson's hesitation cost Sherman an opportunity to put the Confederates in a tight spot. Of equal importance was Sherman's decision not to entrust George H. Thomas with the movement, even though Thomas had originally suggested it. At Kenesaw Mountain he launched a half-hearted and futile assault, rationalizing afterwards that he simply wanted to remind his men of the costs of such an action (as if they didn't know). Finally, although he did succeed in ousting the Confederates from Atlanta, he failed to cripple Hood's army, thus leaving it to live and fight another day.

Opposing Sherman at the outset of the campaign was Joseph E. Johnston. Held in high regard by Grant and Sherman, Johnston, realizing that he was outnumbered, opted to preserve his forces as much as possible while slowing down Sherman's advance by preparing elaborate defensive positions. This, joined with Sherman's preference for maneuver over combat, created the rhythm of the ensuing campaign, described by Shelby Foote as a "red clay minuet." Johnston, however, did not enjoy the full confidence of Jefferson Davis, who saw in Johnston's retreating a recurrence of his withdrawal toward Richmond two years earlier during the Peninsula campaign. In 1862 Johnston had fallen wounded at Seven Pines; his replacement, Robert E. Lee, soon turned the tables on George McClellan's Army of the Potomac, assaulting the Union right and forcing the Yankees back. This time Davis did not wait for the fortunes of battle to make a change; on July 18 John Bell Hood replaced Johnston in command. Lee, consulted about the change, offered that Hood "is a good fighter, very industrious on the battlefield, careless off," adding that William

J. Hardee "has more experience in managing an army." Hood, like Lee, took the offensive; but he was not Lee, and Sherman was not McClellan. In three separate and desperate battles Hood tried to drive the Yankees away, but failed; just over a month later Sherman maneuvered him out of Atlanta, his movements so confusing Hood that for a moment the Confederates thought the Yankees were retreating. In years to come historians would debate the relative merits of Johnston and Hood; it is perhaps best to say that the Confederates tended to retreat when they might have fought and fought when it might have been better to stand fast. It might have been better still to have abandoned Atlanta altogether and instead threaten Sherman's lines of supply much earlier in the year, when farmers' fields could have supported a foraging army advancing northwards. Surely Sherman was blessed in the tactics chosen by his opponents and their decision to make Atlanta a focal point of resistance, since these decisions allowed him to forego (for the most part) assaults, the weakest part of his military repertoire.

For all of its importance as a railroad junction, the fall of Atlanta was most significant for the boost it gave to Abraham Lincoln's chances for reelection. Just ten days before, Abraham Lincoln had privately forecast his impending defeat; jubilant Democrats had just nominated McClellan on a platform widely interpreted as declaring the war a failure. Northerners hardly had time to digest that message when the first dispatches arrived announcing Sherman's victory. Republicans roared in celebration, pointing to the news as the best reply to Democratic charges that the war was a failure. The reaction to Atlanta's fall reminds us how much the Northern public still measured victory in terms of cities taken at least as much as in armies destroyed. The spirit of "On to Richmond!" never quite died; in one of the richest ironies of the Civil War, Sherman's triumph resembled McClellan's way of making war by taking cities. McClellan himself sent along his congratulations to Sherman; Little Mac predicted, "Your campaign will go down to history as one of the memorable ones of the world, & will be even more highly appreciated in the future as it is in the present." In celebrating Sherman as a father of total war, we overlook the rather traditional, almost McClellan-like victory he secured; yet the very type of victory that McClellan relished was decisive in destroying his chances for the presidency in 1864. Sherman, the man who despised politics, had won a victory that was most decisive in its impact upon the minds of Northern voters in that election year.

The political significance of the victory, in fact, overshadows its limited consequences in other ways. Hood's army escaped intact, remaining an offensive threat. As Cox's account makes clear, for the next six weeks Sherman found himself forced to defend his frail supply line, stretching from Atlanta back to Chattanooga, from Hood. Indeed, Sherman found Atlanta something of an albatross around his neck; finding it difficult to shield his supply line and impossible to corner the elusive Hood, he began to ponder his options. The March to the Sea, often hailed as a stroke of military genius, was equally a response to circumstances, for in fact Sherman's other alternatives were to chase Hood or to retreat.

Many historians enjoy comparing Sherman's offensive against Atlanta with Grant's drive against Lee's army and Richmond. Some critics praise Sherman's frugal expenditure of human life as opposed to the lengthy casualty lists from Virginia. Certainly Sherman's capture of Atlanta bolstered public morale, while Grant's inability to bring Lee to climactic battle or to capture the Confederate capital contributed to the Northern public's war-weariness. Yet Grant's campaign, conducted under far different circumstances with an army unfamiliar to Grant against the best army and general the Confederacy had to offer, served to deprive the Army of Tennessee of any reinforcements and took Lee out of the war as an offensive threat. In many ways, although the importance of Atlanta's fall to the Union war effort cannot be underestimated, Sherman failed to destroy his opponent. That would not happen until year's end at Nashville, and it would be George H. Thomas who would get the job done.

"Atlanta is ours, and fairly won," Sherman telegraphed the authorities at Washington on September 2. Readers interested in a short account of how that came to happen will find Jacob D. Cox's account of the campaign a most rewarding one.

Brooks D. Simpson
Chandler, Arizona
January 1994

CONTENTS.

CONTENTS.

CHAPTER VIII.

CHAPTER XVII.

APPENDIX A.

APPENDIX B.

APPENDIX C.

APPENDIX D.

APPENDIX E.

LIST OF MAPS.

ATLANTA.

CHAPTER I.

ORGANIZATION—PRELIMINARY MOVEMENTS.

THE battle of Chattanooga was fought by General Grant as Commander of the Military Division of the Mississippi, which was a territorial command made by uniting under one head the Departments of the Ohio, the Cumberland, and the Tennessee. Arkansas was temporarily united to these, but need not be considered in our present sketch. It will help to a clear understanding of the organization under which the campaign of Atlanta was conducted to recall the general outline of these departments, which, with little change, had been the territorial units of military command from the beginning of the war. The Department of the Tennessee had been Grant's field of operations till Vicksburg was taken, and included the country between the Ohio and Mississippi Rivers on the north and west, the Tennessee River to Decatur on the east, and running indefinitely southward till it should reach country in which troops of the Department of the Gulf might be operating. The Department of the Cumberland was commanded by Major-General George H. Thomas, who had succeeded Rosecrans after the battle of Chickamauga. It in-

cluded middle Tennessee with part of Kentucky, so that
Louisville on the Ohio River was its depôt for supplies, and
the lines of railroad from that city to Nashville, and thence
to Northern Alabama and Georgia, lay within it. Like the
Department of the Tennessee its southern boundary was not
fixed, but would embrace whatever territory its troops
should occupy. The Department of the Ohio was commanded by Major-General John M. Schofield, and included
East Tennessee and the eastern part of Kentucky. Cincinnati was its depôt and its line of posts extended through
Kentucky by way of Lexington and Richmond to Cumberland Gap and the other mountain passes upon the country
roads leading to Knoxville and the Holston valley. Its only
line of railway reached no farther south than Lexington,
though General Burnside had begun the construction of
another, which was meant to extend the Central Kentucky
railroad to Knoxville. Whilst that officer was in command
of the Department in the summer and fall of 1863, he
thought such a line would be necessary, if East Tennessee
was to be firmly held and made the base for movements
looking toward Charleston and Savannah as objective
points. No one doubted that a railroad upon the line surveyed would be of great advantage in military operations if
it were once constructed, but even the enterprise of Mr.
Lincoln's administration, accustomed as it was to gigantic
operations, shrank from engaging in building hundreds of
miles of railway, and Burnside's project was dropped. The
sufferings of the army in East Tennessee during the winter
following proved how inadequate country roads were to
supply an army so far from its depôts, and when the enemy
had interrupted the railway communication of Thomas'
army at Chattanooga with Nashville, Burnside's forces about
Knoxville were reduced to the verge of starvation.

From the sketch thus given it will be seen that the general plan on which the armies between the Allegheny Mountains and the Mississippi worked during 1863 was one in which three parallel columns, each with its own line of communications, were pushing their way toward the Gulf and the ocean. The War Department at Washington and General Halleck, as the President's Chief of Staff, had the task of combining and harmonizing these movements, and of furnishing the material of war and the recruits needed to keep up the strength and vigor of each. The department commanders not only led in person the larger moving forces at the front, they had multifarious duties of administration within their territorial jurisdiction, and the responsibility for the safety of their own communications and lines of supply, as well as for the peace and quiet of the country behind them. It was for them to determine how much the posts and garrisons in the rear could be reduced for the purpose of strengthening the army at the front, and each was independent of the others, except as they were subject to the orders of the President as Commander-in-Chief. Each would naturally be anxious to increase the importance of his own part in the campaign, and to secure all the men and means possible to increase the strength and efficiency of his own army. The emulation was usually generous, a common earnestness of patriotism was felt by the generals in command, and co-operation was sincerely aimed at; but the system had its disadvantages, and the fall of Vicksburg and Port Hudson, with the opening of the Mississippi, gave the opportunity for more unity of effort, and indicated, by a process of natural selection, the officer for the larger task.

In October, Grant was put in command of the military Division of the Mississippi, and Major-General William T. Sherman succeeded him in the command of the Department and Army of the Tennessee. The organization of the military division did not supersede the departments. These remained as before, subordinate, however, to the superior commander, who might modify the control of the department commander on special matters. This power was exercised a little later, in regard to the management of railways; for when the united army became dependent for supplies upon lines of road lying within the Department of the Cumberland, it was necessary that the railroads should be operated by officers reporting directly to the General-in-Chief. A civil engineer and railway expert, Colonel Anderson, was assigned, with military rank, to this duty, and, as Master of Railway Transportation on the Headquarters Staff, issued his orders in the name of the general commanding the military division. This was not done, however, till General Sherman had succeeded Grant in the command, and was preparing for the advance into Georgia.

To complete this view of the military organization it is only necessary to add that the three department commanders were designated as commandants of armies in the field, so that when acting together, the grand army consisted of the Armies of the Cumberland, the Tennessee and the Ohio, constituting the centre and wings of the whole force, and the orders of the General-in-Chief issued to the three army commanders as his immediate subordinates. Questions of precedence were settled by the rule that the assignment by the President of any general officer to the command of an army or a corps, gave him temporary superiority of rank over officers in the same command not so assigned, even though his commission might be junior in date. The positions of army commander and corps commander were thus practically made distinct temporary grades in the army, equivalent to those of general and lieutenant-general in the Confederate service.

The opening of the Mississippi River isolated the country west of it from the rest of the Confederacy. The hostile river navy was destroyed, and the gunboat fleet of the United States, by constant patrol of the water system of the great West, prevented any considerable passage of supplies or of men from one part of the rebellious States to the other. The problem for Grant now to solve, was how to cut another such section from the hostile country, and so to diminish proportionately the strength of the enemy. The Confederate Government felt severely the diminution of its resources; for not only had Texas and Western Louisiana with Arkansas furnished large amounts of subsistence stores to their commissariat, which were now lost, but the enforcement of the conscription became impracticable, and after one considerable effort in the Red River campaign of the spring of 1864, the war in that region dwindled to a partisan conflict, having no appreciable importance. If Mississippi and Alabama could be in a similar way severed from the active theatre of war, it would be very hard for the Government at Richmond to find the means of prolonging the struggle at the East. The winter was spent by General Grant in subordinate operations, tending to simplify the situation, and all looking to a campaign with his united forces against the Army in Northern Georgia, which he had recently defeated, and which was now in winter quarters around Dalton. Thomas, with the Army of the Cumberland, was to occupy the attention of General Joseph E. Johnston, who had relieved Bragg of the command at Dalton; Schofield, with the Army of the Ohio, was to rid East Tennessee, if possible, of the forces operating there under Longstreet; and Sherman, with the Army of the Tennessee, was directed to make a rapid movement from Vicksburg toward Meridian, for the purpose of destroying the railroads and thus to make hostile operations toward the Mississippi so difficult that a small force could protect the great valley and a concentration could be made of the larger part of all the forces under Grant's command against Johnston's army.

It was not to be expected that the Confederates would allow these preliminary movements to be made without resistance; but it was reasonably reckoned probable that if Johnston should concentrate against Sherman, Thomas would be able to push his column southward from Chattanooga toward the important railway connecting points at Rome and Atlanta, and thus secure even greater advantages than could be hoped from Sherman's success.

Thomas, therefore, kept up such activity through the early spring as the condition of his army and the state of the roads permitted, and in fact kept Johnston from detaching any sufficient forces from his command to prevent Sherman from accomplishing his purpose. Meanwhile, the reopening of its railway line of communications relieved the Army of the Cumberland from its long-continued scarcity of supplies; the men were comfortably clothed, the artillery and wagon teams were put in good condition, the cavalry was partly remounted, and the whole force was brought into an excellent state of efficiency and confidence.

Sherman started from Vicksburg on February 3d with about twenty thousand men, organized in two columns, which were commanded respectively by Major-Generals McPherson and Hurlbut. He gave out that he aimed at Mobile, but his real purpose, as previously settled between himself and General Banks, who was in command at New Orleans, was to destroy the railways at and about Meridian. A strong cavalry force, under Brigadier-General W. Sooy Smith, was ordered to march from Memphis simultaneously with Sherman's advance from Vicksburg, to seek and, if possible, to rout the Confederate cavalry under Forrest, then operating in Northern Mississippi and Southern Tennessee, and afterward to join Sherman at Meridian for further operations.

A glance at the map will show the significance and importance of the movement. Meridian is near the eastern boundary of Mississippi, where the railway from Vicksburg to Montgomery and eastward crosses the Mobile and Ohio Railroad. If Sherman's advance should force a concentration of all the available Confederate troops to resist him, it was hoped that General Smith would find little difficulty in making a rapid raid southward from Corinth, destroying railroad bridges and crippling that line of railway to such an extent as to make it useless for military operations during the coming campaign. When Sherman had done the same for the east and west line to Meridian, it was safe to assume that no large column of troops could operate against Memphis or Nashville by way of Northern Mississippi for some months at least, for the experience of the war had demonstrated that no considerable army could subsist, depending upon wagons and common country roads for more than a few miles from railway depôts. A rapid march could be made, living upon the country, if it led to a point where military stores could be reached or captured; but protracted operations were indissolubly tied to the railway and water lines, which could be depended on in all weather and to any extent. Complete success in both parts of Sherman's movement would, therefore, have taken the northern half of Mississippi out of the theatre of active operations, and if Banks could subsequently take Mobile, that port would become a most important base for a new movement co-operating with the one to be made from Chattanooga as soon as the spring should open. Sherman's own part in the plan was the only one successfully carried out; but it was suffi-

cient to secure the principal object, and his subsequent
campaign in Northern Georgia was undisturbed by any formidable demonstrations of the enemy in the Valleys of the
Mississippi and the Lower Tennessee. He reached Meridian
on February 14th, and after tearing up the railways in that
vicinity, burning the ties, twisting the rails, and destroying
the bridges, he withdrew to Central Mississippi. Two divisions of the Army of the Tennessee, under Major-General A.
J. Smith, were detached to assist in Banks's Red River expedition in March, and became permanently separated from
the army in the field. The rest of it was given rendezvous
near Huntsville, Ala., and was gradually collected and prepared for its part in the coming campaign.

CHAPTER II.

EAST TENNESSEE.

THE operations of the Army of the Ohio during the autumn of 1863 have an interest of their own which will justify a little further retrospect. General Burnside had been assigned to the command of the Department of the Ohio in the spring, and at his special request two divisions of the Ninth Army Corps, made up of troops which had been with him ever since his expedition against the North Carolina coast, were sent to him from the Potomac. He began also the organization of the Twenty-third Army Corps, made up in the main of new recruits raised in Ohio, Indiana, Illinois, and Kentucky. These were collected at camps of instruction in Kentucky, with a view to an early movement into East Tennessee. The Holston Valley and the mountain region on either side of it had been the stronghold of loyalty to the Union, and had, in consequence, suffered severely at the hands of the Confederates. Its leading public men had urgently pressed Mr. Lincoln to send an army to its relief, and it was commonly thought a reproach to the Federal Government that so large and important a region in the heart of the South, devoted to the Union, should be left to the mercy of the enemy, who was determined to crush out its loyal men. The difficulty of sustaining an army more than two hundred miles from its base, from which it was separated by rugged mountains, over which there were only a few roads, and these scarce better than pack-mule tracks, was fully felt by all military men who studied the problem ; but the political reasons for making the attempt were imperative, and Burnside prepared for the undertaking. It was concerted between him and Rosecrans that their movements should be so timed as to be mutually supporting, in the hope that the occupation of Chattanooga would make it easy to hold East Tennessee, whilst Burnside's little army at Knoxville would effectually cover the left flank of Rosecrans. On June 2d Burnside was ready to start from Lexington, Ky., with his two corps—the Ninth, under command of Major-General John G. Parke, and the Twenty-third, under Major-General George L. Hartsuff. He himself left his headquarters at Cincinnati to take personal charge of the movement, but was met on the 3d by orders from Washington to send eight thousand men to reinforce General Grant at Vicksburg. The Ninth Corps, being the oldest and best organized force in the Department, was sent at once, and the Tennessee movement was of course delayed till the newer troops should be strengthened and better fitted for their work. The unwelcome delay in Burnside's movement affected Rosecrans's plans of campaign also, and it was not till the 16th of August that the combined advance began, Rosecrans marching from Winchester, Tenn., and Burnside from Lexington, Ky.

Meanwhile the battle of Gettysburg had been fought, and the only formidable invasion of the Northern States had been defeated. Vicksburg had fallen, and the Mississippi was opened to the Gulf of Mexico. The country was full of hopeful excitement, and called loudly on the officers commanding the central columns to do their part in making the whole campaign a great success. The story of Rosecrans's movement is fully told in another of these volumes.

The Ninth Corps divisions had come back from Vicksburg the mere skeletons of their former strength. Being Eastern troops, wholly unacclimated to the Western climate, they suffered fearfully from the malaria of the Yazoo River and the bayous about Vicksburg, and on their return left large detachments in every hospital between the captured city and Cincinnati. Their whole camp was a hospital, and they were necessarily scattered in garrison encampments among the hills of Kentucky till returning health should bring the men back to the ranks. Their return, however, relieved Burnside from the need of keeping other troops in his rear, and enabled him to gather up his detachments of the Twenty-third Corps, and make a moving column of about eighteen thousand men of all arms. Dividing these into several columns, he sent those on his right, under General Hartsuff, by way of Tompkinsville, Somerset, and Chitwoods to Montgomery, whilst he led another through Crab Orchard, London, Williamsburg, and the east fork of the Cumberland River to unite with Hartsuff at Montgomery, whence the whole infantry force moved upon Kingston. He thus turned Cumberland Gap, which was held in considerable force by the enemy, but was obliged to cross the mountains by roads which were considered impracticable for military purposes. Part of the way his own road lay through the gorge of Rockcastle River, whose perpendicular sandstone cliffs, towering a thousand feet above the torrent, simulated the fantastic forms of ruined towers and battlements. The infantry passed the principal range of the Cumberland Mountains, by Emory and Winters's Gaps, whilst the cavalry crossed further to the north by Big Creek Gap and other equally romantic passes and defiles. The last-named of these is a fair type of the wild barriers through which the little army forced its way. At the prin-

cipal ascent of the mountain the teams of two or three guns
had to be hitched to a single cannon to pull up to the summit, and even then were aided by soldiers at every wheel;
but when the summit was reached, a glorious panorama
opened to the east. The circling mountains made a vast
amphitheatre into which the head of column looked down,
whilst directly in front, the rocky strata, upheaved till they
stood vertically on edge, were broken by a gap as regular as
the proscenium of a stage. Through this dashed the blue
stream which gives name to the pass, and beyond, the
beautiful valley of the Clinch and Holston Rivers was seen,
backed in the distance by the peaks of the Great Smoky
Mountains, which here assume more picturesque outlines
than any other mountains of the Allegheny range.

The march had been a laborious one, but it had been
made without resistance. The Confederate forces under
General Buckner retreated southward rapidly. The passes
of the mountains were held, and Burnside entered Knoxville
with his infantry on September 3d, amidst the sincere and
enthusiastic rejoicings of the people, who decorated their
houses with the flags they had carefully concealed against
the time when the Union should re establish its government
among them. From Lexington to Knoxville is two hundred
and fifty miles, much of it the roughest mountain road. To
march it in fourteen consecutive days was good work, and
proved that the regiments of the Twenty-third Corps contained good *cadres* of re-enlisted veterans who had quickly
made reliable troops of the recruits. Its success proved the
excellence of Burnside's plan. He immediately concentrated forces for the investment of Cumberland Gap, hurried in person to the scene, and on the 9th demanded and
received the surrender of the garrison under General
Frazer, 2,500 in number. The little Army of the Ohio and

its commander had earned and received the warm thanks of Congress and of the President.

Rosecrans occupied Chattanooga on September 9th, but Bragg had been reinforced by Longstreet's corps from the Army of Virginia, and was preparing to resume the aggressive. Burnside had naturally turned his attention first to getting rid of the enemy under General Jones, who was farther up the valley, and who would be upon his rear if he moved toward Rosecrans. He pushed him back beyond the Watauga, some seventy-five miles from Knoxville, and burned the railroad bridge there. In consequence of news he received from Rosecrans he ordered the Ninth Corps on the 16th to hasten forward from Kentucky. The battle of Chickamauga occurred on the 19th and 20th, and that disaster to our arms was followed by peremptory orders from Washington for Burnside to drop everything and go to Rosecrans's relief. He was himself at the Watauga, but on the 18th had ordered a concentration of the bulk of his forces at Knoxville and at Loudon, which lay about thirty miles further toward Chattanooga. Before his troops could get beyond these points, Rosecrans's position at Chattanooga was regarded defensible and the urgency ceased. Some weeks passed ; the two divisions of the Ninth Corps, numbering some six thousand effective men, arrived. General Grant had assumed command of the military division, Rosecrans had been relieved, and Mr. Dana, Assistant Secretary of War, was at Burnside's headquarters consulting as to future plans of action. Suddenly, Longstreet, who had been detached by Bragg for the purpose, attacked Burnside's advanced post at Loudon, whilst Mr. Dana was still with him. In consequence of the information carried by the latter, Grant encouraged Burnside's slow withdrawal toward Knoxville, leading Longstreet after him. The affair at

Loudon on November 14th was a lively one, but Longstreet's advance was checked by a division of the Twenty-third Corps under Brigadier-General Julius White. Burnside halted again at Campbell's Station on the 16th, when he again repulsed the Confederate advance in a warm combat. On the 18th he retired within his lines at Knoxville, under cover of a gallant resistance to Longstreet by Brigadier-General Saunders with the rear guard, though with the loss of Saunders himself, who was killed. Longstreet invested the city, and was now beyond supporting distance of Bragg, against whom Grant had concentrated part of the Army of the Tennessee as well as the Army of the Cumberland. The battle of Chattanooga was fought on November 23d and 25th, and Grant's victory rendered Longstreet's return to Bragg impracticable. Sherman, who had marched from the Mississippi to the relief of Thomas, now moved again to the relief of Burnside. Longstreet, learning of his advance, made a desperate effort to carry the works at Knoxville by storm at daybreak of November 29th, but suffered a bloody repulse. His troops assaulted Fort Saunders with the same persistent intrepidity they had shown at Gettysburg and on a score of fields in Virginia, but were driven back from the ditch of the earthwork, with a loss of about a thousand men whilst that of the Union forces was only forty-three. On the night of December 4th, Longstreet raised the siege and retired toward the northeast, taking position in the upper valley of the Holston, near Morristown. Sherman, who was now within supporting distance of Burnside, was no longer needed, and leaving the Fourth Corps of the Army of the Cumberland under Major-General Gordon Granger to assist the Army of the Ohio, he returned to Chattanooga to organize still another distant expedition, which we have already traced. Burnside had asked to be relieved of his command on September 10th, as soon as the complete occupation of East Tennessee was accomplished. His request was then refused, but it was now acted upon and he was succeeded by Major-General John G. Foster, who was soon compelled to retire on account of his health, and was succeeded by General Schofield about the middle of February.

Whilst Longstreet's movement upon Knoxville had been advantageous to the Union armies by rendering the victory at Chattanooga an easier one, it was the cause of a great deal of suffering to the little army of the Ohio. It interrupted the accumulation of supplies during the favorable weather of the autumn, and when winter set in, the mountain roads to Kentucky became impassable, and neither food nor clothing could be looked for in that direction. When the blockade at Chattanooga ceased, and the railroad thence to Nashville was repaired, the single line was overburdened, and could not for some time be made to supply both armies. The important bridge at Loudon had been burned, and though a few light-draught steamboats were pushed up to Knoxville, the navigation of the Holston was very uncertain, and until the beginning of March the forces in East Tennessee suffered the extremest want. A considerable drove of live cattle had been collected at Knoxville before the siege; but they grew thin for lack of forage. The country was stripped bare, and during the month of January the cattle that were turned over to the troops for beef were so poor they could hardly stand up. It is literally true that it was the custom of the commissaries to drive the cattle over a little ditch in the field where they were corralled, and those only were killed which could not get over, their weakness proving that it would not do to keep them longer, whilst the others might still last for future use. Indian corn was ground up, cobs and all for bread.

Bran and shorts were diligently hunted and used for the same purpose. The country was scoured for subsistence stores, and nothing but a patriotism equal to that of the troops made the country people patient under their losses and privations. The new year opened with a furious gale and icy storm, which came as a cyclone from the northwest, reducing the temperature suddenly below zero. The half-naked soldiers hovered around their camp fires, some without coats, some without pantaloons, some with tattered blankets tied like petticoats about their waists. An officer passing among them with words of sympathy and encouragement was greeted with the cheery response, "It's pretty rough, General, but we'll see it through!" Even during that fearful time cheers were heard ringing out from one and another of the regimental camps, indicating that the regiment had "veteranized," as it was called when a majority of the rank and file had re-enlisted for another three years, or during the war. The only inducement the Government offered was that those re-enlisting should, in their turn, and as rapidly as was safe, have a furlough of thirty days at home. This veteran re-enlistment was going on in all the armies among the troops which had been organized in 1861, and must be borne in mind as one of the important factors in military affairs for the year. Its immediate effect was to reduce greatly the effective force of the armies in the field, but it secured, a little later, a body of experienced soldiers who kept the tide of success moving steadily onward to the end.

The military operations in East Tennessee during the winter were unimportant. Longstreet remained in cantonments near Morristown, except for a short time in January, when he marched to Dandridge on the French Broad River. He was met by a counter-movement of our forces under

General Parke, who marched to meet the enemy with his own corps (the Ninth), Granger's Fourth Corps, and the Twenty-third Corps, which was temporarily in command of General Cox, Hartsuff having been relieved at his own request. After a slight affair at Dandridge, the return of storms of snow and sleet made both parties willing to seek their huts again, and they simultaneously withdrew to their permanent camps. General Grant himself made a visit of inspection and of consultation with General Foster, about the 1st of January, but it was plainly seen that the first work to be done was to improve the means of transportation and push forward supplies by way of Chattanooga. This was vigorously done, and by the time Schofield assumed command, the army was in much better case. As soon as railway transportation could be had, that noble organization, the United States Sanitary Commission, sent forward fresh potatoes, pickled cabbage, and other anti-scorbutic articles of food, the full ration was again issued, clothing began to arrive, and before the first of March the pinch was over.

Longstreet now withdrew beyond Bull's Gap, and Schofield advanced to Morristown. In April it had become evident that the great efforts of the year were to be made in Virginia and in Georgia. Longstreet was recalled by Lee, leaving only a corps of observation in the Upper Holston Valley. Schofield occupied Bull's Gap, and just before the concentration of Sherman's army for the great campaign, destroyed several miles of the railroad beyond the pass and began the concentration of the Twenty-third Corps for its movement toward Georgia. The Ninth Corps left East Tennessee between the 17th and 23d of March, proceeding in detachments to Annapolis in Maryland, where it was greatly reinforced, and Burnside again took command of it in person, joining the Army of the Potomac for the memorable campaign of 1864. The Fourth Corps returned to Cleveland, Tenn., where it resumed its place in the Army of the Cumberland. From this time the Army of the Ohio consisted only of the Twenty-third Corps of infantry and artillery, a corps of cavalry under Major-General George Stoneman, and the garrisons and posts in East Tennessee and Kentucky.

CHAPTER III.

THE OPPOSING ARMIES.

GENERAL GRANT was not left to carry out his plan of campaign for the Army of the West. Before the spring opened Congress had created the grade of Lieutenant-General, which was conferred upon him, and he was called to Washington to assume the direction of all the armies of the United States. In accordance with his desire, the President assigned Sherman to the command of the Military Division of the Mississippi, left vacant by his promotion, and the two generals met in Nashville on March 17th to consult as to the immediate steps to be taken. The general purpose was already marked out by the preliminary movements which have been described, and the Confederate army, under Johnston, now lying near Dalton, was the object at which all efforts must be aimed. Some days before, Sherman, with prophetic enthusiasm, had written to his commander of his confidence in the future of the National armies under Grant's direction, and saying, "From the west, when our task is done, we will make short work of Charleston and Richmond, and the impoverished coast of the Atlantic." The public sentiment of the country and of the army concurred with the President in approving Grant's indication of his successor, and from this day to the close of the war the confidence of his army in Sherman and its personal attachment to him never wavered, but only grew stronger from month to month. His

From Chattanooga to Atlanta.

courage and activity had been abundantly proven, but his capacity for the independent command of a large army was to be tested. His nervous and restless temperament, with a tendency to irritability, might have raised a doubt whether he would be successful in guiding and directing men of the capacity of his principal subordinates; but experience showed that he had the rare faculty of becoming more equable under great responsibilities and in scenes of great excitement. At such times his eccentricities disappeared, his grasp of the situation was firm and clear, his judgment was cool and based upon sound military theory as well as upon quick practical judgment, and no momentary complication or unexpected event could move him from the purposes he had based on full previous study of contingencies. His mind seemed never so clear, his confidence never so strong, his spirit never so inspiring, and his temper never so amiable as in the crisis of some fierce struggle like that of the day when McPherson fell in front of Atlanta.

On March 18th Sherman issued his orders assuming command of the Military Division, and Major-General James B. McPherson succeeded him in command of the Department and Army of the Tennessee. McPherson had under his immediate command but two corps, which were, at the beginning of May, scattered by divisions along the railroad from Nashville to Huntsville, and thence to Stevenson. Of these the Fifteenth consisted of three divisions, and was commanded by Major-General John A. Logan, and the Sixteenth, which had but two divisions, was commanded by Brigadier-General Grenville M. Dodge. The difficulty which had been found in supplying Thomas's and Schofield's troops by the single line of railroad from Nashville, made prompt attention to the question of transportation necessary. The plan adopted has already been referred to. The three army commanders were put upon an equal footing as to the right to make requisition for stores and transportation, but the control of the railways and management of the trains was held strictly in hand by the General-in-Chief, and his orders issued through his Master of Transportation at Nashville were absolute. All traffic over the lines by private citizens was forbidden, as was private travel also. No one could travel by rail except by permission specially given or under army orders. Troops *en route* were directed to march, unless in cases of exigency they were ordered forward by rail. In short, the railway trains were strictly devoted to the carrying of army supplies, and every hundred weight the engines could draw was to be made immediately useful to the army. It was estimated that thirteen hundred tons per day must be forwarded to keep the army supplied and accumulate such stores as would be needed in case of temporary interruption of communications by accident or by the enemy's cavalry. The rolling stock and machinery under army control were not sufficient for this, even when posts within a radius of thirty miles from Nashville were ordered to be supplied by wagons, and beef cattle for the army were driven on foot to the front. Sherman then ordered the cars and engines of other railroads coming into Nashville to be held and used for army purposes, and in this way the means of supplying the army were finally secured.

Such vigorous measures were not adopted without opposition, and it seemed to the inhabitants of Tennessee impossible to live under such restrictions; but the military necessity was satisfactorily shown to the Government at Washington, and the Commanding General was not interfered with. New channels of communication were found practicable by citizen traders, and when the army was in possession of a surplus the rules were judiciously relaxed, so that little actual suffering was occasioned. The sufficient answer to all complaints was, that it was the only system under which a forward movement of the army would be possible.

The field transportation of the army was also regulated. Each regiment on the march was allowed one wagon and one ambulance, and to the company officers of each company was assigned a pack-mule in common for carrying their mess-kit and personal baggage. A similar reduction to the minimum reached through brigade, division, and corps headquarters, and the *impedimenta* were everywhere as small as was consistent with the performance of the necessary official work of an army organization. The greater part of all clerical duty was performed at offices in the rear, to which the field reports of various kinds were sent for record and for proper transmission, only the absolutely necessary work being done in the field. The army was thus stripped for its work, and its commander went even beyond what was necessary in setting an example of contempt for personal comfort and convenience, and of the subordination of every other consideration to the single purpose of uniting mobility with strength in the great army.

The plan of campaign which Grant adopted for the year was a simple one, and one naturally growing out of the positions of the Confederate armies. The Lieutenant-General took upon himself the task of pressing Lee back upon Richmond, unless he would accept a decisive battle in the open field. Sherman was to do the same with Johnston's army, for which Atlanta, as a railway centre, had similar importance to that which the capital of Virginia had for Lee. Banks was expected to collect an army of 25,000 men in his Department, and move from New Orleans on Mobile, and, should he take it, operate thence as auxiliary to Sherman. The beginning of May was fixed upon for the general opening of the campaign, and each of the three columns was expected to keep the enemy in its front so fully employed that reinforcements from one to the other of the Confederate armies would be impracticable. The veteran re-enlistments reduced the strength of the National forces at the outset, by reason of the month's furlough given to those who renewed their term of service; but it gave assurance of increased and more valuable disciplined strength later in the campaign, and even from the beginning gave us a considerably larger force than our opponents in each of the moving columns. The days for brilliant detached campaigns, such as Jackson had made in Virginia, were over. Lee, as well as Johnston, settled down to patient defensive operations behind carefully constructed earthworks, watching for some slip in the strategy of the Federal commanders which might give hope of success to aggressive return blows by their smaller forces.

Sherman visited his subordinate army commanders, informed them of his purposes, directed the concentration of the Armies of the Tennessee and Ohio near the respective flanks of the Army of the Cumberland, and fixed the 5th of May for a general forward movement. His first plan had been to make Dalton the point for concentration of his three columns; but the fact that McPherson was unable to concentrate over two-thirds of the Army of the Tennessee, by reason of the absence of the divisions which were with Banks and the large number of furloughed veterans, was the primary reason for changing his orders. The change was in accord with sound military maxims, for Johnston held very strong positions some miles in front of Dalton, and the Army of the Ohio would have been in a dangerously exposed position had it marched upon that place whilst the enemy still held Rocky Face and Mill Creek Gap.

On the 4th of May, Schofield, marching out of East Tennessee by way of Cleveland and the old Federal road, had crossed the Georgia line and reached Red Clay, passing by part of the Fourth Corps, which immediately took up its march and moved to Catoosa Springs, whilst the rest of the Army of the Cumberland advanced to the immediate neighborhood of Ringgold, and the Army of the Tennessee came close upon their right at Lee & Gordon's Mills. Sherman himself was at the centre with Thomas, and the whole army was well in hand, the extreme distance from McPherson to Schofield being about sixteen miles, in a line nearly at right angles to the road from Chattanooga to Dalton, Thomas, whose force was nearly equal to Johnston's, being somewhat advanced beyond the wings.

Sherman entered the campaign with an effective force of nearly 100,000 men and 254 guns. Of these the Army of the Cumberland had 60,000 men and 130 guns, the Army of the Tennessee 25,000 men and 96 guns, and the Army of the Ohio 14,000 men and 28 guns.

The popular tendency to clamor against an unsuccessful general was quite as strong in the Southern States as elsewhere, and Bragg had been relieved in obedience to it after the battle of Chattanooga. He was still strong in the confidence of Jefferson Davis, and was called to Richmond, where he performed the duties of chief-of-staff to the Confederate President. General Joseph E. Johnston was assigned to the command of the army at Dalton, but did not have the full confidence of Mr. Davis, who nominated him rather because public opinion pointed him out as the officer most fit for the command, than because of his own preference. The estrangement between them dated from the first campaign of the war, when Johnston had not taken Mr. Davis as fully into his military confidence as the latter expected, and had

probably hurt the self-esteem of the Confederate President
in a point on which he was understood to be tender—his
judgment and ability in military matters.

The effect of these relations is plainly seen throughout
the campaign. A game of cross purposes began from the
first. In January, Johnston was urged to assume the aggressive, but he somewhat tartly replied by demanding the reinforcements in men and material which he considered
necessary. The correspondence with Bragg, as the mouth-
piece of Mr. Davis, continued through the winter, each trying to put the other in the wrong. Johnston showed that
the army was no fitter for the initiative than when Bragg
was relieved, and the latter endeavored to show a much
more favorable condition of things. Early in March reinforcements, which would raise his army to 75,000 effective
men, were offered him on condition of a forward movement.
He eagerly urged that the increase be given him at once,
but indicated that it was wise to await the advance of Sherman, repulse him, and then assume a vigorous aggressive.
No doubt his army needed rest and recuperation nearly as
much as the Union forces, and the season of bad roads and
wintry weather was profitably employed in bettering the
condition of artillery and train animals, disciplining and
drilling the troops and collecting supplies. At any rate, the
season passed in a tilt at letter-writing between Bragg and
Johnston, and no reinforcements were sent him till Sherman's advance in force compelled it.

Johnston was an officer who, by the common consent of
the military men of both sides, was reckoned second only
to Lee, if second, in the qualities which fit an officer for the
responsibility of great commands. His military experience
and knowledge were large, his mind eminently systematic,
his judgment sound, his courage imperturbable. He was

not sanguine in temperament, and therefore was liable to lack in audacity. Inclined by nature to a Fabian policy, it was a settled conviction with him that in the existing condition of the Confederacy such a policy should be imposed on the most audacious, unless a great blunder on the other side should reveal an opportunity for a decisive advantage. The results which followed a change of policy later in the campaign go far to justify him in his judgment. Right or wrong, he deliberately adopted a plan of carefully intrenched lines, one succeeding the other, as he might be compelled to retire. He practised a lynx-eyed watchfulness of his adversary, tempting him constantly to assault his intrenchments, holding his fortified positions to the last moment, but choosing that last moment so well as to save nearly every gun and wagon in the final withdrawal, and always presenting a front covered by such defences that one man in the line was, by all sound military rules, equal to three or four in the attack. In this way he constantly neutralized the superiority of force his opponent wielded, and made his campaign from Dalton to the Chattahoochee a model of defensive warfare. It is Sherman's glory that, with a totally different temperament, he accepted his adversary's game, and played it with a skill that was finally successful, as we shall see.

It is difficult to determine satisfactorily what was the exact strength of Johnston's army as compared with Sherman's at the opening of the campaign. The Confederate armies never made use of so complete a system of reports as were used among us. Their poverty imposed upon them both the disadvantages and the advantages of an absence of the elaborate bureau organization which we employed. Their field reports of effective strength were almost the only ones upon which their generals relied, and these did not show the whole number of men present and fit for duty, but the actual number of muskets in line after deducting all the slightly sick, the men on special duty of every sort, and all officers and detachments.

This is illustrated by Johnston's statement in a letter to Mr. Davis on January 2, 1864, that the reports and returns for December 20th showed his "effective total of the army (infantry and artillery)" to be "not quite thirty-six thousand; the number present about forty-three thousand; that present and absent about seventy-seven thousand." In comparison with the reports of the National forces the number present affords the best parallel computation, and it will usually be found, as in the example given, to be about twenty per cent. more than their reports of effectives. In commenting upon the expectations of his Government, Johnston complains that they expected him to open the campaign aggressively with sixteen thousand less men than had been named in the proposal in March. That number was 75,000, and would seem to show that he reckoned his force about sixty thousand men when Sherman moved upon Dalton on May 5th, and before Polk's corps joined him. The Richmond administration gave the same figures. Add to this the statement of General Hood, that the Confederate force was 75,000 men in the early part of the campaign, and it is fairly proven that the 44,000 which Johnston gives as his effective force at Dalton on May 1st, is considerably below the number present, as usually computed, and that the additions to his command made soon afterward, would bring it nearly or quite to the figures named by the Confederate General Hood. The chief interest in the question is in its bearing on the statements of "effective" force on the one side, and the "present for duty" on the other, as they appear in the reports of commanding officers of the opposing forces and in the current histories of the time.[1]

Johnston's position at Dalton was not originally selected by himself, for Bragg had gathered his defeated forces there at the beginning of the winter. But the new commander had strengthened the position by fortifications, and prepared it with such skill to resist an attack in front that it was practically impregnable. The key to the topography of North Georgia is the general trend of the great Allegheny range of mountains, which determines the eastern shore of the continent and forms the backbone of the Atlantic States from Vermont to the region we are considering. The general direction of the mountains is northeast and southwest. In the valley between the Cumberland and Great Smoky ranges lie the Holston and Clinch Rivers, which, uniting to form the Tennessee, then turn to the west at Chattanooga, rounding the southern spurs of the Cumberland Mountains. The more eastern ranges continue further south, one after another losing its character as a ridge, till Kennesaw, Pine Mountain, and Lost Mountain, near Marietta, with Stone Mountain, near Atlanta, stand out as isolated highlands in the midst of the broken but not quite mountainous country which is intermediate between the mountains proper and the sandy plains of the Gulf coast. Going south from Chattanooga a number of narrow parallel valleys are drained by branches of Chickamauga Creek, which enters the Tennessee just east of the town, and which heads nearly west of Dalton about twenty miles from its mouth. The eastern barrier of this basin is Rocky Face Ridge, a continuous wall of quartz rock with precipitous faces, flanked on the west by a subordinate ridge, through which, at Tunnel

---

[1] See Appendix A.

Hill, the railway pierces and runs southeasterly through a gorge in Rocky Face known as Mill Creek Gap, the towering sides of which are called the Buzzard's Roost. Mill Creek winds southeasterly five or six miles after passing the gap and flows into a branch of the Connasauga River, a tributary of the Oostanaula. Dalton lies about a mile south of Mill Creek; through it, and upon the same side of the Connasauga, the railway passes, Tilton and Resaca being the neighboring villages and stations, the latter at the crossing of the Oostanaula, and about twelve or fourteen miles from Dalton. Rocky Face extends some three miles north of Mill Creek Gap, or a little farther than Tunnel Hill, where it breaks into separate hills. On the east, Dalton was not covered by any similar natural defence, though the line of Mill Creek and the river could easily have been made strong if Sherman had shown any serious intent to advance on that side. The transportation question, however, was a great obstacle to such a plan, for it required the full capacity of his railway line to keep the army supplied, and the interruption of communications, even for a few days, was not to be considered, except in emergencies. To make Cleveland his base, would be to open the way for Johnston into Middle Tennessee and tempt him to transfer the war into that region, by a movement with his whole force similar to that which Hood made later in the year. He would have been, from the beginning of such a movement, between Sherman and his line of supplies in the lower Tennessee Valley. Johnston rightly judged, therefore, that he must expect his opponent along the line of the railway, and his defences were prepared accordingly. Mill Creek was dammed so as to make a deep wet ditch in a part of his front, and intrenchments made in the Gap connected with the crests of Rocky Face both north and south. Near the northern extremity of this ridge, and about four miles from Dalton, an east and west line of earthworks on a very strong position connected Rocky Face with the high ground commanding the East Tennessee Railway, and the line then turned southward and made a nearly continuous chain of defences east of the town. In front, therefore, and on either flank for miles to the rear, Dalton was so strong as to be safe from a *coup de main;* too strong, indeed, to make it probable that the Federal commander would seriously attack the works, if caution counted for anything in his character. But Sherman was reckoned impulsive and enterprising, and Johnston had hopes that he might dash his army upon these formidable barriers and give the chance for a destructive counter-blow when weakened and perhaps disorganized by an unsuccessful assault.

Before the opening of the campaign, Thomas had called Sherman's attention to Snake Creek Gap as a route by which Resaca or Calhoun could be reached, and the position at Dalton be turned. He had offered to lead the Army of the Cumberland by this defile, whilst the Armies of the Tennessee and Ohio occupied Johnston in front. The positions of his forces, and the desire to have the greater strength of the Army of the Cumberland at the centre and covering his own base, made Sherman modify whilst he accepted the plan. He determined to send McPherson with his two corps against Resaca, whilst he pressed Johnston in front with the superior force, ready to follow him up the moment he let go of Dalton, and before he could seriously damage McPherson.

It is uncertain whether Johnston believed Snake Creek Gap to be a practicable route for a large column. It is hard to realize now how little accurate knowledge either party had of the topography of the country. Maps worthy the name there were none, and the Confederate staff seems to have been greatly inferior to that of the United States Army in working up such material as they had. The fact that the route McPherson followed was almost entirely unguarded gives strong support to the opinion, which was the common one in Sherman's army at the time, that Johnston rested securely in the belief that his position could only be turned by a much longer detour, and one involving many more contingencies for his opponent.

Before extending our examination of the topography, let us return to the military movements of the 7th of May and the week following.

CHAPTER IV.

THE LINES BEFORE DALTON.

On Saturday, May 7th, under orders from Sherman, Thomas advanced the Fourteenth Corps (Major-General John M. Palmer) from Ringgold upon Tunnel Hill, the Fourth Corps (Major-General O. O. Howard) from Catoosa Springs to Dr. Lee's house on the Tunnel Hill road, where it would be in support of Palmer, and the Twentieth Corps (Major-General Joseph Hooker) from Lee & Gordon's Mills southeasterly into Dogwood Valley at and above Trickum, where it would be about three miles nearly due south from the centre at Tunnel Hill.

At the same time Schofield moved the Twenty-third Corps from Red Clay southwest, his leading division (Cox's) to Dr. Lee's, where it was close upon the Fourth Corps, and the rest extending toward Catoosa Springs, McCook's division of cavalry covering Varnell Station and the East Tennessee Railway.

McPherson, with the Army of the Tennessee diverging from Hooker's line of march, moved toward Ship Gap and Villanow, under orders to be near the Gap on the 7th, and the following day to proceed *via* Villanow and Snake Creek Gap, and place himself upon the railroad in Johnston's rear.

These movements concentrated the army on a much shorter line than before, and swung the right centre (Hooker) close to Rocky Face ridge south of Mill Creek Gap,

where he covered the road leading to Villanow. They were
made with no serious resistance, except that at Tunnel Hill
the enemy's cavalry presented a pretty firm front, and delayed Palmer's advance long enough for the deployment of
part of Howard's corps on their flank, when they speedily
retired within the gap.

On the 8th the concentric movements continued. Harker's
brigade of Newton's division, Fourth Corps, scaled the north
end of Rocky Face and moved southward along the crest.
The advance was led by Colonel Opdycke, 125th Ohio, who
drove back the enemy's outposts and skirmishers till the
Confederates were found in force upon a very strong position crossing the ridge at a place where it rose rapidly in
front of Newton's men, an abrupt and rugged rocky barrier,
about a mile and a half north of the signal station at Buzzard's Roost, above Mill Creek Gap. The ridge was so narrow that no deployment could be made, sometimes scarce a
dozen men having room to stand abreast. The progress was
therefore tedious, and numbers gave little or no advantage.
The rest of the Fourth Corps troops connected with Newton
as well as the ground would admit, forming a diagonal line
from the valley on the west up to the summits which Newton held. At the centre, Wood's division of the Fourth,
Davis's of the Fourteenth and Butterfield's of the Twentieth
Corps pushed back the enemy into the mouth of the Gap.
About two miles farther to the south, Geary's division of the
Twentieth Corps made a strong effort to carry the summit
of Rocky Face at Dug Gap,[1] but were foiled by the same
physical difficulties which baffled all other attempts along
this palisaded ridge. The skirmishers advanced, scrambling

---

[1] Van Horne erroneously describes this movement as being against Chattooga
Mountain "separated from Rocky Face by Mill Creek." General Thomas calls it
Chattoogata Mountain, the "ridge running due south from Buzzard's Roost."
Geary's report describes his crossing Mill Creek (which here runs north) before
ascending "Rocky Land Ridge," or Rocky Face at Dug Gap.

over the rocks and through the undergrowth, till already blown and nearly exhausted they found themselves facing a perpendicular wall with only clefts and crevices leading up through it, the narrow roadway which had been their guide being strongly held by the enemy and intrenched.   A gallant effort was made to reach the crest, but the smaller force of Confederates was led by General Hardee in person, and held their natural fortress.

Meanwhile the Armies of the Ohio and Tennessee were also moving forward.   Schofield's left division (Cox) moved a mile eastward to Kincannon Cross Roads, with one brigade a mile farther to the south.   His right (Judah) connected with Newton at the north spur of Rocky Face, and the centre (Hovey) completed the line, covering the roads from Dalton direct to Varnell Station, whilst the cavalry division of McCook watched the flank further to the east.

McPherson, following his orders, pushed forward to Villanow, and on the next day, the 9th, marched through Snake Creek Gap.   At two in the afternoon he was close upon Resaca, and Sherman was full of hope that he would be able to place himself astride of the railway in Johnston's rear.   He was accompanied by Kilpatrick's cavalry division.

Snake Creek is an insignificant branch of the Oostanaula, running southward between high and rugged ridges, which, on the east, are nearly continuous with Rocky Face, and are known by the general name of Chattoogata Mountains.   On the west the parallel range is called Horn Mountain.   A watershed half-way from Tunnel Hill to the Oostanaula separates the sources of Mill Creek from those of Snake Creek, and this divide is properly the gap.   The whole pass, however, is known by this name, and is a wild and picturesque defile, five or six miles long.   Hardly a cabin was to be seen in its whole length.   The road was only such

a track as country wagons had worn in the bed of the stream
or along the foot of the mountain. The forest shut it in,
and only for a little while at midday did the sun enter it.
Near its southern extremity, at Sugar Valley P. O., it
reached the more open country bordering the river, which
here runs for a little way nearly west, and roads branch off
to Resaca eastward, and southward to Calhoun, turning the
south end of the precipitous ridges which guard Dalton on
the west. Resaca itself stands in the elbow at the junction
of the Connasauga with the Oostanaula, and on the north
bank of the latter stream. Camp Creek, another small
stream, flows into the river just west of the village, and the
high plateau bordering it and the more rugged hills between it and the Connasauga a little further north, made it
a very strong place for the intrenched camp which the Confederate commander had prepared there. It was held by
two brigades under General Canty,[1] and such a force could
easily defend it against a very strong column. It was a
well-fortified post, suitable for a safe depôt of supplies;
but it is improbable that Johnston regarded it as a position for his whole army.

McPherson passed the defile without opposition, and
pushed his advance close to the fortifications about the
post. His reconnoissance satisfied him that he could not
carry the works by assault, or that it was at least not worth
the cost in lives which it would involve. He had no accurate knowledge of the topography or of roads by which he
could turn the position and reach the railroad further north.
Neither could he tell to what extent Johnston had already
detached portions of his command to resist him. He there-

---

[1] Some of the accounts speak of only one brigade as the garrison, but Johnston, in his Narrative (p. 316), distinctly says that two brigades defended it
against McPherson.

fore adopted the prudent course of retiring to a strong position at the southern mouth of the gap, where he made sure
of keeping the way open for the whole army, and reported
the situation to his superior. Sherman was disappointed in
this, and when they met, told McPherson that he had lost a
great opportunity; but he carefully spared the feelings of
his subordinate, with whom his friendship was most inti-
mate, and he applied his energies at once to making the
most of the actual situation.

During Monday, the 9th, Thomas and Schofield pressed
Johnston's front at all points. The divisions of Hooker's,
Palmer's, and Howard's corps in front of Buzzard's roost
were all engaged, and whilst there was no combined and determined assault of the Confederate lines in form, the attack
was kept up with well-supported skirmish lines, and Sherman's purpose of keeping his opponent fully occupied was
well carried out. On the north crest of Rocky Face, Harker's brigade of Newton's division made the most serious
effort of the day, and became committed to an attack
which fully tested the possibility of pushing the enemy
away from his stronghold on that summit at Buzzard's
Roost. The brigade was supported by the rest of the division as well as by Judah's division of the Army of the Ohio.
Meanwhile Schofield advanced Cox's and Hovey's divisions
along a lower parallel ridge on the east, nearly two miles,
till they came upon the fortifications extending across the
valleys north of Dalton already described. The works were
found to be very strong, and the enemy was not tempted to
leave them. Schofield's troops were due east from the
crest where Harker was fighting, and from there the view
of the combat above was an exciting one. The line of blue
coats could be seen among the rocks, nearly at right angles

with the line of the ridge, the men at the top in *silhouette*
against the sky, close up to the Confederate trenches, where
their charges were met with a line of fire before which they
recoiled only to renew the effort, till it became apparent
even to the most daring that it was useless to lead men
against such barriers. The orders were not to waste life in
serious assault upon intrenchments, but the zeal of the
troops and subordinate commanders turned the intended
skirmish into something very like a ranged battle, and the
Confederate reports state that five separate and regular
assaults were made upon their lines.

Johnston's disposition of his troops was such as was naturally indicated by the contour of the ground. He relied
upon the inaccessible palisades of Rocky Face to defend his
left rear, and had Reynolds's Arkansas and Granberry's Texan
brigades and Grigsby's brigade of dismounted Kentucky
Cavalry holding Dug Gap and the ridge adjacent. Bate's
division was on the left of the stream in Mill Creek Gap
under Buzzard's Roost, Stewart's on the right of it, Cheatham's continued Stewart's lines about a mile along the crest
to the commanding point attacked by Harker, thence turning down the mountain to the east came in succession Stevenson's, Hindman's, and Cleburne's divisions, crossing
Crow Valley and holding the works in front of Schofield's
Twenty-third Corps. Walker's division was in reserve near
the angle of the Confederate line. Lieutenant-General
Hardee commanded the left wing, and Lieutenant-General
Hood the right. Wheeler's cavalry covered Johnston's right,
and during the day McCook, whose division of horse was
near Varnell's Station, had a lively affair with him. La-
Grange's brigade attacked and drove Wheeler back some
distance to a hill defended by artillery, known as Poplar
Place. Here the enemy resumed the aggressive with supe-

rior force, having two brigades of infantry as well as the cavalry, and LaGrange was routed and himself captured. In this affair the loss in casualties and prisoners was about a hundred and fifty on either side.

During the night the National army rested on its arms, the troops on the mountain sides and crests in line of battle. Rest it could hardly be called, for the surface of the ground was a mass of broken quartz rock, the sharp edges and angles of which had not yielded to weathering, and the bivouac was a rough one.

The 10th, the demonstrations were continued along the line, but with less vigor. Johnston was now aware of McPherson's presence in Snake Creek Gap, and during the night had sent Hood with Walker's, Hindman's, and Cleburne's divisions toward Resaca. The Richmond Government was also awake to his necessities, and Polk's corps was on the way to him. On getting news that McPherson was not pressing an attack upon Resaca but had taken position at the mouth of the Gap, Hood was recalled with Hindman's division, leaving Cleburne and Walker near Tilton, covering the Rome and Resaca roads. Lieutenant-General Polk with his advanced division (Loring's) reached Resaca on the 11th and was authorized by Johnston to call Cleburne and Walker to him in case of need.

During the 10th Sherman became aware that it would not now be practicable for McPherson to reach the railroad in view of Johnston's new disposition of his forces, and that the latter was not yet ready to let go of Dalton. He directed McPherson to strengthen his position, and intimated his wish not to have Johnston hurried in leaving Dalton for a couple of days, till his own arrangements for the larger movement should be complete. Schofield was swung back, marching to the rear in line, till his com·

mand prolonged the line of the Fourth Corps on the ridge of Rocky Face, with his front to the east. Williams's division of Hooker's corps advanced to the support of McPherson on the Villanow and Snake Creek road, and the rest of that corps was ordered to follow. The movement of the whole army by that flank was only awaiting the arrival nearer the front of Major-General Stoneman with the cavalry of the Army of the Ohio, which had been refitting, and which was expected to cover the Chattanooga and Cleveland roads.

On the 11th orders were issued for a general movement on the next day at daybreak : Howard's (Fourth) corps to remain in position, Stoneman's cavalry to take the place of Schofield's Twenty-third Corps, and the rest of the armies of the Cumberland and Ohio to follow the movement by the right flank through Snake Creek Gap. In the afternoon of the 11th, Johnston being anxious to learn whether the National army was in motion, made a reconnoissance in force of Wheeler's cavalry supported by Hindman's division against Schofield's left. The enemy were resisted by the cavalry under Stoneman, and did not reach the infantry lines, which, though called to arms, were not engaged. Johnston was induced by false reports from scouts and country people to believe that Stoneman burned many wagons of the train. The affair was an unimportant one, though causing some scores of casualties on either side.

By sunrise next morning, Thomas, with the Fourteenth Corps (Palmer's), was in motion, closely followed by Schofield, and during the day the whole army, except Howard's corps and Stoneman's cavalry, was concentrated near McPherson's position at the *debouche* of the Gap looking toward Resaca. The troops had ten days' rations, of which three were cooked and in haversacks, all baggage was at the rear near Ringgold, no tents were allowed even to general officers.

The deep valleys and forests west of Rocky Face had perfectly covered the movement, and it was made without the slightest interruption from the enemy. Johnston learned from Polk at Resaca of the gathering forces in front of that place on the 12th, evacuated Dalton during the night, and concentrated his command in front of Sherman. He took his position under cover of the resistance made by Loring's division of Polk's corps to the advance of McPherson's column. His rear was covered by his cavalry which Howard followed on the morning of the 13th, passing through Dalton at nine o'clock and capturing a considerable number of prisoners as he advanced. Wheeler was supported by infantry at Tilton, and by this means was able to delay Howard near that point till night.

The first important step in the campaign had been successfully taken, and the enemy had been compelled to evacuate the impregnable lines about Dalton, with but trifling loss on Sherman's part. Johnston had been disappointed in his hope of making a heavy return blow upon his opponent. The prestige of a fortunate initiative was with the National commander.

CHAPTER V.

RESACA.

THE sketch already given of Resaca will make it easy to understand the position which Johnston took about the place. Polk's corps, which was already on the ground and facing McPherson, naturally became the left of his line, with his left flank resting on the Oostanaula. Next to him was placed Hardee's corps, extending the line northward, and Hood's corps, bending to the east, reached the Connasauga River with his right flank. The valley of Camp Creek was in front of his centre for a distance of two miles or more nearly north and south. Polk had part of his troops on the west bank of the creek near its mouth, because the high hills which he thus occupied covered and protected the railroad bridge at Resaca. This advanced position also enfiladed the upper part of Camp Creek and served as a bastion for the line of works along the east bank of the stream. Further north the Confederate line left the creek and followed the line of high wooded hills facing to the north.

Sherman brought his trains into Snake Creek Gap, Garrard's cavalry picketing the roads to the rear. Schofield left one division (Hovey's) at the mouth of the Gap, one brigade of it being stationed near the rear of the parked trains, about five miles southeast of Villanow. During the day the Army of the Tennessee was advanced to cover the movement of the rest of the forces, Logan's corps being deployed and

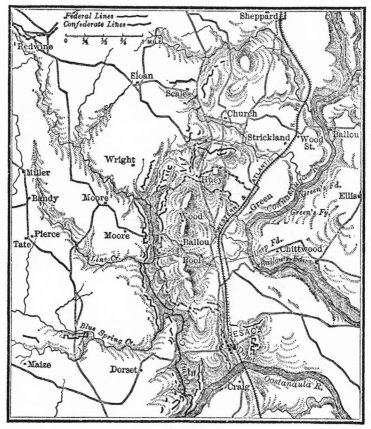

Resaca.

supported by Veatch's division of Dodge's. Logan, who met with a sharp resistance, succeeded in occupying a ridge nearly parallel to that held by Polk in front of him; but as his right did not reach far south of the Resaca road, the division of the Sixteenth Corps was brought up and deployed on his right. This gave the whole army a strong flank resting on the Oostanaula. On the morning of the 14th McPherson was ordered to move straight on Resaca, his right covered by Kilpatrick's cavalry. He was to occupy the line of Camp Creek on its west bank, and endeavor to reach the railroad with his left. The lack of topographical information made it seem possible to do this, but it turned out that the maps were misleading, and the railroad curved eastward above Resaca, behind the enemy's centre. Thomas was directed to take advantage of country roads and paths to reach McPherson's left with the Twentieth and Fourteenth Corps and to form there. Schofield's remaining two divisions, Judah's and Cox's, followed the Rome and Dalton road some two miles to the north, and then struck across country and came in on Thomas's left. The broken nature of the ground made this a difficult march, and it required extraordinary exertions to take the artillery across the ravines and streams which had to be passed. About noon the whole line was facing the valley of Camp Creek, and Howard with the Fourth Corps was about a mile to the north of Schofield's left.

In the deployment, the left of Palmer's (Fourteenth) corps reached nearly to the place where Camp Creek Valley bends to the northwestward, and where the enemy's intrenched line curved away from it to the east. Thomas and Schofield were in person at this point, and word being received that Howard was within supporting distance, the order was given for the line to advance. Along the right the

enemy's skirmishers were driven over the creek, except at
the bridge where the Resaca road crosses it. The defensive
lines on the east bank were fully developed, and the artillery opened on both sides of the valley. Schofield's divisions moved in line across the creek. His left division
(Cox's) carried and held the intrenchments in its front,
driving the enemy from them at a charge after a fierce struggle. His right division (Judah's) marched against the angle
of the Confederate works where these turned away from the
valley. The ground was very difficult there, and the troops
in crossing the valley were subject to enfilade from salients
further to the right as well as to the direct fire in front.
They were unable to get a foothold on the opposite bluffs,
and were repulsed with considerable loss. Meanwhile
Cox's right was exposed to a cross fire of artillery. His men
made use of the reverse of the enemy's captured trench,
strengthening it by such means as were at hand, and Newton's and Wood's divisions of the Fourth Corps marched to
their support. The enemy fell back and established a new
line several hundred yards further in rear. Wood formed
on Cox's left, and Stanley's division was in *echelon*, still beyond Wood's flank.

The movements of the morning had crowded our forces
too much to the right, and Howard's left was in the air.
Sherman directed Thomas to move Hooker's corps to the
left, the Army of the Tennessee and Palmer's (Fourteenth)
corps being able to extend and hold the west bank of Camp
Creek. Johnston also had detected the weakness of our left
flank, and Hood was already marching with Stewart's and
Stevenson's division to turn it. At the same time the effort
was made to drive back all the National forces which had
crossed Camp Creek, and a demonstration was made all
along the line. Stanley was outflanked and was being

pressed back, when Hooker's leading division (V
arrived and turned the tide. The other divisio
corps followed promptly, the enemy was repulseu ᵃⁿᵘ ᵘⁿᵒ
line extended on the continuation of the intrenchment carried by Schofield's men earlier in the day. Cox's division
had exhausted its ammunition about the middle of the
afternoon, and as wagons could not reach him over the
creek, he was relieved, one brigade at a time, by Newton.
In relieving the right brigade (Manson's) by Harker, both
brigade commanders were injured by the explosion of a
shell, and at this point the losses on both sides were
severe.

On the right a brisk skirmish and artillery fight was kept
up, more by way of feints and demonstrations than with the
intention of serious attack. Osterhaus's division of Logan's
corps was upon the principal road leading to Resaca, which
runs through a heavily wooded valley before reaching the
creek. The stream is there deep enough to make a formidable obstacle, and the road crosses it by a bridge. In the
afternoon, during one of the demonstrations, the enemy's
skirmishers showed signs of weakness, and Osterhaus, pushing the advantage with vigor, succeeded in driving them
through the wood and over the bridge. Before this could
be destroyed the Twelfth Missouri was thrown across it and
into the timber on the farther side, where they succeeded in
making and holding an intrenched line as a bridge head.
The Confederates under Polk, in their advanced position on
our extreme right were a good deal weakened in *morale* by
the knowledge that the National troops had thus made
good a foothold in rear of their flank, and between five and
six o'clock Logan ordered forward the brigades of Generals
Giles A. Smith and C. R. Woods, supported by Veatch's division from Dodge's corps. The height held by Polk was car-

ried, and the position intrenched under a galling artillery and musketry fire from the enemy's principal lines. During the evening Polk made a vigorous effort to retake the position, but was repulsed, McPherson sending forward Lightburn's brigade to the support of the troops already engaged. The hill thus carried commanded the railroad and wagon bridges crossing the Oostanaula, and Johnston, upon learning of Polk's failure to retake the lost ground, ordered a road to be cut during the night, and a pontoon bridge to be laid across the river a mile above the town, and out of range of fire.

Early in the day, in pursuance of Sherman's orders, McPherson had sent Sweeny's division of Dodge's corps to Lay's Ferry, with instructions to make a lodgment on the south bank of the Oostanaula and cover the laying of a pontoon bridge by Captain Reese, Chief Engineer of the Army of the Tennessee. Sweeny moved to the river and effected the crossing by one brigade, but on a false rumor of an attempt by the enemy to cross above him, he withdrew to the right bank and retired a mile and a half to a less exposed position. Johnston received the report of this movement from General Martin of the cavalry, whose outposts had been driven off, and marched Walker's division of infantry toward Calhoun in the night; but this officer, finding the south bank clear, reported the alarm a false one, and was at once recalled. Sweeny, however, resumed the movement on the morning of the 15th, got his whole division across and intrenched, and the bridge was laid with comparatively little opposition. The cavalry under Brigadier-General Kilpatrick had been very active and useful in covering the flank of the Army of the Tennessee, and that enterprising officer had been severely wounded in the advance against Polk's lines in front of Resaca.

During the morning of the 15th sharp skirmishing continued along the whole front, but the left flank was that by
which Sherman intended to advance. Hooker's whole corps
was in line, and Schofield's two divisions were withdrawn
from the centre and passed to the extreme left in his support. On the Confederate side Hood was reinforced by
troops from Hardee's and Polk's corps, and made another
effort to swing his right forward. This was shortly after
noon. He was met by a simultaneous advance from Hooker.
Butterfield's division drove back Hood's advance under
Stevenson, the latter being unable to withdraw a battery
which had been run forward to a commanding position.
The guns remained between the armies till night, when they
were taken and brought off by a detachment of the Fifth
Ohio under Colonel Kilpatrick. Hooker's corps made a
strong line of defensive works along its front, Schofield
took position on his flank and rear, and everything was prepared for a still closer investment on the morrow.

Sherman's purpose was to contract and strengthen his
lines as much as possible, so that a considerable part of his
forces could be withdrawn for another flanking movement
south of the Oostanaula. He had laid a second pontoon
bridge at Lay's Ferry, near the mouth of Snake Creek, and
Garrard's cavalry were already operating toward Calhoun,
threatening Johnston's railway line. Johnston's position,
though a very strong one, had the fatal defect of giving him
a river at his back, and a comparatively small force on the
further bank would make his investment complete. He saw
that he could not safely make a longer delay, and withdrew
during the night of the 15th, burning the railroad bridge
behind him. Polk's and Hardee's corps crossed by the railroad bridge and one built on trestles near it, and marched
to Calhoun. Hood crossed on the pontoon laid in the night

of the 14th, and took the road to Adairsville by Spring Place.

In the morning Sherman entered the town, and began at once the work of repairing bridges and putting his columns across the river. Davis's division of Palmer's (Fourteenth) corps was immediately sent to support Garrard's cavalry toward Rome. McPherson was ordered to cross the Oostanaula at Lay's Ferry, Thomas's Fourth and Fourteenth Corps to cross at Resaca, Schofield's Twenty-third and Hooker's Twentieth Corps to cross the Connasauga at Fite's Ferry or Echota, some two miles above. Stoneman, with the cavalry of the Army of the Ohio, was on the extreme left, and Kilpatrick's accompanied the central columns.

CHAPTER VI.

FROM THE OOSTANAULA TO THE ETOWAH.

THE country south of Resaca and between the Oostanaula and Etowah Rivers is much more open and less broken than any other portion of Northern Georgia. The Oostanaula pursues a southwesterly course to Rome, where it is joined by the Etowah running nearly due west, and the two form the Coosa. Taking the two rivers as sides of a triangle, the third side from Resaca due south would be about thirty miles in length. The railway, after crossing the river at Resaca, runs south through Calhoun, Adairsville, and Kingston, then bends eastward through Cassville and Cartersville, and crosses the Etowah at Alatoona, where a spur of rugged and high hills on the south side of the river is traversed by a deep gorge, the famous Alatoona Pass. From Kingston a branch of the railroad ran to Rome, but had not at that time been built farther to the southwest.

Johnston's opinion of the steadiness of the National troops and of Sherman's ability to handle them was, as he says, higher than that which Southern newspaper editors, and even the Richmond Government held, and he was fully resolved not to risk a general engagement in a field where Sherman's superior force could be manœuvred so as to reach his flanks. He sought, therefore, for a position in some valley narrow enough to enable him to rest either wing upon commanding ground which could not readily be turned by ordinary field tactics. He halted, on the 16th, a mile or two south of Calhoun, in the valley of Oothcaloga Creek, where the roads on which Hardee and Hood were moving were only about a mile apart. Cheatham's division of Hardee's corps, with Wheeler's cavalry, formed the rear guard.

The position below Calhoun was not thought a good one, but Johnston's engineers reported that a mile or two north of Adairsville suitable ground could be found. Accordingly he marched on the 17th to the position reported, and halted whilst a careful reconnoissance was made. The breadth of the valley was again found too great, and by this time Sherman was pressing him in front with the Army of the Cumberland, whilst the Armies of the Tennessee and Ohio were moving on his left and right flanks respectively, and he gave orders for a further retreat to Cassville.

But it will be well to follow the movements of the National forces during these two days a little more closely. Sherman's calculation, in his march south from Resaca, was that the Army of the Cumberland in his centre was always strong enough to hold Johnston at bay until one of the wings could attack his flank or rear. This simple plan controlled the whole campaign. The three corps under Thomas pressed constantly and closely against the enemy, keeping him fully employed, whilst McPherson and Schofield alternately threatened to turn his positions.

Garrard had been ordered to move with his cavalry down the right bank of the Oostanaula till near Rome, and then to operate with vigor on Johnston's flank. After the evacuation of Resaca, he was further ordered to leave his artillery at Farmer's Bridge, some eight miles above Rome, so that he might be "flying light," and Davis's division was detached from Thomas, as has been mentioned, to follow

Garrard, take his artillery, and rejoin the Fourteenth Corps at Kingston. This threw that division for the moment beyond McPherson and the river, and gave a very extended front, apparently, to Sherman's movement.

McPherson crossed the Ooostanaula at the mouth of Snake Creek (Lay's Ferry) as ordered, and taking up the pontoon bridges marched to the mill on the Oothcaloga Creek, about a mile southwest of Calhoun. The Army of the Cumberland found it slower work than had been expected, getting its large artillery train over the bridges at Resaca, and the whole of the 16th was used up in doing it. It was for this reason that Hooker was ordered to follow the Newtown road and cross the Oostanaula in the southward bend of the river, near that place. By some error in transmission of orders his leading division took Schofield's route instead, and crossing the Connasauga between Resaca and Tilton, marched to the other tributary of the Oostanaula, the Coosawattee, crossing it at McClure's Ferry.

Schofield's infantry forded the Connasauga at Fite's Ferry, the artillery and wagons being ferried over in a small flat-boat, and Hooker did the same. The water was waist deep, and the men stripped naked, carrying their clothes and arms upon their heads, making great sport at the ludicrous appearance of the column. Neither of these columns had a pontoon train, the only ones with the army being at Resaca and Lay's Ferry. Schofield marched further up the Coosawattee, to Field's mill. Owing, however, to the delay caused by Hooker's column getting on the same road, he was unable to get nearer to Field's than four miles. On the morning of the 17th he built a trestle foot-bridge for his infantry, the Coosawattee being too deep to ford, and ferried the artillery and wagons in a flat-boat. This occupied the day, but as the centre was advancing, Schofield determined

to be in position near Adairsville in the morning, and
marched at ten o'clock at night, reaching Big Spring about
two in the morning, with his advanced guard forward on the
Adairsville road, that village being about three miles distant.

Hooker's advanced division (Geary's) had crossed the
Coosawattee at McClure's, in the night of the 16th, and resting during the morning while the rest of the corps came
over, the whole moved at one o'clock by the direct road toward Adairsville, till they came into close support of Howard's corps at the centre. The latter moved directly south
from Resaca through Calhoun, where lively skirmishing began. In the afternoon, as Howard approached Adairsville,
the resistance of the enemy's rear-guard grew more determined. They made temporary barricades of rails and logs,
behind which they fought, several lines being apparently
formed, the front when driven in retiring through the next
line to the rear, and so on. This made the progress slow,
and at evening the position was reached on which Johnston
had contemplated a decisive engagement. Sherman was
now with Newton's division in the advance, and had a narrow escape from shots of the enemy's artillery as he was reconnoitring, the group about him having attracted their
fire.

McPherson's way diverged from Thomas's as he moved
south, but in the evening of the 17th he was near diagonal
roads leading direct upon Adairsville and upon the flank of
the position of Johnston north of the town.

The appearance of things at nightfall made Sherman hope
that Johnston would offer a pitched battle the next day, and
that the campaign might be at once decided. His orders
were therefore issued for a concentration with that purpose.
When day broke on the 18th, however, the lines in front

were vacant, and the pursuit took a new and somewhat embarrassing shape. Johnston divided his forces at Adairsville, Polk and Hood marching direct to Cassville, and Hardee to Kingston. The movement was so managed as to leave the impression that his principal force had gone toward Kingston, and Thomas with two corps was kept on that road, whilst Hooker and Schofield were ordered to move toward Cassville direct from their respective positions.

We have already seen that the railway makes a considerable curve to the east at Kingston, and as the wagon road does the same, it follows that Sherman's columns in moving from Adairsville diverged rapidly. Cassville was almost or quite as near as Kingston, and if Johnston by rapid marching concentrated there whilst Thomas and McPherson were at the latter point, he could easily turn upon Schofield and Hooker on his right, whilst Sherman with the larger part of the army was some five or six miles off on the left. To add to the enemy's chances of success, McPherson, in trying to reach Kingston by parallel roads on the west, so as not to crowd upon Thomas, was obliged to diverge equally far in that direction, and in the afternoon of the 18th the National army was more scattered than at any time since the 5th, when the campaign opened. Could Sherman have been sure that Johnston would not cross the Etowah at Kingston, he would have kept McPherson on the road to Adairsville according to his first orders, pushed the whole of the Army of the Cumberland and that of the Ohio straight on Cassville, and given McPherson the road from Adairsville to Kingston. But the maps of the country were almost worthless, and were often misleading; the inhabitants were hostile and gave false reports, and Sherman thought the " broad trail " of Johnston's army proved that the whole had followed the railroad.

It was in the hope of this that Johnston had made his
plan in leaving Adairsville, and so far things seemed to
work as he wished.   His corps commanders halted in
front of Cassville after they had crossed Two Run Creek, a
considerable stream at right angles to the Adairsville road,
which, after flowing past the town to the southwest, turns
west and empties into the Etowah at Kingston.

During the 18th Thomas advanced from Adairsville with
the Fourth and Fourteenth Corps to within three miles of
Kingston.   Hooker with his Twentieth Corps marched by
Adairsville and out on the direct Cassville road as far as
Spring Mills, some two or three miles beyond.   Schofield
continued his march in the general direction of Adairsville
eight miles, being hindered and delayed by the cavalry of
Stoneman, which passed his column under orders to try to
break the railroad near Cartersville.

The next day Thomas occupied Kingston and marched
Howard's and Palmer's corps eastward till, toward evening,
after sharp skirmishing, Hardee's rear guard was driven into
Cassville.   Hooker had also advanced, skirmishing on his
road, and when near its crossing of Two Run Creek, his
right formed connection with Howard.   Schofield moved
across country parallel to Hooker, driving back the cavalry
which covered the enemy's flank, crossed the upper branches
of Two Run Creek north of Cassville, and before evening
the line was complete and advanced close to the enemy's
works, which stretched along a commanding chain of hills
back of the town and running nearly north and south.
McPherson with the Army of the Tennessee was halted at
Kingston.

Johnston says it was his intention to advance Hood and
Polk on the 18th, in the expectation of overwhelming Schofield, at least, before the centre and right of Sherman's army

could come up. He declares that he ordered Hood to move
in the afternoon by a country road to the north, then to
turn west and fall upon the flank of the advancing column.
Polk was then to advance against the front of the same force
by the Adairsville road. Hood denies that any combined
advance was planned, and says that he asked permission to
move Hindman's division in the manner stated, but that he
had proceeded only a little way northward when he found
himself outflanked by the National forces in motion, both
infantry and artillery, and was obliged to return. If the incident occurred on the 19th it would exactly correspond
with the advance of Schofield and Hooker on that evening ;
but it is certain that none of Sherman's infantry was in the
position Hood indicates on the 18th. Stoneman was operating in that direction with cavalry alone in his efforts to
reach and cut the railway.

The 19th had been spent by the Confederates in making a
strong line of intrenchments. Johnston issued a general
order saying that the retreat had gone as far as was necessary for strategic purposes, that the time had come for
trying conclusions with the National army and he would
give battle where he was. No sooner had the left of
Sherman's army pushed into position and the batteries
opened fire than Hood and Polk protested against the tena-
bility of their position on the ridge, a large part of Polk's
line being, as they thought, enfiladed by our artillery.
Hood was on Polk's right and Hardee on the left. A controversy arose, and Johnston, putting upon his subordinates
the responsibility of thwarting his plans, and unwilling to
go into battle under their protest, gave orders to retire from
the place and march through Cartersville to the Etowah,
which was crossed the next day. Hood asserts that he
urged an aggressive concentrated movement on the day

before, when alone there was a chance to take Sherman at
any disadvantage, and blames strongly the strict defensive to
which Johnston adhered. The only thing that is certain in
the matter is that their dissensions prolonged the campaign
by postponing the decisive engagement, as to the result of
which Sherman was justly confident. So eager was he to
bring on a battle in the comparatively open country north
of the Etowah, that he had ordered his subordinates not to
hesitate to engage the enemy without reference to supports,
feeling sure that he could at any time concentrate with
rapidity enough to secure the victory.

Johnston's only chance of securing any important advantage would have been to have forced the marching of Hardee's corps on the 18th till he concentrated everything at
Cassville, and then turn with all his force upon Sherman's
left wing. The country between the Kingston and Cassville
road and the one leading from Adairsville to the latter place
is a high gravelly plateau, becoming rough and broken in
its southern part. Sherman would have been obliged to
traverse this region to get to the aid of Schofield and
Hooker if they had been attacked in force; but he had
every reason for faith that his subordinates would be watchful, and by taking advantage of the defensible positions
everywhere to be found, could hold Johnston at bay, or
slowly retreat by converging movements till he could come
to their assistance. Although he was in the dark, therefore,
as to the position of Johnston on the 18th, his apparent
carelessness was a calculated audacity, willing to take some
risks for the sake of tempting his adversary to a general
engagement with him there. His despatch to Schofield
late in the evening of the 18th said : "If we can bring
Johnston to battle this side of Etowah we must do it, even at
the hazard of beginning battle with but a part of our forces."

On the 20th Schofield advanced Cox's division to Cartersville, a rear guard of the enemy disputing the movement.
The Confederates were driven back without serious resistance,
and crossed the Etowah River, burning the railroad bridge behind them. A show of force was made in the enemy's front
at this place, whilst Reilly's and Casement's brigades of Cox's
division were sent several miles up the river and destroyed
the important iron works and other factories situated there.

We have seen that Davis's division had been sent to support Garrard's cavalry in a movement down the west bank of
the Oostanaula, whilst the forward movement from Resaca
was taking place. His orders were to find a bridge or easy
ford of the Oostanaula, and bring into the central column
Garrard's artillery and trains, whilst the cavalry, unencum-
bered, should operate rapidly against the flank of Johnston.
Garrard, finding no bridges or satisfactory crossing, and
believing that to continue on to Rome would separate him
too far from the head of column, returned by the route
he had travelled and crossed at Lay's Ferry. Davis determined to continue on to Rome, and on the 18th took that
place after a sharp engagement, losing in killed and
wounded about one hundred and fifty men. The town was
a considerable depôt for army supplies, and contained important factories and the repair shops for ordnance. The
capture in supplies and material of war was not very great,
but the occupation of the town was opportune, and by giving a broad front to Sherman's movement, handsomely
covered his principal columns and imposed upon the enemy.
As Major-General F. P. Blair was at this time at Decatur,
Ala., moving to the front with two divisions of veteran volunteers of the Army of the Tennessee, he was ordered to
march by way of Rome, and General Davis was directed to
hold the place till Blair should relieve him.

Sherman secured in the vicinity of Kingston two good bridges over the Etowah, and being thus sure of his ability to deploy on the south of that river, he gave his army a few days of rest, during which the railroad was repaired and pressed to its utmost capacity to accumulate supplies for another advance.

The losses in the engagements about Dalton, and in the battle of Resaca cannot be accurately given, as the system of reports covered the casualties of a month, in most cases, instead of stating them after each engagement. The brigade and division reports enable us to approximate it only. There were not more than six or eight hundred killed and wounded in front of Dalton. At Resaca the Army of the Cumberland lost about a thousand, the two divisions of the Army of the Ohio which were engaged lost nearly a thousand, the casualties in the Army of the Tennessee cannot be accurately given, but they were fewer than in either of the other armies. A comparative view of the losses on both sides can be better made at a later point in the campaign, for the reason already stated.

CHAPTER VII.

FIELD LIFE—RAILWAY REPAIRS—MAP-MAKING—MARCH ON DALLAS.

When the movement of May 7th began, preparation was made for four days of extreme exertion, and under the imperative orders of General Sherman all baggage had been left behind. When the four days' cooked rations were exhausted, the advance through Snake Creek Gap was just beginning, and an issue of the most necessary supplies was all that was possible. Till the army reached the Etowah River the same condition of things existed. A tent-fly—a single sheet of light canvas—was the only shelter for division and brigade headquarters; mess-kits there were none, and the superior officers were even worse off relatively than the company officers and the privates. The company pack-mule carried the simple cooking utensils and compact kit which experience had shown to be best for the bivouac; and the mule, driven by a negro servant, could keep up with the company, on or off the roads, and would not be far at the rear even when the command was under fire. The private soldier carried his shelter-tent or rubber blanket, and he and the comrade who was his "partner" made of the two a comfortable protection from the weather. His haversack contained his rations, his canteen and a small tin coffee-pot or pail clattered at his belt, and, in half an hour of halt, the veteran knew how to prepare a wholesome and abundant meal. The ration of meat, bread, coffee, and sugar was a large one, and of excellent quality, and by foraging or traffic extras could be added to it on the way.

The general officers could not manage in quite the same simple style. From the adjutant-general, the surgeon, the quartermaster, the commissary, the ordnance and mustering officers regular statistical reports were required by army regulations, and enforced by stopping the pay of delinquent commands. At each headquarters, therefore, a good deal of business had to be transacted, and much clerical work had to be done in the intervals of fighting. The order to leave all baggage behind for four days implied only a short interruption of the usual routine, but when it was, by the circumstances, extended to nearly a month, it involved no small trouble and privation. But the weather at this time was good, each day was full of excitement, the enemy was retreating, and it would be hard to find anywhere a merrier company than assembled each evening around the headquarters camp-fires. Necessity was the mother of invention, and at Cartersville the mess at a division headquarters boasted that, beginning with nothing, they had accumulated a kit consisting of a tin plate, four tin cups without handles, three round oyster cans doing duty as cups, two sardine boxes for extra plates, and a coffee-pot! Pocket-knives were the only cutlery needed, and for dishes nothing could be better than one of the solid crackers familiarly known as "hard tack." This outfit they declared was luxurious compared with that of the General-in-Chief.

Good weather, however, could not be calculated upon to last forever. The orders issued at the Etowah were to be ready for twenty days' separation from the railway, and everybody prepared for contingencies as fully as was consistent with the utmost mobility, and in the best manner that experience and ingenuity could devise.

The railway repairs of the army were under the management of Colonel Wright, a civil engineer, with a corps of two thousand men. The efficiency and skill of this branch of the service was beyond praise. The ordinary wooden bridges of the railway were reconstructed, where destroyed, of a standard pattern of truss, of which the parts were interchangeable, and the prepared timbers were kept in stock at safe points in the rear. By this means a bridge could be renewed as if by magic, and perhaps nothing produced more moral effect upon the enemy than hearing the whistle of the locomotives in rear of our lines within a few hours after they had received reports that the railway had been broken so thoroughly as to cause us great delays. But the triumph of energy and mechanical skill came when, as at the Chattahoochee, great trestle bridges, hundreds of feet long, and near a hundred high, were flung across a chasm with as little delay or trouble as an ordinary pioneer corps would make in bridging a petty stream. The construction corps and the railway transportation department, under Colonel Anderson, worked in complete accord, and at no time during the campaign was there the slightest anxiety about supplies, whilst a reduction of the ration was very rare.

For instantaneous communication between the Commanding General and his principal subordinates the military telegraph was organized. A light train of wagons carrying wires and insulators moved with the headquarters; the forest trees were used as poles; an operator with his instrument accompanied each army commander, who could thus converse directly with the central station and with General Sherman himself. This was supplemented by the ordinary flag signals used by the Signal Corps, whose officers pushed to the very front, and, from any commanding hill or tree·

top, waved their flags, conveying information or orders by
means of a code of cipher signals, of which the key was
frequently changed to prevent its interpretation by the
enemy.

Another part of the administration of the army deserves
mention also. The topography of the country was almost
unknown. The maps in common use were erroneous and
misleading to a degree that was exasperating. They gave
the outlines of counties, the names of towns and villages,
and some remote approximation to the courses of the principal streams. The smaller creeks and watercourses were
drawn at random, as if to fill up the sheet, and were uni-
formly wrong. A few principal country roads were laid
down, but so incorrectly that every attempt to calculate distances upon them or between them was sure to lead to
trouble.

To meet these difficulties each division commander was
ordered to detail a competent officer as acting topographer,
reporting to the engineers at corps and army headquarters.
It was the duty of these officers to make an itinerary of
every march, to sketch all roads and streams, hills and valleys, woods and open land; to collect from citizens and
negroes all possible information as to distances, names of
residents and the like; to accompany reconnoitring parties
and extend their topographical knowledge with diligence
and enterprise. They were furnished with a few portable
instruments, always carried on their persons. The information thus obtained was consolidated and connected; improved sketch maps of the vicinity of the army were thus
made, and by a simple photographic process they were mul-
tiplied and distributed to the proper officers of the command. New editions were issued from time to time, with
bulletins giving newly discovered information, and thus the

effort was made to supply the army with the knowledge vital to its success.

The changes in the relative strength of the opposing armies had been in Johnston's favor during the preceding part of the campaign. French's division of infantry and Jackson's of cavalry had joined Polk's corps at Adairsville, so that the three Confederate corps were now full, and the local militia were being organized and used to cover the lines of communication and perform duties which on the National side required detachments from the army in the field. Johnston's line was being shortened whilst Sherman's was stretching out. The one was picking up his detachments, the other was constantly making new ones. From the 15th of May for a month the forces of the two armies were more nearly equal than at any other time in the campaign, and no opportunity so favorable could again occur for Johnston to make an aggressive movement, as he had whilst crossing the open country between the Oostanaula and the Etowah. That he did not do so was accepted by the officers and men of the National army as proof that he would not be likely to attempt it in the more difficult country they were now entering, and their operations were carried on with a confidence which was in itself a guaranty of success.

The Resaca bridge had been rebuilt in three days, and on the 22d of May, rations for twenty days had been issued to the divisions. Kingston was announced as the base of supplies until the railroad should be reached again at some point south of the Alatoona Pass, and orders were issued for a forward movement.

Johnston had crossed the Etowah at the railway bridge and occupied the high rocky hills facing northward, whilst he placed the greater part of his army a little in rear, ready to meet his opponent as soon as Sherman's line of advance

should be developed. The new theatre of operations lay
between the Etowah and Chattahoochee rivers, and like the
last was a strip of country of which the features were determined by the general trend of the mountain ranges pointing
to the southwest. The Alatoona Hills, Kenesaw Mountain,
Pine and Lost Mountains lay near the line of the railroad
and necessarily formed the most important strategic points
for both armies. The town of Marietta, just south of Kenesaw and about midway between the two rivers, became at
once Johnston's new base of supplies, as Kingston was
Sherman's. Dallas is a village lying nearly south of Kingston and west of Marietta, about twenty-five miles from the
first and nearly twenty miles from the other. A line running southwesterly from Marietta, a little south of Dallas,
marks sufficiently well the watershed of this region, separating the streams flowing north into the Etowah from those
running south into the Chattahoochee. For several miles
west of the railroad the hills are high, the mountains, however, standing out commandingly above them, giving to
Johnston the most admirable points of observation, from
which the smoke of Sherman's camp fires revealed every
movement that was made. Farther west the hills diminished, the line of the watershed was a rolling sandy region,
and the streams, cutting their way in pretty sharp ravines,
ran through forests and thickets of the loblolly pine, often
growing almost as closely as a cane-brake, and nearly impenetrable for man or horse. The creeks form frequent
ponds, called lagunes in the country, full of quicksands, in
which wagons or artillery were likely to be hopelessly mired.
The more important roads, besides the railway and the
wagon roads near it, are those that lead south from Kingston
through Stilesboro and Burnt Hickory to Dallas, east from
Dallas to Marietta, and east from Burnt Hickory to Ack-

worth, a station on the railway between Marietta and Alatoona.

Sherman's centre being at Kingston, the topography of the country determined for him his line of march, which was to move southward to Dallas, and then east to Marietta, or some other point on the railroad near there.

There was little danger that Johnston would meet him near the Etowah in front of Kingston, for the Confederate commander could not afford to divide his army, and had he massed in front of Kingston, Sherman would have pushed his left wing over the river at Alatoona, and seized at once the line of the railroad. This was what would have pleased Sherman most, and would have shortened the campaign. Johnston wisely determined to make the Pumpkin Vine and Alatoona Creeks the cover for his front, and to meet his opponent with strong entrenched lines across the Dallas and Marietta road, or that from Burnt Hickory to Ackworth, as Sherman should choose either for his principal line of advance.

The fact that the Dallas and Marietta road followed very nearly the line of the watershed made it naturally the easier one, and Sherman resolved to try for it, and if he were too stubbornly met there, to swing his left flank forward by the Burnt Hickory and Ackworth road, forcing Johnston back and establishing himself afresh upon the railway as soon as possible. Accordingly, on May 22d, Sherman issued his orders directing his centre, under Thomas, to move southward on parallel roads through Euharlee and Stilesboro on Dallas, excepting Davis's division of Palmer's corps, which, being at Rome, was ordered to move direct to Dallas by way of Van Wert. The Army of the Tennessee, keeping to the right of Thomas, was to move from near Kingston to Van Wert and thence to Dallas. Blair's corps (the

Seventeenth), had not yet joined it, being on the march
toward Rome, which it was ordered to garrison with about
two thousand men, and then march to Kingston. The garri-
soning of Kingston, meanwhile, and of Resaca (the latter
being the principal depôt of supplies) was left to Thomas'
army of the Cumberland. Schofield's Twenty-third Corps was
to cross the Etowah at any point above Euharlee, then take
roads on the east of those occupied by Thomas, to Burnt
Hickory and thence to the left of Dallas. His cavalry,
under Stoneman, was ordered to cross still further up the
Etowah, and cover the movement on that flank. Kilpatrick's division of cavalry was left on the north bank of the
Etowah to cover that line. Garrard covered the movement
of the columns on the right, and McCook the centre.

On the evening of the 22d the cavalry of the Army of the
Ohio marched to Milam's Bridge on the Etowah, where the
roads from Cassville and Cartersville to Stilesboro cross
the river. The enemy's cavalry retreated, burning the
bridge; but Stoneman was able to cross by a ford above
the mouth of Raccoon Creek, and cover the laying of two
pontoon bridges on the following morning.

Early on the 23d McPherson crossed on the bridge
which had been secured at the mouth of Conasene Creek.
Thomas crossed Howard's and Palmer's corps at the bridges
on the direct road from Kingston to Euharlee; but Hooker,
instead of waiting his turn at these, in accordance with
orders, moved further to the left and crossed at Milam's
Bridge on the pontoons laid down for Schofield. When
the latter, therefore, marching from Cartersville, reached
the river, he found both pontoons already occupied, and the
whole afternoon was lost waiting for Hooker to cross and
get out of the way. This was a repetition of what had occurred at the Oostanaula, and was characteristic of Hooker,

who was apt to be reckless of what interference he made with any plan, so that he got a road or a position which better suited him. By this means he anticipated the rest of the army of the Cumberland in crossing the Euharlee Creek toward Stilesboro, and camped in the advance, followed by Howard and Palmer.

McCook's cavalry advanced to Stilesboro, which he found occupied by the horsemen of the enemy, supported by infantry, and was unable to make further progress before night.

Next morning Thomas ordered one division of Hooker's corps (Geary's) to cross Raccoon Creek on the Alatoona road, and cover the way leading up the creek till relieved by Schofield. The other divisions of the Twentieth Corps marched through Stilesboro to Burnt Hickory, preceded by McCook's division of horse, which skirmished with the enemy's cavalry under Jackson as they advanced.

Schofield crossed at Milam's Bridge at daybreak, followed the Alatoona road till he relieved Geary, who rejoined his own corps. He then marched up Richland Creek to Sligh's Mills, at the forks of the roads leading to Ackworth and to Burnt Hickory. Stoneman's cavalry covered the advance and the flank toward Alatoona, skirmishing as he went.

Johnston was still, on the evening of the 23d, a little uncertain whether Sherman had crossed the Etowah with his whole force, and therefore hesitated about his own movements, fearing to leave his right flank weak till he knew there was no danger from that quarter. He therefore ordered Wheeler, who had forded the Etowah the day before, to push in on Cassville with his division of cavalry and to discover and report what was there. This was done on the 24th. Wheeler found that the whole army had moved toward

Kingston, but part of the supply train was still at Cassville
with a small train guard. By crossing several miles to the
right he had eluded Kilpatrick and made an easy swoop
upon the wagons and quartermaster's men who were thus
delaying in the rear. He claimed to have captured seventy
wagons with their teams, and a hundred and eighty-two
prisoners, besides burning some other wagons. He certainly
did some mischief through the negligence and tardiness of
those who were in charge of the trains, and who had been
ordered to Kingston as soon as the infantry had moved. By
this time Johnston was getting reports from Jackson's cavalry toward Stilesboro, and hardly needed the news from
Wheeler. He now knew that Sherman was over the Etowah
and evidently pushing toward Dallas. On the afternoon of
the 23d he ordered Hardee's corps to march by New Hope
Church to the Stilesboro and Dallas road, Polk's corps to
move in the same direction but a little further south, and
Hood's corps was directed to follow Hardee the next day.
On the 25th the whole command was in line. Hardee's left
division (Bate) was placed across the Stilesboro, Dallas, and
Atlanta road, south of Dallas, where it crosses over the
ridge which there forms the watershed already referred to.
Hood was put upon the right, his centre at New Hope
Church, and his line in front of and covering the road
leading from Dallas to Ackworth. Polk's corps constituted
Johnston's centre, but closed up upon Hood, leaving a
somewhat thinner line between himself and Hardee. In
front of New Hope Church was a valley wooded along the
road, but with open fields a little further to the north, and
the stream, which is a branch of Pumpkin Vine Creek, flows
northeastwardly at that place, parallel to Hood's front.
The banks sloped easily on either side, and were some fifty
feet in height. The whole of Johnston's line was admirably

chosen for defence, occupying as it did a series of ridges covered with wood on their summits, but having open valleys in front, over which attacking forces must advance without shelter. It covered the roads leading from Dallas to Atlanta, to Marietta, and to Ackworth, as well as those passing near New Hope Church in the same directions. He says that only a part of Hood's front was protected by breastworks, and these only of logs thrown hastily together; but the reports of his subordinates, on which his statement is based, may properly be taken with many grains of allowance. They had intrenched at Dalton and at Resaca, at Adairsville and at Cassville, and certainly nothing had occurred to increase their confidence as they had retreated step by step south of the Etowah. When they were forced to evacuate these lines a little later, they were found to be of the most solid character. They had been some hours in position, with full opportunity to intrench, and it would be every way strange and contrary to their already fixed habit if they had not done so. The circumstances, therefore, all sustain the reports of Hooker's division commanders that they drove the Confederate advance guard and skirmishers within intrenched lines. But we are anticipating the current of events.

CHAPTER VIII.

NEW HOPE CHURCH—COMBATS AT PICKETT'S MILL AND BEFORE DALLAS.

On the morning of Wednesday the 25th of May, Sherman's extreme right under McPherson was near Van Wert, some sixteen miles north of west from Dallas, where it had struck into the Rome and Dallas road, and met Davis's division of Palmer's (Fourteenth) corps on its way to rejoin the Army of the Cumberland. McPherson kept on by the direct road, but Davis, to get clear of his column, turned east, taking a by-road over the hills which he found passable, and which enabled him to rejoin his corps before evening. At the centre, Thomas sent forward the Army of the Cumberland on several roads from Burnt Hickory. The corps of Palmer and Howard (Fourteenth and Fourth) made a detour to the right by country roads, intending to reach the Van Wert and Dallas road three or four miles out from the latter place. Hooker's corps (Twentieth) took the direct road to Dallas with his centre division (Geary's), Butterfield's and Williams's divisions taking country roads on the left and right respectively.

The infantry of the Army of the Ohio (Twenty-third Corps) was ordered to rest near Burnt Hickory during the day, whilst the cavalry under Stoneman scoured the roads to left and front. Garrard's cavalry had pushed back the outposts of Bate's division of Hardee's corps near to Dallas the preceding evening, and camped at Pumpkin Vine Creek, about three miles from the town. McCook's cavalry, in front of Hooker's column, had captured an orderly with a despatch from Johnston to General Jackson, who commanded the mounted troops in his front. The message informed

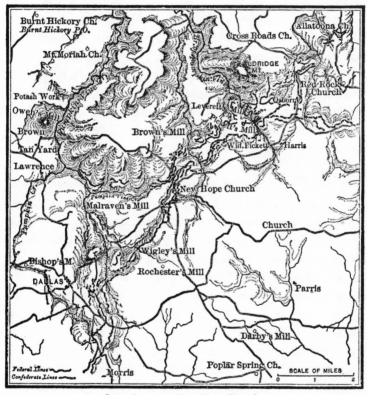

Operations near New Hope Church.

Jackson that the Confederate army was moving toward Dallas. It was this information that led Sherman to hold back his left a little, till the Army of the Tennessee could come forward on his right, and by a partial wheel, his front would be brought nearly parallel to Pumpkin Vine Creek, whilst

he still concentrated toward Dallas. When Geary's division
reached the Pumpkin Vine near Owen's Mills, the bridge
was found burning, but the enemy's cavalry was driven off,
the fire put out, and the bridge repaired. The appearances
convinced Hooker that the stronger force of the enemy lay
in the direction of New Hope Church, and Geary was ordered to take the fork of the road leading there. Ascending
the hill on the east side of the stream with his front covered by the Seventh Ohio regiment deployed as skirmishers, Hooker found the infantry advance of Hood's corps. It
consisted of the Thirty-second and Fifty-eighth Alabama
regiments and Austin's Sharpshooters, under command of
Colonel Bush Jones. It had been ordered to make a stubborn resistance, and did so with such gallantry as to force
Geary to support and extend his skirmish line greatly, and
produced the belief that he was dealing with a larger force.
This sharp contest continued for half a mile or more.
Geary deployed Candy's brigade, and repulsed several determined counter-charges made by the enemy in his front.
He had now reached the ridge facing that on which Hood's
line was deployed in force, and had driven the advanced
guard in upon Stewart's division, to which it belonged. He
threw together such logs as were at hand, and made a
breastwork of them for temporary cover. At the sound of
the firing Sherman had hastened to the front, and directed
Hooker to call in his divisions from right and left, and to
attack and develop the force before him. Williams had
advanced well toward Dallas, but being recalled, faced
about and crossed the creek at Owen's Mills. He came up
with Geary about five o'clock,[1] marching left in front so as

---

[1] General Thomas's report states that Williams and Butterfield joined Geary
about 3 P.M., but Geary says it was five, and that hour best agrees with the time
when heavy firing was heard by Schofield's column.

to enable him more quickly to take position on Geary's right. Butterfield arrived about the same time; the three divisions were formed in columns of brigades and moved forward to the attack. They bravely assaulted the ridge, moving through a dense wood which covered both slopes of the intervening valley. In the midst of their fight a thunder-storm came up, followed by a pouring rain, which lasted through the night. The noise of the storm mingled with the roar of the artillery, but it was the continuous rattling and volleying of the musketry, heard more than half way to Burnt Hickory, that told the columns in the rear there was sharp work at the front. Hooker's columns assaulted Hood's position again and again, each division by a brigade front, and the several brigades relieving each other by passing lines; but the position was too strong to be carried by assault, and was hourly becoming stronger. They persisted in their efforts, however, till darkness shut down on the field, when, gathering up their dead and wounded, they retired to the ridge behind them.

Thomas was directed to bring Howard's corps (Fourth) to Hooker's support, and by six o'clock Newton's division was up and went into position on Hooker's left, the rest of the corps following as fast as Hooker's trains, which filled and blocked the road, would let them. They were all on the field by morning and extended the line still further to the left. Davis's division of Palmer's corps (Fourteenth) was coming over from Van Wert, as we have seen, and was ordered forward on the Dallas road to support the Army of the Tennessee and feel forward toward Hooker's right. Baird's division was left at Burnt Hickory to protect the trains, and Johnson's, which could not get over the blockaded roads during the night, was ordered to come up in the morning, and was then placed in reserve.

McPherson hastened forward from Van Wert with the
Army of the Tennessee, moving direct on Dallas, which he
reached early on the 26th, and took position facing Hardee,
putting Davis's division of the Fourteenth Corps on his left,
a gap of two or three miles still being between this division
and the rest of the Army of the Cumberland, to which it belonged. McPherson's line was about two miles in front of
Dallas. He placed Logan's (Fifteenth) corps on his right,
with its flank reaching across and a little beyond the Villa
Rica (Atlanta) road, whilst Dodge's (Sixteenth) corps connected on the right with Logan, and on the left with Davis.
Beyond Logan, on the extreme flank of the army, Garrard's
cavalry picketed the country, and maintained an active
skirmishing warfare with Jackson's division of the Confederate horse.

Schofield marched at five o'clock in the afternoon of the
25th, upon getting news that Hooker's advance guard had
found the enemy. He left Hovey's division to cover and
protect the trains, and with Hascall's and Cox's divisions,
took, by Sherman's directions, the road from Sligh's Mills
to Burnt Hickory, and thence by the Dallas road to Owens's
Mills. As he was now getting in rear of two corps of the
Army of the Cumberland, and Hooker's wagons were imped-
ing everything, the progress was slow and tedious. The
storm came up and the men plashed along through the mire,
throwing down fences and marching in the fields, or thread-
ing their way among the mule teams on the road. After
passing Burnt Hickory the musketry firing was plainly
heard, and the column pushed along in the drenching rain
till midnight, when they were still west of Pumpkin Vine
Creek. Halting the troops by the roadside, and directing
them to bivouac where they were, Schofield himself rode
forward to learn the situation and receive further orders

from Sherman.   The night was utterly black in its darkness
and storm, and trying to pick his way around some wagons,
his horse fell with him into a gulley, and he was so severely
injured that he was forced to relinquish his command for
several days.   Orders were sent back to the senior division
commander (Cox) to continue the march.   Having had only
an hour's rest, the corps moved again and reached the field
at break of day.

Sherman, who had rested beside a log in the woods during the night, himself met the head of column of the
Twenty-third Corps, and directed it to move to the left
toward Brown's saw-mill on Little Pumpkin Vine, and
thence swing forward upon an extension of the Fourth Corps
line.   Cheery and undisturbed, as if the most ordinary business were going on, the General sat upon a log and sketched
upon a leaf of his pocket memorandum book a map of the
supposed situation, for the use of the officer leading the
column.   Its firm delicate lines, and neat touches, even to
the fine lettering of the names of houses and roads, showed
how completely his nerves were unaffected by the night of
battle and storm, and the map is still preserved as a precious
memento of the scene.   The corps moved northeast through
a wood so tangled with undergrowth that the direction of
column could only be kept by the compass ; then advancing
to the right, the position of Howard's corps (Fourth) was
reached, and forming on its left the two swung forward to
the right, reaching the open ground.   They crossed Little
Pumpkin Vine Creek at the saw-mill and continued the
wheeling movement until the extreme left crossed and covered the Dallas and Alatoona road.   The whole front of the
two corps was along the crest of a series of hills, a narrow
open valley intervening between this wing and the right of
the Confederate lines.   The movement was made with con-

tinuous hot skirmishing, and the hostile lines were at nightfall intrenched so close to each other that for several days a
bickering fire was almost incessant from the breastworks on
both sides, and skirmishers could only be relieved in the
darkness; indeed they could only be kept out at all by making each man cover himself by means of a pit, or by help of
a log or a few fence-rails. Casualties were of frequent oc-
currence within the lines; and there were openings between
the knolls across which no mounted officer could ride without being a target for the enemy's sharpshooters, who were
constantly on the watch for an opportunity to pick off who-
ever came within range.

During the 26th a similar skirmishing fight ranged along
the whole line. McPherson pressed in close to Hardee's
works on the extreme right, and found that flank of the enemy somewhat refused, running a little east of south after
passing a salient angle immediately in front of Dallas.
Our superiority in numbers made it plain that the intrenchments could be held with less than the whole force, and a
part of it could be withdrawn for a flanking movement.
Sherman was determined in his plan by the fact that at the
close of the day, and at the extreme left, the Army of the
Ohio already covered the direct road to Alatoona; and he
had only to extend by that flank to reöpen communications
with the railroad south of the Etowah. He therefore directed
General Thomas to withdraw Wood's division of Howard's
(Fourth) corps from the line, supplying its place by the
greater extension of the other divisions, and that it, supported by Johnson's division of Palmer's (Fourteenth) corps
(which was already in reserve) and by McLean's brigade
from the Army of the Ohio, should make a vigorous effort
to turn the right flank of the enemy. McCook's cavalry had
been operating in that direction during the day, and had a

lively combat with part of Wheeler's horse, in which Mc-
Cook had been the victor, inflicting considerable loss and
capturing some fifty prisoners. This affair and the statements of prisoners seemed to indicate that only Wheeler's
cavalry were holding the enemy's flank beyond the left of
the Army of Ohio.

During the forenoon of the 27th, Wood's division was
drawn out and formed in a column six lines deep, in rear of
Schofield's extreme left. Passing northward on the Alatoona road beyond our lines it faced eastward and advanced. Its skirmishers, however, soon developed a line of
strong intrenchments reaching beyond its front, and as the
orders to the division were to avoid a direct assault on
fortified lines, it was withdrawn from the sight of the enemy. Wood now moved about a mile still farther to the
left, his supports doing the same, and he again formed,
Hazen's brigade being in front and facing nearly south.
This time the reconnoissance by Generals Howard and Wood
seemed to show that they overlapped the Confederate line,
and Howard determined to attack. Johnson's division was
in echelon on Wood's left, Scribner's brigade in front, and
was to advance also, keeping its relative position. McLean's
brigade, the support on the right, was ordered to show itself
in an open place in full view of the enemy's works, to attract their attention and draw their fire. When the preparations were complete, and the troops had rested a few
minutes, the order to advance to the attack was given.
Hazen led boldly forward, and the enemy's skirmishers
were quickly driven within the works, which he promptly
assaulted. His left seemed still to outflank the position,
and it pushed forward confident of success. The movement
of Johnson's division still farther to the left brought it near
to Pickett's Mill on a tributary of Pumpkin Vine Creek, and

the leading brigade (Scribner's) receiving a fire in flank
from across the stream, halted and faced in that direction to
protect itself. This left that flank of Wood unsupported,
and he too was met with a withering fire from that direction. Through some mistake McLean's movement on the
right did not result as expected, and Wood's column was
assailed with a furious cross-fire of artillery and musketry
in front and on both flanks. Wood was forced to retire,
which he did deliberately, and halted upon a ridge a little
in rear and on the right ; Johnson connected with him, continuing the line, with the left curving backward and making a strong refused flank in the direction of the mill and
the creek.

Whilst this movement was in progress a strong demonstration was making by Newton's and Stanley's divisions of
Howard's corps, to keep the enemy occupied in their front,
though no serious attack was made. Cox, temporarily commanding the Twenty-third Corps, swung his left forward
as Wood advanced. Hascall's division, which had been
refused, now straightening out, and the whole advanced,
pivoting upon the right of the corps, into a new position
continuous with the advanced ground which Howard had
gained, but with a considerable gap between. McLean had
left Howard's command when the attack had been abandoned, regarding his connection with it as limited to the
day, and his men being without rations. Howard, with
some reason, complained of this, and McLean's brigade was
placed by the Commandant of the Twenty-third Corps in
rear of the gap in the line, with orders to support either
command in case of need, and the whole front was covered
by a strong connected chain of skirmishers and pickets.

The affair was a costly one, for Howard reported a total
loss of about fifteen hundred. The ground gained was

nevertheless very valuable, for it enabled the whole left
wing to swing forward so far as to cover and conceal the
extension of Sherman's line toward the Ackworth road, and
protected the Alatoona road upon which his cavalry were
operating.   Howard supposed that he had brought off all
his wounded, but Johnston claims that seventy fell into his
hands, being concealed in a little hollow close to the enemy's
line, and covered by the fire of his troops, and that a hundred and forty prisoners were taken at the same place.
This very closely agrees with General Wood's list of missing.

The Confederate accounts of the affair show that what
Howard and Wood supposed to be the extremity of the
enemy's line was only an angle of his works, which there
made a sharply refused flank.   Cleburne's division had been
sent from Hardee's corps to reinforce Johnston's extreme
right, and on the approach of Wood's division, Cleburne
moved out in rear, taking position where Wood, to reach
him, must expose his right flank to the fire of Hindman's
division of Hood's corps, which held the re-entrant at the
angle referred to, where was also a battery of artillery.
Granberry's brigade of Texans checked Hazen in front,
whilst Wheeler's dismounted cavalry made the flank attack
upon Johnson's division at Pickett's Mill.   This gave time
to move other troops of Hood's around Cleburne to attack
Wood on his left flank also.[1]   Had Johnson noticed that he
was first attacked in flank by cavalry only, and pushed
Scribner's brigade straight on in support of Hazen, whilst
he took care of the horsemen with another brigade of his
division, the determined attack of the Fourth Corps men

---

[1] General J. E. Johnston in his Narrative says that Polk had been transferred
to his right, and that Polk's, and not Hood's troops supported Cleburne.   On this
point, however, Hood's circumstantial statement seems the more accurate one,
and is supported by other probable evidence.

would probably have been successful. The ground, however, was a dense wood broken into ravines, where nothing could be seen, and where the embarrassments were scarcely less than in a night attack. Under the circumstances the wonder is, not that the attack failed, it is rather that Howard was able to withdraw in order, carrying off his wounded; and that he did so proves the magnificent steadiness and courage of his officers and men.

The attack of Hooker at New Hope Church, and this of Howard at Pickett's Mill were both made in column of brigades or demi-brigades. The result in both cases demonstrated that in a difficult and wooded country, and especially against intrenched lines, the column had little, if any advantage over a single line of equal front. It could not charge with the *ensemble* which could give it momentum, and its depth was therefore a disadvantage, since it exposed masses of men to fire who were wholly unable to fire in return. Since the office of breastworks is to give the defence an advantage by holding the assailant under fire from which the defenders are covered, the relative strength of the two is so changed that it is within bounds to say that such works as were constantly built by the contending forces in Georgia made one man in the trench fully equal to three or four in the assault. Each party learned to act upon this, and in all the later operations of the campaign the commanders held their troops responsible for making it practically good. The boasts, on either side, that a brigade or division repulsed three or four that attacked it, must always be read with this understanding. The troops in the works would be proven to be inferior to their assailants if they did not repulse a force several times greater than their own.

From this time till Hood succeeded Johnston in command

of the Confederate forces, troops were almost never massed
for an assault on either side. The attack near Kenesaw on
June 27th is perhaps the only exception. The usual formation was in two lines, the second only half as strong as the
first and kept under cover from fire till the front line needed instant help. Coming up then with a rush, it would
sometimes give the advance a new impulse which would
carry it over obstacles that it could not otherwise have sur-
mounted. On the other hand, an attack in column was
quickly seen to have only a narrow front, and the right and
left of the defensive line was stripped of troops to strengthen
the point of danger, or to attack in flank the advancing
column. So far was this practice carried that a line of
earthworks was often held by a skirmish line alone, with
such reserve of troops near at hand as could quickly move to
and fill the trench at a menaced point.

The character of the intrenchments changed by the natural increase of experience and the education which it gave.
It did not take long to learn the advantage which cover
gave, when rifled arms had more than doubled the range of
effective fire. In the open, a covered line could be sure of
crippling an attacking force whilst it was passing over eight
hundred or a thousand yards, so that its power to harm
would be gone before it reached the ditch. In the woods,
an abattis or entanglement in front of the breastwork produced the same effect by delaying and holding the enemy
so long under fire that he was no longer formidable when
the obstruction was passed.

From the combat at New Hope Church onward, it may be
said that every advanced line on both sides intrenched itself
as soon as a position was assumed. On our side the practical method was this. A division having been moved to a
place it was expected to hold, the general in command, by a

rapid reconnoissance of the topography, determined the
most available line for defence, and directed brigade commanders to form their troops upon it, following the outline
of the ground and making such angles, salient or re-entrant,
as it required. The skirmish line was kept in front, the
rest stacked arms a few paces in rear of the intended place
for the breastwork, intrenching tools were taken from
wagons that accompanied the ammunition train, or were
carried by the troops in the movement, and each company
was ordered to cover its own front. Trees were felled and
trimmed, and the logs, often two feet thick, rolled into the
line. The timber revetment was usually four feet high, and
the earth thrown from the ditch in front varied in thickness
according to the exposure. When likely to be subjected to
artillery fire it was from ten to thirteen feet thick at base,
and three feet less on the upper line of the parapet. Skids
or poles, resting on the top of the revetment at right angles
to it, sustained a head-log, a horizontal loophole for firing
under it being about three inches wide. The skids, when
left in place, served to prevent the head-log from falling
upon the men in the line if it were knocked off by a cannon-
ball. The timber in front was then slashed so as to fall out-
ward, making an entanglement which was too heavy for removal, and which utterly broke the formation of any line
attempting to pass it. Indeed, it would be only painfully
and slowly that single men could clamber through it. As
the troops became familiar with the work, they were able to
cover themselves with an intrenchment of this kind within
an hour from the time they stacked arms.

Circumstances would, of course, vary the character of
these lines, and in special cases the engineers would plan
particular works. The usual custom, however, was that
stated, and the intelligence of the soldiers was such that

their eye for a position was often as quick and keen as
that of any of their officers. Foreign officers, visiting the
army, often expressed their amazement at seeing the troops
of the line doing instantly and without engineering assistance what was elsewhere done by a corps of sappers under
direction of the scientific staff.

The Confederate troops were differently situated and proceeded a little differently. Anticipating the necessity of retreating to a new line, Johnston directed his Chief Engineer,
Colonel Prestman, to prepare it beforehand. It was carefully surveyed and marked from near Powder Springs to
Lost Mountain, thence to Pine Mountain and Kenesaw;
making a curve facing the northwest, and six or seven miles
in rear of the lines at New Hope Church. Still another line
was afterward located in the same way along Nickajack Creek,
and yet others at the Chattahoochee, Peach Tree Creek,
and Atlanta. In the construction of these the Confederate
engineers used the Georgia militia and impressed negroes;
and in some respects they were even more elaborate than
those built by the National army. At exposed places they
were covered by *chevaux-de-frise*, made of logs pierced with
sharpened spokes, and by sharpened palisades along the
ditch. This, however, was exceptional, and the general
character of the works was the same on both sides. No clear
understanding of this remarkable campaign can be had, unless the difficult character of the country and the formidable nature of these artificial defences are remembered. It
has seemed worth while to anticipate a little in order to give
an idea of their construction, and to save recurrence to the
subject.

The fighting of three days had fully developed Johnston's
line, and proven to Sherman that the three Confederate
corps were all in his front, with defensive works which it

was unwise to assault. He determined to transfer troops
from his right to his left, and by crowding in beyond Johnston's right flank, gain control of the Ackworth road. When
this should be done, Blair's (Seventeenth) corps of the Army
of the Tennessee could be moved from Rome, which it was
approaching, and be used to effect the occupation of Alatoona Pass and the rebuilding of the railway bridge over
the Etowah.

In the extension of the line to the left, divisions had been
used wherever they were at hand, without reference to corps
or army organizations. Howard's corps was on both sides
of Schofield, and Johnson's division of Palmer's was at the
extreme left, whilst Davis was with McPherson at the right,
several miles away. McPherson was therefore ordered to
relieve Davis, sending him back to Thomas, and to take
ground farther to the left, relieving part of Hooker's corps,
which in its turn could take the place of Schofield's (Twenty-
third), and this, passing beyond the Army of the Cumberland, would become the extreme left flank again. Supply
trains were ordered to be concentrated at Burnt Hickory, so
that Baird's division of the Fourteenth Corps, which was
there, could protect them all, and Hovey's division of the
Twenty-third could be brought to the front.

It happened that as McPherson was preparing to execute
his part of this plan, on the afternoon of the 28th, Johnston,
suspecting that our right was withdrawing, had directed
Hardee to make a forced reconnoissance of the lines in his
front and ascertain if they were still strongly held. Hardee
ordered Bate's division out for this purpose, and the latter
formed his three brigades in separate columns. Bate ordered
his brigade commanders to await a given signal, which was
to be given, it seems, by Armstrong, whose brigade of cavalry, dismounted, tried to penetrate between the National

cavalry and the right flank of Logan's corps. On hearing the signal they were to advance rapidly against the lines before them. Armstrong was received with a cannonade and fire of musketry so spirited that each of the brigade commanders supposed that all of the troops but his own were engaged, and ordered the assault of the works. The error cost them dear.

Logan's corps was formed with Harrow's division on his right, that of Morgan L. Smith in the centre, and Osterhaus on the left. The road from Dallas to Marietta ran out through the centre of the corps, and the Villa Rica road on the right. The latter ran up a ridge curving toward the south, and continued to ascend for a considerable distance after passing beyond Logan's line. McPherson had not thought it practicable to extend his flank far enough to include the highest crest of the ridge, and Bate's left brigade charged along the line of the road, coming down hill upon Walcutt's brigade which held that part of Harrow's line. Three guns of the First Iowa battery had been run out near the skirmish line, and their supports being driven back, the guns were temporarily in the enemy's hands, though they were unable to carry them off. The assault was made in column of regiments, and was only checked close to Walcutt's breastworks, by the withering front and flank fire of the division. The combat raged for half an hour, when the enemy retreated, having suffered terrible loss. Similar attacks upon Smith's and Osterhaus's divisions followed within a few minutes, but they also were repulsed. The enemy, however, charged up to Smith's breastworks with the most determined courage, and though suffering terribly, was not driven back till he had inflicted considerable loss upon us, some of our bravest and best officers being among the killed and wounded. Logan reports that he buried over 300 of the

enemy in his front and took 97 prisoners. He estimated the
whole of Hardee's loss at 2,000, which would not be exces-
sive if the usual proportion between killed and wounded was
maintained. The losses of a Kentucky brigade, one of the
assaulting columns, were so great that the memory of the
engagement, as one almost destructive to it, was treated as
a cause of special sorrow by the Confederate officers and
soldiers long after the war. The reports to Johnston, however, do not seem to have been full, for he speaks of Bate's
loss as "some three hundred, killed and wounded."

To cover the withdrawal of Bate's division, Hardee sent
forward other troops, and McPherson reported the engagement as an active one along the whole extent of the Fifteenth and Sixteenth Corps. Logan's loss aggregated 379
killed, wounded, and missing; those of the Sixteenth
Corps were not separately enumerated in the reports. In
the evening, after the affair was over, McPherson wrote to
Sherman that he regarded it impracticable to move that
night in pursuance of the previous plan, unless imperative
necessity demanded it, and by the direction of the General-
in-Chief the movement was delayed for a few days. In the
interim the time was improved by the Army of the Tennessee in preparing interior lines by means of which they
were able to withdraw without difficulty when the order was
finally given.

Davis's division was also unable to withdraw on the 28th,
though he had, after sharp skirmishing, put Mitchell's brigade in a strong position half way between himself and
Hooker, where he was very useful in covering the subsequent transfer of troops from the right flank. The Confederate attack from Hardee's corps was accompanied by strong
demonstrations all along the line, made by well-supported
skirmish lines, though there was no other serious attack.

The same night Hood's corps was moved out from its place
in line, and passed to the rear beyond Johnston's right flank
with the purpose of attacking Sherman's extreme left. His
place was filled by Polk and Hardee, the whole Confederate
army thus taking ground to their right to meet the parallel
movement of Sherman. Hood had supposed that Thomas's
left was over the creek at Pickett's Mill, but, learning that
it was not, he did not pursue his march, and was recalled. The hostile lines were so closely applied to each
other that this night movement was discovered, and all were
on the alert. The night following (May 29th) another effort
was made against McPherson, and the alarm ran down the
whole line. Nearly all of Johnston's batteries opened from
right to left, and skirmish lines were pushed up close to
Sherman's works. The night was dark, and along the centre,
where the valley was open, the flashing artillery from the
hill-tops and the flying and bursting shells made a magnificent spectacle, but it ended in display. It drew fire enough
from McPherson to prove that he was still there, and this
was probably all that the enemy intended by it. Along the
rest of the line the batteries responded and the troops were
on the alert, but in an hour or two the noise subsided, except that a desultory picket-fire was kept up till morning.

In the midst of these incessant alarms the positions of the
corps were rectified, and those minor changes made which
were necessary preparations for extending the National lines
eastward ; but the month closed upon a situation substantially the same. Sherman was sure of being able to transfer
his forces systematically from one flank to the other, he was
ready to seize Alatoona Pass with his cavalry, and a new
base upon the railroad was practically secure. It had been
a hard month's work. Every day had brought its combat,
and, in the latter part of it, the army had lived day and

night under fire. The gains had been solid, however, and the country felt that the campaign was, so far, a success. The losses had been 9,000 in all forms, of which less than two thousand were killed, and a large part of the wounded soon returned to the ranks.

Johnston gives the number of his killed during the month of May as 720, and his wounded as 4,670, but this is in his infantry alone. Add to this the prisoners captured by the National forces, which ought to appear in his report as "missing," and which Sherman states at 3,250, together with his cavalry losses, Wheeler's 420, and Jackson's at least as many, and his total loss amounts to 9,480. Hood and Jefferson Davis make a larger estimate, but the figures given show that his losses were numerically greater than those of the National forces, and, of course, much larger in proportion to the size of his army.

CHAPTER IX.

On the 1st of June, Stoneman occupied Alatoona with his cavalry, and, taking a strong position in the pass, was able to cover the repair of the railway from Kingston to the Etowah, which was immediately begun. The next day Sherman resumed in earnest his flanking movement to the left. McPherson's Army of the Tennessee relieved Hooker's corps, and with Davis's division occupied the whole line which Hooker and Schofield had held. Schofield having all three of the divisions of the Twenty-third Corps united, moved to the vicinity of the Burnt Church, at the crossing of the Alatoona road with that leading from Burnt Hickory to Marietta. Here he formed the corps in line, Hovey's division on the right, Cox's in the centre, and Hascall's on the left. Hooker's corps meanwhile had come up and was in support of Schofield. The latter then advanced, guiding his left by the Marietta road. The movement was sharply contested by the Confederates, but Schofield pressed steadily forward till his centre division crossed Alatoona Creek close to the Dallas and Ackworth road. Here he came upon an intrenched position of the enemy covering the forks of the road. The men dashed through the creek in the midst of a furious thunderstorm, which made it difficult to distinguish between the discharges of the enemy's artillery at close quarters and the rattling thunder. The slope beyond was

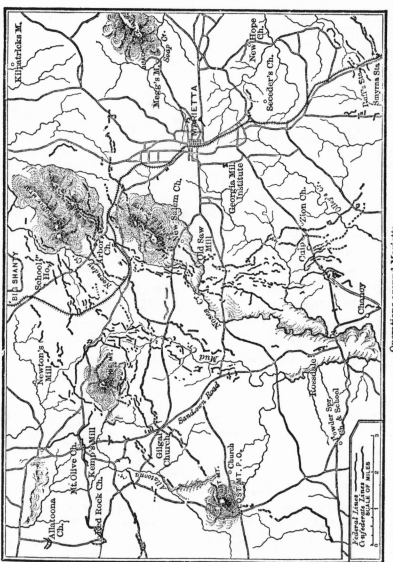

Operations around Marietta.

wooded, and the fortified line was found to be a hundred and fifty yards beyond the top of the bank. Cox's division was halted and ordered to intrench where it was, facing southeasterly. Hascall's, which had been left a little in rear by the swinging movement, advanced till it came into line, and intrenched also. The same was done by Hovey's division on the right. The movement had been followed by Hooker in support, and Butterfield's division was placed in echelon on Hascall's left.

So dense had been the wood through which the centre moved that skirmishers two hundred feet in advance of the line could not be seen, and the direction could only be kept by compass. Even then the skirmish line took ground to the left, and partly uncovered the front without being aware of it. The Division Commander, noticing that the dropping skirmish fire was ceasing, spurred forward to see if the skirmishers were in position. Crossing a little ravine he was met by the fire of the enemy's picket at pistol range, and Captain Saunders, the Division Adjutant-General, fell mortally wounded. To wheel, meet the line and deploy forward a fresh line of skirmishers was the work of a moment; but the incident proved how precarious and blind all movements in such a tangled wilderness must be, and what constant risk there was of accidents like that which befell McPherson later in the season.

The second line was halted on the north bank of the stream, but the storm changed the creek in half an hour into an unfordable torrent. The knowledge of this gave speed to the exertions of the first line to strengthen their breastworks, and they did so under a galling fire of both cannon and small arms. The density of the wood made this but random firing in the main, and the position was held through the night with comparatively little loss.

Whilst Schofield and Hooker were thus advancing on the
extreme left, Thomas threw forward Baird's division of
Palmer's corps beyond Pickett's Mill, and Johnson's (which
had bent back along the creek) was swung out to keep pace
with Baird, so that at the close of the day the whole line
had been extended to the left some three miles, and the divisions were intrenched securely upon it.

The Confederate trenches east of Pickett's Mill following
the commanding lines of the ground, ran nearly due east for
a mile and then almost directly north to the point which
Schofield had reached.   One line of this angle could be
enfiladed by the Army of the Cumberland, and the other by
the Army of the Ohio.   When therefore on the following
day (June 3d) Hooker extended Geary's and Butterfield's
divisions along the Ackworth road, McCook's cavalry being
still further east, Johnston became satisfied that he could no
longer hold the line of New Hope Church.   McCook's and
Stoneman's troopers reached Ackworth on the 3d, capturing
a few vedettes, and finding the town already abandoned.
The same day Schofield transferred Hovey's division to
his left, Hooker's command being still farther out on that
flank, and the enemy abandoned the works in the immediate front of the Twenty-third Corps, falling back into intrenchments which were the continuation of that above
Pickett's Mill, and facing due north.

This was only preparatory to abandoning the whole line
in front of New Hope Church, which was done in the night
of the 4th, and Johnston retreated to the new positions
which his engineers had selected between Lost Mountain
and Brush Mountain, two or three miles north of Kenesaw.
On this line, Pine Mountain, a high, isolated hill, formed a
salient near the centre, but as it was somewhat exposed on
the west, an advanced line was occupied southwest of it,

crossing the Burnt Hickory and Marietta road a mile or more north of Gilgal Church. This road crosses, at the church, the so-called Sandtown road, which from this point continues in a southerly direction to the Chattahoochee, reaching the town from which it is named, and thence going on toward Atlanta.

As soon as it was known that Johnston had been manœuvred out of his position, Sherman at once took steps to reach the railroad at Ackworth. Schofield was ordered to stand fast, whilst the Army of the Cumberland followed Hooker, and the Army of the Tennessee moved somewhat in rear of both, until the positions of June 2d were reversed, Schofield becoming the right of the whole army as he had before been its left.

On the evening of the 7th McPherson had reached the railroad in front of Ackworth, Thomas was south of him with his right on the Sandtown road; and Schofield remained in his former position, covering the transfer of the hospitals and trains to the railroad. The weather was showery and the roads were becoming very bad. This made the change of base all the more opportune, for the way from Kingston was long and the mud deep. By driving beef cattle " on the hoof" there had been no lack of rations, except of bread, of which the allowance was short in some of the camps.

Another step in the campaign was thus successfully taken, and the army buckled to its work again with unbounded faith in its commander and in itself. Sherman ordered Blair to hasten forward from Kingston with the Seventeenth Corps, saying he wanted "to go to Marietta on Wednesday or Thursday." Several Wednesdays were destined to pass before Johnston's skilful and obstinate defence should be overcome, but every man in the National army felt that it was only a question of time. The certainty of

ultimate success was undoubted.   From the 5th to the 9th
of June the several corps were ploughing through the mud
toward the railroad, taking and rectifying their positions in
line.   Schofield kept one of his divisions (Cox's) near the
crossing of the Dallas and Burnt Hickory roads to cover the
movement of the hospitals and trains, and new field depôts
were established for the several commands as follows : Mc-
Pherson's at Big Shanty Station on the railroad, Thomas's at
Ackworth, and Schofield's at Alatoona.   Pontoons were laid
at the Alatoona crossing of the Etowah, and Colonel Wright
promised to have the railway bridge rebuilt by the 12th.
Blair reached Ackworth with his Seventeenth Corps on the
8th, leaving a brigade as a garrison at Alatoona.   He
brought about nine thousand men in his two divisions, and
the reinforcement was almost exactly equal to Sherman's
losses up to that time.

When Johnston evacuated his lines before New Hope
Church, the first impression in the army was that his next
line would be the Chattahoochee River, and Sherman shared
this belief.   Reconnoitring parties soon brought information that the enemy held Pine Mountain and a chain of
hills eastward, and made it plain that another prolonged
contest must be had around the commanding spurs of the
mountains that covered Marietta on the north and west.
Alatoona Pass was fortified under the direction of Captain
Poe, Chief Engineer, and remained an important post during
the rest of the campaign.   Garrard's division of cavalry was
ordered to report to McPherson, and to cover the operations
of the Army of the Tennessee on the left flank ; Stoneman's
was already attached to the Army of the Ohio and covered
the extreme right; and McCook's, of the Army of the Cumberland picketed the rear, protecting the crossing of the
Etowah and covering the fords of that river.

On Thursday, June 10th, in accordance with orders issued the evening before, the whole army moved forward, feeling for the enemy. McPherson, putting Blair's corps on his left, marched down the Ackworth and Marietta road through the village and station of Big Shanty, and found the Confederates occupying Brush Mountain in force. In the deep valley in front of these heights runs Noonday Creek, first eastwardly and then north into the Etowah. A branch of the same stream is found behind Brush Mountain, separating it from the three peaked ridges of Kenesaw and a line of hills east of it. Logan's and Dodge's corps of the Army of the Tennessee were on the right of McPherson, but the troops of this wing were kept a good deal massed, so that they might rapidly extend farther to the left if circumstances should make it of advantage to do so.

Thomas divided the Army of the Cumberland into three columns, Palmer's corps on his left, keeping connection with McPherson and following the road to Newton's Mills, Howard's in the centre, and Hooker's on the right, moving straight upon Pine Mountain. The country in which Thomas was, included the upper waters of Proctor's Creek, which takes its rise in the highlands between Kenesaw and Pine Mountain, and runs nearly midway between Noonday and Alatoona Creeks, all three seeking their outlets in the Etowah.

Schofield followed the general course of Alatoona Creek, marching from Mount Olivet Church, on the Marietta road toward Gilgal, known in the neighborhood as Hard Shell Church. His Twenty-third Corps was consolidated into two divisions, Hovey having become discontented and asking to be relieved. Hascall's division followed the road southward from Kemp's Mills, and Cox, on the extreme right of the army, marched from Alatoona Church by the

Sandtown road. On this flank the enemy was found in position just over Alatoona Creek, in a line of intrenchments facing northwest, about a mile in front of Gilgal Church. Stoneman's cavalry reconnoitred toward Lost Mountain, where lines' of intrenchments were also found, though they were not held by infantry.

Johnston seeing the movement of the National forces by their left flank, rightly interpreted its meaning, and concentrated his infantry between Gilgal and Brush Mountain. Hardee's left was at the church, Bate's division occupied Pine Mountain and constituted the right of that corps. Polk's corps extended from that point across the railway to the Ackworth and Marietta wagon road, where his right rested, Noonday Creek covering part of his front. Hood's corps was the Confederate right, and was massed behind Noonday Creek and along the base of Brush Mountain, awaiting events. Wheeler's cavalry covered the Confederate right, and Jackson's was on the left.

In front of the centre and left of the National army the country was rough, almost mountainous. On the right it was hilly, but less difficult. The Confederate lines toward the southwest followed the line of the watershed, heretofore described, and could only be approached by crossing the ravines, which were generally parallel to Johnston's front. The general trend of the mountains is continued in the lower ridges, and the watercourses furrowing their way between the hills find outlets to the north or the south, whilst the prevailing course of these valleys continues to be nearly northeast and southwest. The country to the east of Marietta was in some respects the most favorable for Sherman's approach, and his movements showed that he thought seriously of using it ; but the line of the railway from Kingston would have been a good deal exposed, for it ran parallel to the river for several miles, and had the National forces moved to the east of Marietta, Kingston and the Etowah with its numerous fords would have been nearer to Johnston than to Sherman. These considerations settled the question of strategy, and determined the National commander to operate by his right flank.

Continuous drenching rains and storms had lasted from the 4th of the month, and the roads were fast becoming impassable. Streams were up and the woods and fields so soaked with water that activity was impossible. Singularly, too, the winds were chilling, even cold, blowing from the east and bringing from the ocean an endless succession of pouring showers. The Northern troops were finding their summer in Georgia quite unlike their anticipation of the " sunny South," but waited patiently, strengthening their lines whilst the bickering skirmish fire went on. On the 11th, the Etowah bridge was completed, Colonel Wright having more than made good his promise, and the next day the whistle of the locomotive was heard at Big Shanty, notifying friend and foe that Sherman's supplies were now close in rear of his line.

On Tuesday, the 14th, there was a partial cessation of the rain, and Sherman directed strongly supported skirmish lines to be advanced, and the whole front to be moved as close to the enemy's works as possible, but without direct assault of fortifications unless some specially favorable opportunity should occur. Thomas pushed forward the right of Palmer's corps and the left of Howard's into the re-entrant angle between Pine Mountain and the Confederate works east of it, advancing until the forces on the mountain were in danger of being quite separated from the rest of the line. The right and left wings of the army drove back the outposts and pickets in their front, and made new

IX.—5

trenches for themselves close to the enemy. As the high
points held by the Confederates overlooked the camps of
our army, the artillery were ordered to open upon groups
which seemed to be reconnoitering. It happened that
Johnston with Hardee and Polk were upon Pine Mountain
during the movement of the 14th, and Lieutenant-General
Polk was killed by a cannon-ball from one of General
Thomas's batteries. The conference between the Confederate generals had been at Hardee's instance, as he thought
Bate's division in danger of being cut off, and the advance
of Thomas's troops only confirmed the opinion. During the
night the position was abandoned and Bate's division placed
in reserve. General Polk, a Tennesseean, had been Bishop
in the Protestant Episcopal Church before the war, but he
had received a military education in early life, and that
circumstance led him to tender his services as a soldier to
the Confederate Government. His influence was large and
his example influenced a multitude of followers in a State
where Union sentiments had prevailed down to the actual
beginning of hostilities. A cousin of a former President
of the United States, his position in Church and State made
him an important personage in the Confederacy. A higher
military rank was given him than his experience or abilities
as a soldier would alone have warranted, and it was rather
as a citizen than as a general that his loss was severely felt
in the South. Loring, his senior division commander,
succeeded temporarily to the corps, but General S. D. Lee
was soon after assigned to the permanent command.

On the morning of the 15th, Thomas moved his line forward beyond Pine Mountain. The advance guard of the
enemy held the trenches connecting their principal lines
with Pine Mountain and some other detached works which
had been made to cover these. Hooker's corps marched

against these works, and after a sharp engagement carried them. He then pushed Geary's division against the principal line, but found it too strong, and after a gallant effort Geary was forced to retire with a loss of several hundred men.

Meanwhile Schofield ordered Cox's division of the Twenty-third Corps to try the works in his front, supported by Hascall. A line of the enemy's skirmishers was driven from a hill beyond Alatoona Creek which proved an excellent position for artillery, a cross fire being obtained and directed upon the Confederate intrenchments, and under cover of this the division was able to carry the line with comparatively small loss, capturing a number of prisoners. On this flank Johnston's troops were now driven back into their principal defences at Gilgal Church.   Stoneman's cavalry was skirmishing and advancing toward Lost Mountain, to which the enemy still held fast.

Thomas's centre and left drove back Loring's corps from a similar line of outworks, making more than a mile of progress, and, connecting with McPherson, applied the National line so closely to that of the enemy that there was the same constant and irritating skirmish going on which had been so marked near New Hope Church.

Blair's freshly arrived corps formed the extreme left of McPherson, and simultaneous with the advance of the rest of the line on the 14th, the Army of the Tennessee moved forward. Force's brigade of Leggett's division was the flank of the movement, and Force, pushing forward the Thirtieth Illinois with a dashing charge, carried a spur of the hills before him, taking in reverse a long line of intrenched skirmishers of Hood's corps, and forcing the whole to fall back behind Noonday Creek.   On the 15th, a division of Logan's (Fifteenth) corps was passed to the left of

Blair, and the extreme flank of the Army of the Tennessee on that side was well lapped beyond the Confederate right.

In the advance of McPherson's left, which immediately followed the gaining of the hill by Force, his line ran over and captured the Fortieth Alabama regiment, 320 strong.[1]

Johnston's left had now become the weak part of his line, for his troops were not numerous enough to enable him to hold the trenches beyond Gilgal Church in any great force, though Hardee made that position very strong by recurving his line and making an interior retrenchment covering the first on the extreme flank. Jackson's cavalry had to be depended upon to hold Lost Mountain, and to guard the line between there and Gilgal, and Stoneman was keeping them busy. On the 16th, Schofield moved Hascall's division to his right, some distance clear of the rest of his line, and then sharply advancing the left brigade of that division, and swinging forward the right of Cox's at the same time, got possession of high ground, from which his artillery was able to enfilade a good deal of Hardee's line, taking part of it in reverse, and also to sweep the road from Gilgal to Marietta for a considerable distance.

With his usual prudence and foresight, Johnston had prepared for this contingency, by constructing in advance a new line of earth-works behind Mud Creek. These trenches left the old line near Hardee's right, and bending south from a high point on the watershed, followed the east bank of the creek far enough to cross the direct road from Marietta to New Hope Church by way of Lost Mountain. Hardee was drawn back into this line on the night of the 16th. His extreme left, by this wheel to the rear, was retired about three miles from its former position.

Thomas and Schofield were both on the alert, and early on the next morning the right wing of the National army

---

[1] In Sherman's despatches (Report of Committee on Conduct of the War) this regiment is said to be the 14th—probably an error in copying. The 14th Alabama

followed Hardee vigorously, brushing away Jackson's cavalry, which was hardly able to retard the advance noticeably, and only enlivened it by a skirmishing opposition, the noise of the batteries, as they moved southward from hill to hill, telling plainly of the advance of Sherman's right along the Sandtown road. Near Derby's house the road to Marietta was reached, and Schofield ordered his advanced division (Cox's) to take it and try to find the enemy's flank. The valley of Mud Creek was soon reached. The stream flows nearly due south in a deep valley which here widens out, a bend of the creek washing an almost precipitous cliff, on which Hardee had posted his extreme left with batteries of artillery in position. This fortress covered a mile or more of the open bottom land through which the road ran; but between the two hilly banks the erosion of the stream had left a bare rounded hill nearly as high as the others. Schofield's men advanced rapidly across the open ground to the protection of this *mamelon*, where the division was deployed in two lines, and made to lie down in close support of Cockerill's battery of Ohio artillery, which unlimbered just below the crest that made for them an admirable parapet, over which nothing but the muzzles of the guns were visible from the front. Soon after a battery from the Twentieth Corps came to the same position, but, not taking the precaution to use the cover of the crest of the hill, suffered so much from the enemy's fire that it was forced to withdraw. Cockerill maintained the artillery duel in a most brilliant manner for an hour, when he silenced the guns opposed to him, and the deployment of the infantry went on. Hooker's corps occupied the whole front of Hardee's left, and Schofield advancing Hascall's division in close support of the other, gained the crest between Mud Creek and Noses Creek. Hardee drew back his left flank, making a sharp

was in Lee's Army of Northern Virginia. McPherson's prisoners, mostly taken by Walcutt's brigade of Harrow's division, were of the 31st and 40th Alabama.

crotchet in his line, the angle being at the fortified point
above described, and hung on to his position during the
next day.

In front of Palmer's and Howard's corps of the Army of
the Cumberland, the union of Hardee's new line with the
old intrenchments was found to make a salient angle, and
hills in front were so situated that Thomas's batteries might
succeed in getting an enfilading fire upon the faces of it.
Johnston, therefore, regarded it untenable, and Colonel
Prestman, his engineer, was already at work on the 17th,
tracing a new contour for fortifications destined to be the
last of the lines around Marietta, though not the last north
of the Chattahoochee. He was not allowed the opportunity
to retire at leisure, however, for on the 18th, early in the
morning, upon indications that the enemy was preparing to
withdraw, Howard threw forward Wood's and Newton's divisions, whose strongly supported line of skirmishers were
able by a rush to carry the line in their front, capturing
about fifty prisoners. Several counter-charges were made in
the hope of regaining the line, but they were repulsed.
During the day and night batteries were worked into the
commanding positions above referred to. As soon as the
skirmishers of the two divisions had gained the enemy's
works in the morning, Harker, of Newton's division, without
waiting for orders, deployed two regiments to hold and secure the ground that was gained, and Howard, seeing the
advantage, ordered up the whole of Newton's division in
their support. The line thus carried was the trench at and
near the junction of the old works with the new, and which
was held by the enemy as an advanced line before their
principal intrenchments, in a position they could not afford
to abandon on account of its relation to the salient already
described. During the night, Newton's men made the posi-

tion strong, and before morning were firmly placed within about a hundred yards of the main line in their front.

These advantages were decisive, and Johnston lost no time in getting his forces into the trenches which his engineer had marked out still closer to Marietta. They moved to the rear during the night, leaving, as usual, a strong skirmish line with supports to hold the old works and delay the advance of the National army. The key of the new Confederate line was Kenesaw Mountain, which is the summit of the watershed, and whose wood-covered sides, breaking down into deep ravines, made an impregnable military position, whilst its summit, overlooking the country in all directions, made concealment of movements on Sherman's part next to impossible. The railway coming from the north turns back to the northeast between Kenesaw and Brush Mountain, till passing beyond the flank of the former it again curves to the south, a couple of miles north of Marietta. The mountain was occupied by Loring's (formerly Polk's) corps, French's division holding its southwestern slope and part of the crest, Walthall's continuing the line along the ridge, and Loring's own (commanded by Featherston) reaching down the northeastern slope to the railroad. Hood's corps held the high upland east of the railway, looking down into the branches of Noonday Creek, which skirted the eastern part of Brush Mountain, and facing the ridge of that hill. Hood's troops were not deployed as much as Loring's, though their right reached far enough eastward to cover the Marietta and Canton wagon road. The divisions were massed, ready to be used promptly as a moving column if necessary. Hardee's corps was the left of the Confederate army, and his divisions from left to right were Cheatham's, Cleburne's, Bate's, and Walker's, the latter connecting with Loring at the base of Kenesaw.

From the mountain southward his front was covered by Noses Creek, now swollen to the dimensions of a river by the incessant rains. The road from Marietta to Lost Mountain ran through the intrenchments near Hardee's right, and his left rested on high ground above a branch of Noses Creek, which rises in the town. A glance at the map will show that in these retreating movements the contour of the country made it necessary for Johnston to retire his left more than his right, Hardee having swung backward six or eight miles, whilst Hood had not needed to move more than two. The curve of defensive lines about Marietta had now become nearly a semicircle facing the west, but considerably nearer the town on the north. In front of the principal line was even more than the usual number of lunettes and advanced works on spurs and commanding hills, and a marvellous industry had been used in covering the whole with abattis and entanglements of slashed forest trees.

As soon as the movement of Johnston was known, early on the 19th, the centre and wings of the National army were all in motion likewise. The pouring rain had not ceased since the beginning of the month, and the whole country was a quagmire. Streams that were ordinarily dry at this season of the year were now formidable obstructions. The "lagunes" in the hollows were dangerous quicksands in which artillery and horses were in peril of being utterly engulfed. The supply trains for Thomas's right and for Schofield toiled painfully along wherever solid ground could be found, leaving the impassable roads for new tracks, which a few trains made in their turn impassable, until the whole country between Alatoona and the centre and right of the army was a wilderness of mire in which the original roads could not be traced.

The 19th of June was occupied in a skirmishing advance,

driving the enemy's rear guard from the old trenches and feeling the way forward to new positions. The next day Blair's corps was advanced strongly on McPherson's left, Leggett's division being on the extreme flank. Force's brigade was directed to occupy a hill somewhat east of the direct line of advance, and marching rapidly forward, after a brisk skirmishing fight carried the crest, and found that they were overlooking a combat between Garrard's cavalry and Wheeler's, which was one of the most fiercely contested of the campaign. General Leggett being informed of this, succeeded in getting a battery up the hill, and opening with spherical case shot on the Confederate horsemen, was able to give Garrard timely assistance. But Leggett's divergent movement had carried him so far to the left and front that the other wing of the corps took him to be the enemy, and opened with artillery upon him, till a messenger going at speed explained the mistake, and the firing was stopped before serious mischief was done. Logan's and Dodge's corps (Fifteenth and Sixteenth) moved forward, keeping pace with Blair's, developing the enemy's new position on Kenesaw, and advancing close to them under a hot fire. In the Army of the Cumberland Palmer's corps was on the left and moved up close to the base of the southern spurs of the mountain. Howard was on the west bank of Noses Creek, his centre on the road from Gilgal Church to Marietta. In front of Hooker's corps the creek made a considerable bend to the west, where the road from Lost Mountain to Marietta crosses it, and the principal Confederate lines being farther from the stream, Geary's division had been able to cross, using a bridge which the swollen stream was constantly threatening to carry away. Butterfield's and Williams's followed, and the whole of the corps took positions, massed by brigades with the front covered by skirmishers.

On the 20th, Howard sent Wood's division and a brigade of Stanley's to relieve the left of Hooker's corps (Williams's division), which in its turn was moved to the right. Stanley got his other brigades over the creek, and in the afternoon occupied two hills in his front. The hill on the right was a bald knob and was occupied by Kirby's brigade, but not in force. The other was wooded and was quickly intrenched by Whittaker's brigade, and held despite the vigorous efforts of the enemy to retake it. Kirby was not so fortunate, and his skirmishers and pioneers were driven off. During the 21st, part of the Army of the Cumberland was relieved by McPherson, and the process of taking ground to the right continued. Palmer's corps relieved the left of Howard's, and Newton's division of the latter moved to the right and relieved part of Hooker's, which was extended still farther toward that flank.

Howard determined to take again and to hold the bald hill in front of Stanley's right. The left brigade of Wood (Nodine's) was ordered to co-operate with Kirby, and a concentrated artillery fire was directed upon the hill for half an hour. The advance by the two brigades was then made, the enemy was driven off with a loss of some prisoners, and the knob was intrenched under a hot fire from the Confederate batteries in front. Wood was enabled at the same time to march two regiments against another height still farther to the right and front, which he occupied, thereby forcing the abandoning of a long intrenched skirmish line and enabling the whole of the right of Howard's corps to move forward across an open field several hundred yards. Hooker's corps advanced at the same time, occupying important positions on hills upon Culp's farm, and connecting with Howard on his left.

Schofield had marched on the 19th along the Sandtown

road some three miles, meeting with no serious opposition
till his head of column reached the crossing of Noses
Creek. Here the planking of the bridge was found to be
removed, the stream was up so that the water was over
the bottom land skirting it, and the enemy's cavalry with
artillery disputed the passage. The two principal branches
of the creek unite before crossing the road the Twenty-
third Corps was now marching on, and the road from Powder Springs Church to Marietta crosses it on a ridge just
beyond the creek. As the position was about two miles
from the flank of the Army of the Cumberland, Schofield, in
accordance with instructions from General Sherman, made
no serious effort to cross the stream, but kept the enemy
amused whilst Stoneman was operating with his cavalry
toward Powder Springs. The village of Powder Springs
is three or four miles south of the church of the same name,
and the road from Marietta to this village forks near the
Culp farm, the northern branch being that which has already been mentioned as crossing the Sandtown road just
south of Noses Creek, and the other fork crossing the same
road a mile and a half farther south at Cheney's farm. On
the 20th, the enemy still showed a bold front to Schofield's
advanced division (Cox's), and Cameron's brigade was ordered to make a serious effort to cross. The creek being
unfordable, and the dismantled bridge covered by artillery
fire, the task was a little difficult, but the bushes bordering the stream were filled with sharpshooters, a battery was
advanced to a knoll close to the creek, and under protection
of the fire of both cannon and small arms, Colonel Casement
of the One Hundred and Third Ohio succeeded in getting
a small party across, running over on the timbers and
string-pieces of the bridge. The party being deployed and
advancing under cover of the bank were able to drive back

the enemy's skirmishers from the bridge head, and the Confederate artillery, being overmatched, drew back also.
The remainder of the brigade was quickly put over, the
bridge repaired, and the crest beyond was intrenched.
The 21st, the whole of Cox's division, was over the creek,
Hascall's division was moved up in close support, sending pickets to the left between the forks of Noses Creek,
where they connected with the right of Hooker's corps.
The Confederate cavalry under Jackson showed an aggressive disposition in the direction of Powder Springs, and
on word from Colonel Adams, who commanded Stoneman's
detachment on that road, that he was hard pressed, a
regiment of infantry and a section of artillery was sent from
Cox's division to his support. With this help Stoneman
drove back his assailants, but the enemy's activity indicated
a nearer support of his infantry.

Johnston had begun to be concerned for the Marietta and
Powder Springs road, for Hooker's right was close to it, and
Schofield's movements were threatening to put him astride
of it. Hardee had stretched his lines quite as far as was
safe, and the Confederate commander determined to move
the whole of Hood's corps from the right to the left flank.
Ordering Wheeler to show a bold front and make as strong
a fight with his dismounted cavalry as he could, Johnston
left these, with such help as could be got by stretching
Loring's corps to the right, to fill the trenches out of which
Hood was drawn. The movement was made in the night of
the 21st, and by the next morning Hood was upon the Powder Springs road, near Zion church, about a mile east of
Culp's farm. With his characteristic aggressiveness he sig-
nalized his appearance in front of our right wing by a fierce
attack, which was made with his whole corps, Hindman's
and Stevenson's divisions in front, supported by Stewart.

This attack was not made, however, till the middle of the afternoon, and meanwhile important changes had occurred on the extreme right.

During the morning Schofield ordered Cox's division to march southward on the Sandtown road, toward its crossing of the road from Marietta to Powder Springs village, at Cheney's house. Hascall's division had directions to follow across Noses Creek, turn to the left on the road from Powder Springs Church to Marietta, and go into position on Hooker's right, near Culp's. Hascall was in his appointed place about noon, and Cox had reached the forks of the road at Cheney's, which he found to be in rear of commanding ground overlooking the crossing of Olley's Creek, the next of the nearly parallel streams flowing southwest from the plateau at Marietta. Reilly's brigade was moved forward to the heights bordering this valley, and the other three brigades of the division (which was a large one) were arranged to cover well both flanks and rear, as the position was isolated.

Hooker's corps front consisted of Geary's division on the left and Williams's on the right. Butterfield's was in line with Howard's corps further to the left. At Geary's right was an eminence facing open fields, partly in front of Williams, and this right was strongly intrenched and held by well-supported artillery. It had been occupied only a little before, for Hooker had swung his whole command forward at the same time that Schofield advanced on his flank, and the new positions had barely been assumed when the storm Hood was preparing burst upon them. Williams had advanced with his division massed by brigades, Robinson's on the left, Knipe's in the centre, and Ruger on the right, reaching to the Marietta road at Culp's, where connection was made with Hascall's division of the Army of the Ohio.

Ravines with small marshy brooks ran down between Geary and Williams into Noses Creek behind them, and there were similar depressions between Williams's brigades. The Marietta road was on the ridge, and Hascall's division was over it to the south, his right facing the valley of Olley's Creek and covering the road from Culp's to Cheney's, where Cox's division was, though with a gap of nearly two miles between.

In the sharp skirmishing which had accompanied these movements, some prisoners had been taken, and these were found to belong to Hood's corps, and reported both Hood and Hardee prepared to attack. Hooker immediately ordered Williams to deploy the whole division and throw up breastworks at once. Schofield gave the same orders to Hascall. The deployment was just completed, and a beginning made in throwing up breastworks, when Hood advanced with his usual impetuosity. The conformation of the ground gave Williams a convex front, his centre brigade being in advance of the others. The same circumstance made Hood's advance somewhat divergent, his right division (Hindman's) striking the centre of Williams and the right of Geary, whilst his left (Stevenson's) attacked Hascall's division of Twenty-third Corps, on the south side of the Marietta road. Knipe's brigade maintained its ground, but the enemy gained some advantage in the hollow between Williams and Geary; but this only brought him into open ground. From the hill on Geary's right the Thirteenth New York Artillery opened a rapid fire on the charging lines. Winegar's battery of three-inch rifles, and Woodbury's of light twelves joined in the cannonade from Williams's left and front, and the converging fire of canister and case shot played havoc with the exposed enemy. Williams's and Geary's lines were reformed, and after the exchange of a few volleys of musketry, the repulse of the Confederates was complete and they retreated to their intrenchments. When the attack was made, Hooker called upon Howard for Butterfield's division. It was so placed in the trenches that it could not be instantly relieved; but Howard sent reinforcements of such regiments as were in reserve, and relieved Butterfield and sent him to Hooker early in the night. As Williams's division connected with Hascall's of the Twenty-third Corps, Butterfield was put in reserve.

The ground along the Marietta road was thickly wooded, and Hood's left, passing quite by Ruger's brigade, came in contact with Hascall's division.

Hascall had gone into position on the right of Hooker, and upon the continuation of the ridge held by him, and was, as we have seen, covering both the road upon which he had marched and one which, branching from it, ran directly to Cox's position at Cheney's. The two divisions of the Twenty-third Corps therefore occupied two angles of a triangle formed by the diverging roads upon which they had travelled and that which connected them in the manner just stated. Hascall found, however, that a ridge just in front of him was a desirable position to hold, and would soon be needed for a new line when an advance should be made. He therefore ordered his skirmish line, supported by Colonel Gallup's Fourteenth Kentucky Regiment to advance and occupy it. His three brigades, Strickland's, McQuiston's, and Hobson's, began throwing up breastworks on the main line. Gallup captured some prisoners in his advance, and learned from them that Hood's corps had just come from the enemy's extreme right and was preparing to assault. He reported the fact to Hascall, with whom Schofield was in person. The news was immediately followed by the attack; but Gallup had succeeded already in making a slight barricade, and for

some time resisted obstinately the Confederate onset, which
was made by part of Stevenson's division. He had been
ordered to retire to the principal line when hard pressed,
but stimulated by the terrible effect of their own volleys
upon the advancing enemy, and not realizing that his flanks
would soon be turned, his men held on till peremptory
orders were given him to retire. He then came back in good
order, the enemy following, and nearly sixty Confederate
dead still lying on that part of the field the next day, attested the gallantry with which this little advanced guard
had done their duty. As soon as Gallup was within the
lines, Shields's and Paddock's batteries, which had been
placed in well-selected positions, opened with canister upon
the Confederate lines, and with the fire from the breastworks
soon cleared the front.

But Hood's attacks had been so determined and persistent
that, at half-past four, Schofield ordered Cox to leave but one
brigade in front of Cheney's, and with the rest of his division
move by the direct road from Cheney's to Culp's, to Hascall's
support. This was promptly done, but by the time the
march could be made, the brunt of the attack on that front
was over. The three brigades of that division were put in
the line, however, with the right refused, covering the open
ground in the valley of Olley's Creek, and extending pickets
and patrols to watch the interval of a mile still remaining
between them and the brigade of Reilly on the far right and
front.

Johnston admitted a loss of " about a thousand " in this
combat, which seems to have been made by Hood upon his
own responsibility. He evidently hoped that he could outflank the National army on that side, and by catching them
in motion by columns, could gain some decided advantage.
That he was disappointed does not detract from the good

generalship of the effort. He had moved by an interior line from the front of McPherson, Hardee had been able to extend his line as far as Hooker up to the day before, and on every theory of probabilities he had the right to calculate upon finding an inferior force in his immediate front on that flank. The extension of our own lines in the same direction, which has been detailed, upset his calculations. He found at every point an array of men every way equal to his own in courage and self-reliance, and handled with intelligent skill; and he withdrew his battered divisions, covering his defeat as well as he could by a report which tried to diminish the importance of the engagement.

Williams reported a loss of only 130 men, Geary's was trifling, and Hascall's about the same as Williams's. The affair throws instructive light also on the relations of attack and defence in such a country as that in which operations were going on. The weight of the attack on the north of the road fell upon Knipe's brigade, and there was hardly a score of casualties in the rest of the division. So on the south of the road, Hascall's left, which was the most advanced, had sustained a fierce and determined attack, and the rest of the division was able to inflict great loss by a flanking fire upon the enemy whilst suffering very little in return. It would be in strict accordance with the style of the Confederate reports of similar affairs to say that Hood's corps attacked two brigades and were defeated. The truth, however, is that in every such attack in country where the whole field is not visible, the obstinate defence of any salient position checks a whole line, or makes its momentum so weak as to be easily stopped. The fear of being themselves taken in flank produces great caution when officers and men hear sharp fighting in rear of a point they have reached, especially in a thick wood. In such circum-

stances they rarely go far after their connections with lines
right and left of them have been broken. On the other
hand, the advanced brigade which holds its defensive position is strengthened by the consciousness of strong cover
for its flanks. This reciprocal support is a large element in
the chances of battle, and it is every way fairer, in such
cases, to consider the forces of both attack and defence with
reference to the whole numbers within supporting distance
on both sides.

During the evening after the engagement, and acting upon
second-hand information from prisoners (to which Geary also
refers in his report), Hooker reported to General Sherman
that he had been attacked by three corps, but had repulsed
them, and was only anxious about his right flank. The
General-in-Chief, who had been near the centre of the whole
line, at his signal station, was concerned lest Schofield had
not fully met the spirit of his instructions, and next morning went in person to the little church in the woods near
Culp's, where he met both those officers. On his way Sherman had passed through Ward's (Butterfield's) division, and
learned that it was in reserve. Schofield, on being informed
of the despatch sent by Hooker, indignantly declared it in-
excusably wrong, and invited both officers to go to Hascall's
front and see whose dead lay farthest in advance. Sherman, reminding Hooker that three corps was the whole of
Johnston's army, which, if it had attacked, would have
made itself felt along a larger front than two or three brigades, indicated his dislike of such sensational reports, and
especially of the unjust insinuation as to Schofield. After a
repulse of the enemy, and with Butterfield's division of his own
corps still within reach, he thought an officer of Hooker's experience should not have been so anxious about his flank as to
have sent the despatch, even if Schofield had not been there.

The incident was a personal one which might well be omitted from history, but as it had its influence upon the subsequent relations of these officers, and upon General Hooker's withdrawal from the army, it is necessary to notice it.

Hood's attack had been accompanied by a fierce cannon-ade along nearly the whole front, and lively demonstrations were made on both sides from right to left; but no material change in positions or in forces was discovered, except the transfer of Hood's corps. It is uncertain to what degree Loring's corps had been extended to Johnston's right to supply the place from which Hood had been taken; but it is hardly credible that Wheeler's cavalry alone had been able to impose upon McPherson, who certainly believed and reported that the intrenchments in his front were held by infantry.

CHAPTER X.

KENESAW.

SHERMAN's embarrassments at this juncture were almost altogether due to the trouble in keeping his army supplied. The extraordinary and still-continuing rains made it impossible to lengthen the distance between the troops and their depôts, and so long as Johnston held fast to Kenesaw, no nearer points than those in use could be selected for the issuing of stores. Besides this, his long line of railway was tempting the Confederate commander to more vigorous efforts to cut his communications, and several cavalry raids had partial success in destroying bridges, tearing up rails, and burning one or two small trains. Torpedoes—a favorite weapon with the enemy—had been used to blow up a passing train, and Sherman was forced to threaten that he would test the safety of the track by an advance train of prisoners. He rightly distinguished between the use of mines and torpedoes to defend a position attacked, and the efforts to blow up railway trains upon roads far in the rear. The former is legitimate warfare; the latter, like disseminating contagion or incendiary burnings of towns beyond the theatre of war, is a barbarism which could legitimately be met by the means he threatened to use, but did not find necessary, the threat itself having the desired effect.

The affair of the 22d decided Sherman that his best course was to bring McPherson from the left, where the

ground in his front seemed peculiarly difficult; and he notified that officer in the evening to be ready for a transfer
to the extreme right.   To do this required, however, an accumulation of supplies, and getting ahead of the daily demand was slow work in the condition of roads and railways,
though from June 23d the weather improved.   Impatient at
the obstacles which seemed to bring everything to a stand-
still, and disappointed that the attack by Hood had made it
necessary to call back Schofield's advanced division from a
very promising flank movement on the Sandtown road, the
mind of the National commander naturally recurred to the
chances of breaking through a line which he was sure could
not be so strong as his own.   Although it was certain that
great efforts were making to reinforce Johnston, and the
Georgia militia under General G. W. Smith, a full division at
least, were known to be in the field, it still seemed probable
that the enemy's whole line must be very attenuated, and that
the rugged character of the mountain must be greatly relied
upon by Johnston for his security on that flank.   Hood was
known to be in front of Schofield and part of Hooker's
corps; Hardee must be well stretched out to hold the centre against the rest of Hooker's, Howard's, and Palmer's
corps, so that it seemed probable that somewhere along the
lines weak places might be found, where a determined attack might break through.   Johnston's line, from the
southern spurs of Kenesaw to his extreme right, including
the mountain, was held by Loring's corps and whatever reinforcements he might recently have got.   Abundant military experience proved that strength of position often begot
a careless security in the defenders, and the assault of what
were considered almost inaccessible cliffs has very often
turned out to be the most brilliant success.   Lookout Mountain had been an example of this in the very last campaign,

where, by that fortune which in war so often favors the
bold, a so-called impregnable position had been carried with
surprisingly little loss. There was hope, therefore, that
Kenesaw itself might be captured while the attacks were
progressing on other parts of the front.

One of two things Sherman must do. He must either
confess that in stretching his right to Olley's Creek he had
gone as far as possible, and must therefore wait patiently
for good weather and better roads, till with accumulated
stores he could swing McPherson's command quite to the
south of the enemy as he had done at Dalton, or he must
make a bold effort to break the lines before him. Thomas
suggested an approach to the enemy's works by regular sap,
but Sherman replied that when that slow process had carried one line, our experience showed that two or three
equally strong would be prepared behind it. Hitherto the
army had steadily gained ground, and had seen successive
lines of formidable works abandoned by their opponents.
To let it feel that it had gone the full length of its tether,
and must halt whilst the enemy redoubled his efforts to in-
terrupt our supplies would be demoralizing. There was a
fair chance to carry some point in the enemy's line. If
an assault succeeded it would be a decisive event. If it
failed, the venture would at least be justified on sound military principles. Sherman therefore determined on a serious effort to break through Johnston's intrenchments, and
made his preparations accordingly.

He fixed upon Monday morning, June 27th, at eight o'clock,
for a general advance. McPherson was ordered to make a
feint with his extreme left, keeping Garrard's cavalry also
demonstrative and busy, whilst he made an attack at the
south and west of Kenesaw. Strong skirmish lines were
to take advantage of the combat elsewhere to seize the crest

of the mountain if possible. Thomas in the centre was ordered to select a point in his front for an assault, masking it by such other demonstrations as would assist it. Schofield, on the right, was ordered to attack some point near the Marietta and Powder Spring road, whilst he threatened the extreme flank of the enemy. All were to be prepared to follow up rapidly any advantage that might be gained.

On the 26th, Schofield was directed to make a demonstration with his right which should attract the enemy's attention, and possibly induce him to strengthen that wing at the expense of his centre and right, when Thomas and McPherson would attack on the morrow. Schofield accordingly ordered General Cox to push Reilly's brigade, which was still in front of Cheney's, to Olley's Creek, and make a lively demonstration on anything he might find in his front, supporting the movement, if successful, by another brigade from the division. Reilly advanced, and, after a brisk skirmish, occupied the hills close to the stream under cover of a cannonade by Myers's Indiana Battery. He found Jackson's cavalry dismounted, and occupying a commanding hill on the right of the road beyond the creek, where they had artillery intrenched in a very strong position. This fortified hill was nearly on the prolongation of the line of the ridge beyond Olley's Creek and separating it from the Nickajack. Reilly was directed to take forward his battery, intrench it and his brigade as near the enemy as possible, and keep up the artillery fire. Meanwhile Byrd's brigade was taken from the right of the line near Culp's, marched down the creek till within about a mile of Reilly. There it made a bridge, crossed the stream, and occupied a hill northeast of that held by the enemy in Reilly's front, and which was directly connected with the line of heights east of Olley's Creek, on which Hood's left flank rested. A depression in the ridge partly isolated this hill from the rest of the high ground, and made it defensible. Byrd was ordered to intrench immediately on all sides, and hold the place against all comers as a separate redoubt, connecting his front by a chain of pickets, however, with both Reilly on his right, and with the rest of the division in Schofield's line on his left. The space between was the open valley through which the creek ran, and the Twenty-third corps batteries, which had been used to cover Byrd's advance, were disposed so as to search this interval with their fire. The Confederate reports show that these movements caused much uneasiness, but the activity of skirmish lines along the whole army front made both Johnston and Hood feel that they could not afford sufficiently strong detachments to successfully resist them. Sherman warmly approved what was done on this flank, but warned Schofield of the necessity of extreme watchfulness for brigades so far from support. He directed that Byrd's bridge be made good, and operations on that flank resumed early in the morning. Schofield accordingly determined to let Cox continue the movement down the Sandtown road next day with three of his brigades, whilst Hascall's division, as the extreme flank of the continuous line, should try to advance toward Marietta on the road from Culp's.

McPherson selected a point at the south and west of the principal crest of Kenesaw for his attack, and committed the details of the plan to Logan, whose corps lay opposite the point chosen. Blair and Dodge were ordered to assist Logan by active feints and demonstrations along the fronts of their respective corps. Logan ordered the attack to be made by the division of Morgan L. Smith, consisting of the brigades of Giles A. Smith and Lightburn, assisted by Walcutt's brigade of Harrow's division. The attacking troops

were ordered to form in two lines, and to move simultaneously with the columns of the Army of the Cumberland,
when the signal should be given.

Recent changes in the line of the Army of the Cumberland in taking ground farther to the right had put Palmer's
(Fourteenth) corps in the centre and Howard's (Fourth) on
the left. The only points which seemed at all favorable for
an attack were in front of Stanley's division of Howard's
corps. There the conformation of the ground separated the
hostile lines more than at other places, and room could be
found for forming the troops for the attack outside of our
own works and yet under cover. To Howard and Palmer
was committed the duty of selecting the positions to be
carried, and detailing the troops for the assault. Howard
ordered General Newton to prepare for an advance in the
morning from the left front of Stanley's division in two
columns of attack. Newton arranged his division with
Harker's and Wagner's brigades in front, and Kimball's in
reserve. They were formed in two columns, having each a
front of a regimental division, the columns being about
one hundred yards apart. Portions of the divisions of
Stanley and of Wood were held in readiness to support the
movement.

General Palmer had likewise, with General Thomas's approval, selected his point for attack in front of Stanley's
division and some distance to the right of that chosen by
General Howard. Palmer therefore withdrew the division of
General Davis from its place in line on the evening of the
26th, and it lay in bivouac in rear of Stanley during the
night. Soon after daybreak Davis reconnoitred the front with
his brigade commanders, and determined to assault in front
of Whittaker's brigade of Stanley's division. There the
enemy's line coming forward on a ridge, presented a salient

IX.—6

which was not covered with the usual abattis and entan-glement. Davis formed his division in front of Stanley's trenches, and about six hundred yards from the Confederate fortifications, that being as near as they could be placed with-out being in view and subject to fire. His formation was sim-ilar to Newton's; McCook's and Mitchell's brigades were in advance, and Morgan's brigade in reserve. Baird's division of the same corps supported the whole, and Hooker's corps, still farther on the right, was in readiness, under General Thomas's orders to assist either Palmer or Howard, or to take advantage of any favorable contingency that might arise.

The movement on the right of Schofield's corps which had been made on the 26th so far indicated that better results could be attained by pushing forward Cox's divi-sion in that direction, that, with Sherman's approval, the attack which Schofield had purposed to make with Has-call's divisions was limited to a strong demonstration, whilst the divergent movement down the Sandtown road was made by Cox.

In the orders for the day on Monday morning, the first aggressive movement was on the extreme right, and in con-tinuation of that which has been already described as oc-curring on the preceding evening. At daybreak Cameron's brigade of Cox's division crossed Olley's Creek by the bridge Byrd had made the day before, and marching through the valley ascended the slopes in rear and to the right of the position Byrd's brigade already occupied. At the same time Reilly's brigade resumed its efforts to cross Olley's Creek near the Sandtown road, and both movements were covered and assisted by the fire of the division batter-ies. Byrd, who was left on the ridge during the night fa-cing in all directions, reformed his lines, straddling the hill,

and pushed a strongly supported skirmish line up the creek
toward Hood's refused line of works. Cameron at the same
time changed direction to the right, down the stream, facing
the enemy's detached works in front of Reilly, who was held
at bay by the artillery which commanded the road and the
broken bridge across the stream there. A portion of Reilly's
brigade deployed as skirmishers kept up a lively fire at the
road and in its vicinity, whilst the rest of it was moved in
rear of some hills further down the creek, which there runs
nearly parallel to the Sandtown road, until a good position
for a battery was found, quite on the flank of the Confederate intrenchment. Under protection of its fire Reilly's men
waded a swamp, forded the stream, which is there shallow,
and pushed up the farther bank. Cameron moved forward
simultaneously so as to threaten the other flank, and after a
sharp resistance the enemy broke and fled. Reilly at once
occupied the abandoned position and intrenched it, fronting
to the south, and soon afterward Cameron formed connection on his left, reaching along the ridge till he joined
hands with Byrd who was on the higher eminence northward.

This had all occurred before the hour fixed for the attacks
on the main line, and whilst Cox was strengthening the
position of his division the roar of a general engagement
was heard far off to the left and rear. Advantage was taken
of this to move Reilly's brigade forward, following Jackson's
retreating cavalry some two miles farther, where a cross
road rounding the south spurs of the hilly ridge separating
Olley's Creek from the Nickajack, leads into the principal
road from Marietta to Sandtown on the Chattahoochee River.
The importance of the position was evident as soon as seen.
The trend of the hills bordering the Nickajack made it
plain that the Confederate line could not be extended south

in this direction with any real continuity, and that a way was open to the railroad near Smyrna, five miles south of Marietta. The position itself was defensible also. The spurs from the principal ridge ran southward in such a way that Byrd's position could be connected with Reilly's by a strong line, though too long for a single division. Calling to him Cameron's brigade, the Division Commander put it on Reilly's left, connecting it by outposts with both the other brigades; and on reporting the situation to General Schofield he was ordered to intrench the line and hold it firmly. An advanced hill a little up Nickajack Valley was intrenched with a lunette, which was occupied by a battery and a regiment of infantry, and the greatest industry was used to make the position of the whole division tenable against an attack in front or flank, separated as it was by a long interval and by Olley's Creek from the rest of the army.

But whilst this skirmishing advance had been making on the right, a bloody engagement was going on elsewhere, and one assuming the character of a general battle. McPherson's batteries opened with rapid and continuous firing upon the works of the enemy situated at the southern end of the rocky ridge known as Little Kenesaw.

The attack by the detachments from the Cumberland army was substantially along the Burnt Hickory and Marietta road, the same which leads from Gilgal Church to Marietta. Like McPherson's, it was preceded by a general artillery fire along the line for about fifteen minutes, and then, at a signal preconcerted between Howard and Palmer, a little before nine o'clock the columns advanced. At the same time the skirmish lines of the whole army pushed forward also and engaged the enemy, but on the selected routes the narrow heads of column rushed to the front, cheering as they went, and led with as devoted courage as soldiers ever showed. Newton's columns were not checked till they reached the entanglement in front of the enemy's works. Here the formation necessarily lost its order in struggling through and over the trunks and interlaced branches of felled forest trees, and the concentrated fire of infantry and artillery became too hot for endurance. The advance was checked, and the men deploying as they could, and taking advantage of such shelter as the ground and the felled timber afforded, opened a returning fire upon the Confederates within their works. General Harker, with a gallantry already famous in the army, attempting to renew the assault, was mortally wounded, and hundreds of brave men and valuable officers fell on every side.

From Palmer's corps Davis's division made an equally heroic effort with no better result. Indeed, the Confederate reports award to all the columns the merit of the most determined and persistent bravery in their attack. Davis's men had to pass over rocky and rough ground, part of it covered with the forest and tangled with undergrowth. In their enthusiasm they took too rapid a pace at the start, and by the time they had traversed the third of a mile between them and the enemy's works the men were so blown that they had not the strength called for in the final effort to carry the parapet before them. Colonel Daniel McCook and his second in command, Colonel Harmon, both fell in the assault, and both brigades had a heavy list of casualties among field and company officers as well as of private soldiers. They reached the trench in front of their objective point, but the narrow front of the column now stood revealed to the enemy, who were able to concentrate upon them also a storm of rifle-balls and canister which made farther advance impossible. Lying upon the ground within the range of musket-fire from the works, they covered themselves as they could, and finally, by General Thomas's consent, intrenched themselves under a terrible fire, the open ground over which they must retreat making it safer to stay than to return. The cover they were able to make enabled them to hold on till night, and then their works were so strengthened that they were permanently held, though for several days and nights the troops could rest only by sleeping on their arms.

Simultaneous with the rest, the lines of Smith's division of the Army of the Tennessee had marched upon Little Kenesaw. They crossed Noses Creek, carrying the intrenched lines of the enemy with a dash. Beyond these the slope of the mountain was steep and rocky, and felled trees formed so thick an entanglement that the advance became slow, the men climbing rather than marching toward their foe.

Logan's attack had fallen upon the left of Loring's corps (French's and Walker's divisions), Howard's upon Cleburne's division, in Hardee's centre. Loring had a strong skirmish line in rifle-pits six hundred yards in advance of his principal works, and these kept up a rapid fire upon Smith's column till it was within pistol-shot, and then rapidly retreated to the principal line. The National troops advanced steadily till it met the fire of the infantry in the trenches, and received in flank the cannonade of four batteries of artillery. This checked their advance, but with a steadiness and determination which extorted the admiration of their enemy, they held the ground they had gained, remaining more than an hour under the storm of shot and shell, the nature of the forest-covered ground saving them from utter destruction. Logan then ordered Smith to withdraw the division to the line of rifle-pits they had first captured, and these were put in a defensible condition and held. Seven commanding officers of regiments fell in this charge, one of them, Colonel Barnhill of the Fortieth Illinois, within thirty feet of the enemy's principal works.

Howard's columns met a similar opposition from Cleburne's division, and a similar concentration of artillery fire, the batteries of the Confederate lines having been so intrenched as to sweep the front.[1]

Palmer's attack fell upon Cheatham's division of Hardee's corps, and at one time threatened to penetrate between Hardee and Hood, but this was repelled by Cheatham's reserve brigade, which was brought into line.

Sherman's losses during the day were about twenty-five hundred in all, and Johnston admits over five hundred casualties. The latter professes to think that the courage and character of Sherman's attacks warrant the belief in a much greater loss to the National forces. The returns are, however, fairly reported, and a little consideration will show that they would in no way impeach the conduct of the attacking columns, even if all the Confederate reports had not testified admiringly to their gallantry, and to their marvellous steadiness, which enabled them to hold and intrench positions close to the works from which they refused to retreat.

It must be remembered that only three points in the enemy's line had been selected for assault. The middle of these was attacked by two columns, having each a front of two companies only, and those on right and left did not show a greater deployment than a regimental front. By the time each column had been checked by the obstructions in its way, and the terrible concentric fire to which it had been subjected, conscious of having lacked the impetus

---

[1] French gives, in his report, a very vivid description of his position on the mountain, and of the perfect way in which every movement of our forces, even to the occasional change of a headquarters camp, and the coming and going of our orderlies, could be watched and noted from his rocky outlook.

necessary to carry the works before them by the first effort, the experience of the division commanders taught them that further efforts at those points would only be destructive, and they allowed their brigades to seek such cover as they found at hand, maintaining so rapid a fire that any counter-charge by the enemy was not thought of. Except at a very few open points, the forest came up to the verge of the *abattis* covering the trenches, and once within its margin, the timber, the undergrowth, the rocks, all gave such shelter that the loss was slight to soldiers who knew how to take cool and intelligent advantage of them.

From the moment that the heads of the attacking columns were well developed, the enemy knew that these alone needed serious attention, and understood as well as our own officers, that the rest was only a demonstration to cover these real assaults. They, too, were brave and ready, and instantly concentrated both artillery and musketry upon these three points of danger. Reserves within the lines were hurried hither, and unless the first rush were successful, everybody knew that there would not be one chance in a hundred for a second attempt. It would have been easy to have doubled or trebled the numbers of killed and wounded that covered the narrow space where each assault had been made; but it was impossible that columns should be better led, and they did not stop till further progress was out of the question. The one chance to break through had been bravely tried and lost, and it would have been criminal in the commanders to have caused a further carnage that would have been futile. About eight hundred men had fallen at the head of each of these three assaults before its progress was stopped, and on so contracted a front this was proof that they had done enough to test fully the impregnable nature of the Confederate defences, and the vigilance of the troops that held them.   Each of the opposing armies had tried the same experiment, and each in turn had found that with the veteran soldiers now arrayed against each other, one rifle in the trench was worth five in front of it. The attacking columns saw little more before them than a thin and continuous sheet of flame issuing beneath the head-log of the parapet, whilst they themselves marched uncovered against the unseen foe.   In this case, as has already been said, the exigencies of the situation, and the chance of finding an open joint in the harness had warranted the effort, but the division and corps commanders were wise in judging when the effort had failed.

The evidence which the assaults by both armies near New Hope Church gave of the tactical weakness of narrow and deep columns of attack against such fortifications in such a country, is greatly strengthened by the experience in front of Marietta.   Our books of tactics, copying from the French, had taught that the regimental column of divisions of two companies, "doubled on the centre," was *par excellence* the column of attack.   In spite of the fact that Wellington in the Peninsular war had shown again and again that such a column, even over open country, melted away before the "thin red line" of British soldiers armed only with the old "Brown Bess" with its buck-and-ball cartridge, the *prestige* of Napoleonic tradition kept the upper hand.   We made our attacks in this instance (excepting Logan's) in a formation which did not give front enough to have any appreciable effect in subduing the enemy's fire; which by its depth offered the greatest possible mark to a concentric and flanking fire of the enemy ; and which the obstructions in its way deprived of all the impetus to pierce an opposing line, which is the only merit of such a column.   So hard it is to free ourselves from the trammels of old customs and a mistaken practice !

CHAPTER XI.

ACROSS THE CHATTAHOOCHEE.

SHERMAN lost no time in unavailing regrets over the failure of the effort to break Johnston's lines, but frankly said that among the chances for and against success, the unfavorable ones had prevailed, the enemy having been found vigilant and prepared to hold the works at all the points assailed. For similar reasons the lesser demonstrations had also produced no results, except on the Sandtown road, where Schofield's position beyond Olley's Creek he regarded as really important, and described it as "the only advantage of the day." Probably this advantage would not have been attained but for the hot work going on along the line, which so thoroughly occupied Johnston that no detachments could be spared to help Jackson, whose cavalry was waging an unequal contest on the extreme flank; for not only was Schofield's infantry engaging them in front, but his cavalry under Stoneman was actively demonstrating toward Powder Springs village.

The necessity of holding Johnston with such a grip that he could not detach aid to Lee in Virginia was one of the motives for active operations in front and continuously; but on the 28th Grant despatched Sherman that this consideration might now be dropped out of the calculation. Sherman at once resumed the plan for the flank operations he had conceived before, and an inspection of the position occupied by Schofield's advance determined him to move McPherson's Army of the Tennessee bodily to the right flank, as soon as a few days' supplies could be accumulated. The rains were over, and a scorching sun was rapidly drying up the more open country. A movement became daily more practicable, and as soon as the army could get out of a region so utterly cut up by wagon trains as that they were now in, the supply question would be a much less formidable one.

Johnston had not failed to see the fact that his position was already turned, and his engineers were already at work on the 28th with heavy details of the Georgia militia and of impressed negroes, fortifying two lines north of the Chattahoochee. One of these crossed the railroad at Smyrna on a ridge running northeast and southwest, but which about three miles from Smyrna on his left curved south, following the line of Nickajack Creek. The other was closer to the river covering only about two miles of the railroad on the hither side of the Chattahoochee bridge, which was in a deep southerly bend of the river. On the northeast it was protected by the deep ravine of Rottenwood Creek which enters the Chattahoochee with a southeast course. Turning nearly at right angles, the line then, crossing a ridge, reached the Nickajack again, which here runs for several miles above its mouth nearly parallel to the Chattahoochee and about a mile distant from it.

At the same time a good deal of work was doing at Atlanta, where fortifications had already been made ; but these were greatly strengthened and extended in anticipation of the necessity of making a final stand there, if the line of the Chattahoochee should be broken.

All these intrenchments were made with a thoroughness and skill which was admirable, but the improvement in the weather and the use of better roads gave Sherman a freedom of movement which enabled him to manœuvre the enemy out of these formidable positions with an ease and rapidity that astonished and alarmed the Richmond Government, and led to an early change in commanders for their army.

Already in the night of June 28th the sounds of moving railway trains between Marietta and the river were heard so continuously at Schofield's advanced position as to indicate that stores and material of war were being sent by Johnston to the rear; but Sherman meant to move with rations enough to accomplish something decisive, and the two or three days necessary to get up his supplies were spent in preliminary movements. The Army of the Cumberland stretched its lines a little more to the right, so that Hooker relieved Hascall's division of the Army of the Ohio, and this was marched down the Sandtown road till it covered all the direct roads to Marietta and to the railroads in the Nickajack Valley. This threw the whole of Schofield's corps together on a strong line reaching from the ridge beyond Olley's Creek on the left, to some hills near the Nickajack, where the Marietta and Sandtown road runs into that on which his movement had been made. On July 2d Smith's division of Logan's corps marched from the old position of the Army of the Tennessee and reported temporarily to Schofield to strengthen the right flank. Stoneman's cavalry was able to reach the Chattahoochee near Sandtown, and the whole of McPherson's command was moving to the right, leaving Garrard's cavalry to cover the roads to Marietta near the railroad.

That night Johnston evacuated the works at Kenesaw and along the whole front, falling back into the intrenchments prepared behind the Nickajack. Sherman now orders Thomas to advance directly through Marietta and along

the railway, and his columns reach Ruff's station, developing the line which has been already described.   The Army
of the Tennessee reaches the extreme right, and bivouacs
near Schofield's position.   On the 4th, McPherson advances
Dodge's corps well forward on the Sandtown road, whilst
with the rest of his command he unites his lines with
Thomas's half way to the railroad.   In this movement, by
Sherman's special orders, the skirmish lines are greatly
strengthened and the advance has nearly the weight of a
line of battle.   Dodge pushes over a line of Hood's rifle-
pits in spite of fierce resistance, but with heavy loss.   In
the attack, Colonel E. F. Noyes, leading a demi-brigade,
falls severely wounded.   This moving forward of a strongly
reinforced right flank by Sherman brings him nearer to Atlanta at this point than Johnston, and the latter sees that if
he is to make any stand at the Chattahoochee he must be
near enough to guard its ferries and fords.   He does not
wait in his new lines, but in the night of the same day
leaves these also, and before daybreak his troops have entered the works on the north bank of the river.   Again all
the National forces except Schofield's corps are in motion, a
brisk cannonade tells of a sharp affair of advanced guards.
Stoneman's cavalry push boldly in on Johnston's left near
the river, take some prisoners and a black flag which a
Texas regiment of horse was carrying.

Information of the lines along the Upper Nickajack had
reached Sherman's army, but the intrenched position at the
crossing of the river was unknown.   Sherman was at first
unwilling to believe there was anything there ; but a strong
reconnoissance quickly showed the heavy earthworks, the
abattis in front, the batteries arranged for cross fire and all
the most elaborate of the Confederate preparations for defence.   The length of these lines was five or six miles, and

in spite of all the activity Sherman and his subordinates could use, the hope of catching the enemy in the midst of a movement was disappointed, and the problem now before them was not only the flanking of an intrenched army, but the crossing of a river in his presence.

Sherman had said to Halleck in a despatch of the 8th of June, that if Johnston should select the line of the Chatta-hoochee he "must study the case a little," before commit-ting himself. McPherson was put in position on the ex-treme right, covering Turner's Ferry, which, however, like other crossings for a dozen miles along the river, was guarded by a detached fortification on the south side. Thomas, with his three corps, completed the investment of Johnston's position, Howard's corps being at Pace's Ferry, where one of the principal roads from Marietta to Atlanta crosses the river, that near McPherson's flank being another, with a third near the railway bridge. Schofield with the Twenty-third Corps was moved to Smyrna Camp Ground, near the railway, and held as a movable column ready for use in any direction. Stoneman's cavalry was kept active, looking for fords or crossings down the river, and Garrard's was sent some eighteen miles above to seize the Roswell factories and hold also, if possible, a bridge over the Chattahoochee there.

Meanwhile some breaks in the railway were to be repaired, steam communication to be again brought to the camps, and the "case" was to be "studied a little." Sherman estab-lished his headquarters for a few days at Vining's Station, and from a hill near by could see the distant town of Atlanta, the coveted prize of the campaign. There, too, could be seen the preparations Johnston was making to re-sist his crossing of the river, and the general features of the country for some miles south of the river could be observed.

A little more than a month had passed since the Etowah was crossed. It was a month of continuous sharp skirmishing combat, with occasional severer engagements. It was a month in which the troops had been day and night under fire, and the incessant strain on nerve and brain had never for a moment been relaxed. It was a month of continuous pouring rains, converting the camps into mire and the roads into almost impassable sloughs; making insignificant streams as obstructive as rivers, and multiplying the discomforts and the perils of duty in the trenches or on the picket. That such a month's work was rapid education to soldiers hardly needs telling. The ordinary experience of a year was condensed into a few weeks, and the army of veterans became consolidated by a true unity of feeling; confident in itself as a whole, and the several corps in each other as parts, every portion of it could be trusted to uphold the credit and rival the soldierly conduct of the rest.

The monthly returns for June show that in killed, wounded, and missing the army had lost 7,500 men. Of these the Army of the Cumberland reported 5,500, the Army of the Tennessee 1,300, and the Army of the Ohio about 700. As the attack upon the Confederate lines on the 27th of June was the only departure from the usual method of vigorous advance of skirmish lines and extension of flanks beyond the enemy, it will be seen how fierce a bickering fire that must have been which was constantly kept up. Day by day the losses averaged nearly two hundred men, and nearly every day had its success in the carrying of some new hill, the crossing of some contested stream, or the intrenching of some closer position in the enemy's front.

Johnston gives his hospital returns as showing a loss of 4,000 in killed and wounded during the month of which we are speaking; but this is of his infantry alone, and excludes prisoners. Sherman rightly estimates the proportion of prisoners taken during the month at 2,000, out of the whole number captured in the campaign, and putting the proportion of cavalry losses at the same ratio to infantry as Johnston gives for the month of May, another thousand must still be added. The Confederate losses are thus found to have been 7,000, with a probability of their having exceeded that number. Each army had in its turn tried the strength of the other's lines by assault, and each had experienced the disproportionate losses which come of assaulting such intrenched positions. It was not only the principal lines which were of the formidable character that has been described, but, to use the words of Hardee, "it soon became customary, in taking up a new position, to intrench the skirmish line, until it was only less strong than the main one. This line was well manned, and the roar of musketry on it was sometimes scarcely distinguishable from the sound of a general engagement." [1] Such was the skirmishing which lasted incessantly for months!

After occupying the line of fortifications covering the crossings of the Chattahoochee by the railway and two of the principal wagon roads leading to Atlanta, Johnston sent his cavalry to the south side of the river to operate on the same flanks as before: Jackson to cover his left, watching the ferries and bridges below, and Wheeler on the right, looking after the upper ones. The usual method of crossing the river was by ferries, or flat boats pushed over by poles. The Roswell bridge, some twenty miles above, was the nearest structure of that kind, and this was burned by Wheeler before it could be reached by Garrard. Johnston

---

[1] Johnston's Narrative, p. 357.

speaks of the fords as numerous and easy, but whatever might be the case ordinarily, the almost constant rains of June had swollen the river so that there were very few places where a practicable ford could be found. Instead of making an intrenched camp for his whole army north of the Chattahoochee, it would seem more in accordance with sound strategic principles to have held only a bridge-head there, and to have placed the greater part of his command in such a position behind the river that he could strike with overwhelming force any head of column that should attempt a crossing.

The two days prior to the 7th of ·July sufficed to make the repairs in the railway, so that supplies were delivered on Sherman's lines. Garrard had occupied Roswell, where he found very extensive cotton, wool, and paper mills, running at their full capacity and till the last moment, turning out supplies for the Confederate government. The nominal proprietors attempted to protect them with a thin veil of neutrality, alleging French ownership and hoisting the French flag; but Garrard, with Sherman's approval, burned the mills and sent the owners and employees under guard to Marietta. He found the bridge burned, and made a careful reconnoissance for practicable fords.

Sherman sent General Schofield in person on the 7th to make a reconnoissance of parts of the river between Pace's Ferry and Roswell, and in consequence of his report determined to make a crossing near the mouth of Soap Creek, if possible. Although the crossing was not opposed by any force worth naming, being in fact a complete surprise, this could not be anticipated, and the operation, being one of the picturesque incidents of the campaign, may be worth describing.

Soap Creek enters the Chattahoochee about six or seven

miles above Pace's Ferry and Vining's Station, where General
Sherman's headquarters were. It was about the same distance from the camp of the Twenty-third Corps at Smyrna
Camp Ground. Early in the morning of the 8th, the corps,
with Colonel Buell's pontoon train, moved by roads some
distance from the river to the paper mill near the mouth
of the creek. The leading division (Cox's) was ordered
to take position as close to the river as was consistent with
remaining unseen, to permit no camp fires and no exposure of men to view. The river was to be picketed, but the
vedettes to conceal themselves from the opposite side. A
fish-dam was found half a mile above the creek, which had
been made by piling rough stones across the current in such
a way that at low water the stream was confined to the middle of the ordinary channel by diagonal wing-dams. In the
condition of the river on that day, this was a difficult and
dangerous ford, but it was determined to use it in connection with the pontoon boats, as will be seen presently.

The creek runs for a considerable distance near its mouth
parallel to the river, and then turns into the larger stream
by a short curve. Between the river and the creek is a high
ridge, two or three hundred feet in height, which is about
the altitude also of the hills bordering the river on the opposite side.

In the reach of the creek thus shielded from view, the
canvas pontoons were set up and launched, a detail of five
hundred men from the infantry helping in the work. Byrd's
brigade was ordered to lead in the crossing by the pontoons,
the Twelfth Kentucky regiment to be ferried over in the
boats, the rest of the brigade deploying and advancing to
the river's edge on the run when the boats should start, so
as to cover them with their fire.

Cameron's brigade was ordered to cross Soap Creek at the

paper mill, and concealing his men near the fish-dam, push an advanced guard over it, if possible, at the time appointed, and if the ford proved practicable, follow it with the brigade and make a junction with those who should cross below in the pontoon boats. Soap Creek, near the mill, runs in a rocky gorge with precipitous sides, and Cameron's men had to cross it by clambering down the dangerous rocks and by picking their way along the edge of the slippery dam above.

Half past three o'clock in the afternoon was the time set for the crossing. At that hour a careful reconnoissance from the top of the ridge showed that there were no symptoms of alarm on the opposite bank. A cavalry outpost with a piece of artillery was all that seemed to oppose the movement, and these were on the heights immediately in front of the mouth of the creek, at what was known as Phillips's Ferry. The signal to advance was given. Cameron's advance guard, led by Colonel Casement, One Hundred and Third Ohio, entered the water at the fish-dam, scrambling along the broken rocks in the swift current. Immediately twenty white pontoon boats shot out from the mouth of the creek, pulled by expert oarsmen selected from Hascall's division, and loaded with Colonel Rousseau's Kentuckians. The rest of Byrd's brigade, which had been deployed under cover of the woods along the base of the hills, rushed forward across the bottom land and lined the margin of the stream. A single cannon-shot was fired from the enemy's outpost, and the gun was reloaded and run forward to fire again; but so completely was it now covered by the rifles of Byrd's men, that no one could aim it or fire. The mounted men, conscious of their inability to cope with the force before them, galloped away to carry the news. A few moments sufficed to put the boats over, and Rousseau, mounting the steep hillside, captured the gun without the loss of a man, the gunners following the horsemen in quick retreat. Cameron's brigade, coming down from the fish-dam, joined Rousseau and took post on the ridge covering the ferry. The boats were kept running till the whole of Byrd's brigade was ferried over, whilst the work of laying the pontoon bridge was also begun with other boats, and before dark one bridge was completed and a second progressing.

It was found that the ridges on the south side of the Chattahoochee were so shaped as to make a natural bridge-head and an admirable place of defence; and the whole of Cox's division was immediately intrenched upon it, Cameron's, Byrd's, Barter's, and Reilly's brigades in line, and Crittenden's brigade of dismounted cavalry in reserve.

The character of the surprise was well indicated by an incident which brought the private and personal experiences of war into interesting comparison with its exterior glitter and excitement. In the deserted camp of the outpost, in which even the half-cooked supper was left, an unfinished letter from one of the Confederate soldiers to his wife was found. In it he calms her fears for his safety, saying that he was now almost as free from peril as if he were at home on his plantation: that the solitude about them was rarely broken, even by the appearance of a single horseman on the opposite side of the river. But the incomplete sentence was broken by the apparition of the crowded boats and the hostile line of infantry on the river bank, and the letter, by war's strange fortune, reached other eyes than those for which it was written.

Johnston lost no time in testing by cavalry reconnoissances the strength of the National forces now holding the bridge-head, and realized the fact that the crossing of the Chattahoochee was secured to Sherman. Wheeler withdrew from the upper river, and next morning Garrard found no force in his front at Roswell. Sherman immediately ordered Newton's division of the Fourth Corps and Dodge's (Sixteenth) Corps of the Army of the Tennessee, to march to Roswell and fortify the hills opposite the ford on the south side of the river, now held by Garrard's cavalry. Dodge was also ordered to build a trestle bridge there on the site of that which the enemy had burned.

From his hill near Vining's Station, Sherman was able to see, on the 9th, "a good deal of flutter in the enemy's camps," and movements of troops to the eastward, which might mean either a concentration to attack the force already over the river, or preparations for taking a new position. He needed a few days, however, for the accumulation of supplies, and wished also to give time for a cavalry expedition under Major-General Rousseau, starting from Decatur, Alabama, to reach the railroads between Montgomery and Atlanta near Opelika. Stoneman was at the same time ordered to make his cavalry active along the Chattahoochee toward Sandtown and Campbelltown, and if he could secure the ferry at the last-named place, he too was directed to strike out for the railroads southwest of Atlanta, on a "raid" of four or five days.

On the night of the 9th of July, Johnston moved his infantry across the Chattahoochee, the country bridges, with that of the railway and his pontoons, giving two bridges to each of his three corps. He had maintained a bold front up to the last moment, holding off the vigorous attacks by skirmish line which Thomas and McPherson kept up during the movements going on up the river. In the morning the pontoons had been removed, and his rear guard retired, burning the railway and wagon bridges.

Sherman immediately ordered Howard to march his corps

(Fourth) to support Schofield at Phillips's Ferry, leaving
Newton's division with Dodge at Roswell. McPherson was
directed to keep up for two or three days his demonstrations
of a purpose to cross at Turner's Ferry near the mouth of
the Nickajack, so as to leave as much doubt as possible by
which flank the National Army would now move. Schofield
was ordered to build a bridge at his position, so that the
pontoons could be used elsewhere if needed. The division of the Twenty-third Corps, already over the river,
was strengthened by two more brigades and moved out to a
ridge a mile south of the crossing, intrenching a very strong
position across the bend of the river and covering both the
ford and the bridges. Dodge made a similar advance at
Roswell and hurried the building of the bridge, 650 feet
long—the ford, " the best on the whole river," being belly-
deep for horses and very rough.

The plans of the National commander were announced to
his principal subordinates on the 10th and 11th. Thomas
was to lay a pontoon bridge at Powers's Ferry on the night of
the 12th, and fortify a bridge-head on the south bank there.
On the 13th, McPherson was to join Dodge with Logan's
Corps, and Newton's division would rejoin Howard at Phillips's Ferry, behind Schofield. Blair's Corps would await
Stoneman's return from his raid, and then march to Roswell.
Stoneman did not succeed in reaching the railroads near Atlanta, but destroyed bridges and boats between Campbelltown and Newnan, and was back by the night of the 15th, so
that on the 16th everything was ready for a general advance.

The northern part of Georgia had been made a military
district under command of Major-General Steedman, so that
the protection of Sherman's communications might be sys-
tematized under a responsible head. The mounted infantry
of this district, under Colonels Watkins and Croxton, had

given a good account of itself in the latter part of June, by defeating a Confederate force under General Pillow, which had advanced to Lafayette, in an effort to reach the railway. On the 28th of June, Brigadier-General John E. Smith's division of the Fifteenth Corps arrived at Chattanooga and was divided into several parts, guarding the more important posts and bridges along the line to Alatoona.

CHAPTER XII.

JOHNSTON SUCCEEDED BY HOOD—PEACHTREE CREEK—
CLOSING IN ON ATLANTA.

IT was by no means a simple or easy matter for Sherman to decide whether he would attempt to cross the Chattahoochee by his right or his left flank. From the Roswell factories to the railway crossing, the course of the river is very little west of south, Roswell being in fact a little north of Marietta when parallels are drawn. Below the railway bridge the course of the river is nearly southwest, Sandtown being about as much south of Atlanta as Roswell is north of Marietta. Atlanta itself is about ten miles from the river, by the railroad, and is upon a high plateau, from which the streams descend in all directions; or more accurately stated, Atlanta and Decatur are both on the watershed separating the tributaries of the Chattahoochee from those of the Ocmulgee, which flows southeastward to the ocean. The line of the watershed is nearly parallel to the Chattahoochee, and southwest of Atlanta the valleys of the smaller streams are on the short line from the river to the town. For this reason it would be difficult for Johnston to make any defensive line on that side much closer to the river than the city, because it would have been crossed by deep ravines perpendicular to his fortifications, which would make it hard to move supports from one part of the line to the other. The railroads leading from Atlanta to Montgomery and to Macon run out of the city by the same route to the southwest for several miles, till they reach East Point, where they separate, the former continuing its course nearly parallel to the river, and the latter turning away at a right angle to the southeast. On this flank, therefore, lay the shortest route to Johnston's southern communications, and the National Army once on the south of the Chattahoochee, between Sandtown and Campbelltown, would have been already in rear of Atlanta. The Confederate commander must then have evacuated the town, or have changed his base, making the railway through Decatur and his communications with Richmond his line of supplies and, if necessary, of retreat.

Turning now to the country northeast of Atlanta, it will be seen that the *terrain* is a different one. The streams, instead of flowing into the Chattahoochee by valleys at right angles to the river, are found between ridges parallel to it, and after getting a few miles south of the bank, are branches of one larger creek, the Peachtree, of which the northernmost, called Nancy Creek, is parallel to the river; the middle one, called Little Peachtree, has nearly the same course; but the southern, which is the larger and principal stream, runs nearly west, covering both Decatur and Atlanta, and entering the Chattahoochee by a wide and muddy bed, very close to the railway bridge. The ridges parallel to the river on this flank afforded admirable lines for the Confederate Army, but fearing the interposition of part of the National forces between him and the railway, Johnston selected the south bank of Peachtree Creek, nearest Atlanta, for his next defensive line, if Sherman should cross above him.

As Sherman, however, could not know that his adversary would not meet him earlier in his march, as he had done at

New Hope Church, that contingency had to be considered in his study of the problem. The upper route was plainly the longer and the more difficult one in itself : but there were other considerations which became decisive. To adopt the lower route was to leave the enemy's cavalry the opportunity of crossing the river at points practically in our rear, for the purpose of breaking the railway, and stopping supplies ; and the reasons which prevailed to make Sherman operate by his right at the Etowah, were still more potent at the Chattahoochee. The ever-lengthening single line of communication could not be exposed for twenty or thirty miles of its flank till the Confederate Army should be driven within the lines at Atlanta and the bridge across the Chattahoochee rebuilt. Besides, Grant telegraphed that it was not improbable that Johnston would be reinforced by the troops the Richmond Government was withdrawing from the Shenandoah Valley, supposed to be twenty thousand or more, and this made an additional reason for cutting the Georgia Railroad near Decatur as soon as possible, thus preventing that direct line to Richmond from being made of use to the enemy.

Sherman therefore determined that the longest way round would prove the surest, and took the chances of the difficult ground near the river on his left flank. He ordered Schofield to move out from the river by way of Cross Keys toward Decatur, McPherson to keep farther to the left, with Garrard's cavalry on his flank cutting and destroying the railroad between Decatur and Stone Mountain, whilst Thomas with more than half the whole army marched by several roads from Pace's and Phillips's Ferries on Atlanta, his left following the road by Buckhead. Approaching the town with the right of his army, Sherman would then wheel the whole to the right, letting this wing cover the railroad, as his left had done at Ackworth, while the bridge at the Chattahoochee should be rebuilt and fortified.

In this movement McPherson would have three or four times the distance to travel that Thomas had, and there would be the danger that the enemy might attack the right flank, which was thus presented to them; but the Army of the Cumberland was a single organization of nearly fifty thousand men, and with Thomas's great and deserved reputation for military skill, unflinching courage, and steady persistence, Sherman felt confident that he could hold the whole Confederate Army at bay till the manœuvre should be completed.

Johnston had the important advantage of knowing the country by occupation, and not from imperfect maps. He reckoned with confidence on the probability that Sherman's right wing would be separated from the centre when it should cross Peachtree Creek, and planned an attack upon it with the greater part of his own forces when it should be thus exposed and while it should be in motion. His fortifications began at the railroad about two miles from the river, and extended some six miles east till they reached the Pea Vine Creek at its junction with Peachtree. There the line turned south along Pea Vine Creek till it reached the Georgia Railway between Atlanta and Decatur. The ground was well chosen and the intrenchments were of the formidable character with which we are already familiar.

But Johnston was not to deliver battle upon the ground he had selected. On the 17th of July he knew that the National Army was advancing from its bridges in several columns and was making his preparations for the next day's work, giving instructions to his Chief Engineer with no thought or warning of change in his own relations to the army, when he received telegraphic orders from Richmond

to turn over the command to General Hood. General Bragg,
who was then acting as Chief-of-Staff to the Confederate
President, had visited the army two or three days before,
but had given no intimation to Johnston of the dissatisfaction of the Richmond government or of the intended change.
The ostensible reason was his failure to defeat Sherman, and
his unwillingness to give assurance that he could even answer for the permanent safety of Atlanta and its important
railway connections. In obeying the order, as he did
promptly, Johnston with great justice called attention to the
fact that Lee's retreat in Virginia had been quite as rapid
as his own and quite as far: and intimated that the resistance his army had made was better evidence of the probable future than any sounding promises in words. It is now
well known that Mr. Davis did not like Johnston, and he
was no doubt influenced by his prejudices to believe that a
more aggressive policy would do for Georgia than Lee found
practicable in Virginia.

It is certain that the change of Confederate commanders
was learned with satisfaction by every officer and man in the
National Army. The patient skill and watchful intelligence
and courage with which Johnston had always confronted
them with impregnable fortifications, had been exasperating. They had found no weak joints in the harness, and no
wish was so common or so often expressed as that he would
only try our works as we were trying his. It was now known
that this was likely to come, not only because Hood's character as a soldier implied it, but because the reasons for the
change were known to be based upon a determination to
pursue a more aggressive policy. It was understood that
hard blows were to be received ; but Sherman's whole army
was supremely confident in its ability to take such prompt
advantage of natural and artificial means of defence, as to

punish aggression on the part of the enemy severely enough to reduce his strength with great rapidity. It is not over-praise of the National Army to say that its veterans were panic-proof; and its well-tried courage was so intelligent and quick-witted that the smallest detachments could be relied upon to do a wise and bold thing in almost any juncture.

If aggression was to be tried, it would be hard to find any commander better fitted than Hood to test it. He had gained renown as a division commander under Longstreet in Virginia, and at Gaines's Mills,. Second Manassas, Antietam, and Gettysburg he had shown the kind of courage and dash which made him to be looked upon as a soldier of the Jackson school. It was a fatal error to suppose that the Army in Georgia could afford to take the kind of initiative now intended; but it was the error of the Richmond government, and Hood, though he had been freely critical of Johnston's cautious strategy, seems to have been sincerely reluctant to take the command under the implied conditions.

Johnston tells us that he fully informed Hood of his plans, both for attacking Sherman at Peachtree Creek, and then of moving the bulk of his troops south and east of Atlanta and striking a blow upon the other flank. Whether the details of Johnston's method would have been the same as Hood's is uncertain, but Hood adopted the general ideas of his predecessor in both parts. The promotion of Hood was accompanied by changes in the command of two of the three corps which composed the Confederate Army. General A. P. Stewart was assigned to what was formerly Polk's corps, General Cheatham took Hood's, and Hardee retained his own. On the morning of the 20th July, these were in the Peachtree Creek intrenchments, Stewart's on the left, nearest the Chattahoochee, Hardee in the centre, and Cheatham on the right, with the Georgia State troops under General G. W. Smith still farther on that flank.

General Thomas had not been able to get a pontoon bridge at Pace's Ferry laid at as early a day as Sherman's order of the 14th contemplated. On the 17th, Wood's division of Howard's corps, which was then at Powers's Ferry, the next ferry below Phillips's, marched down the left bank of the river, driving off the enemy's skirmishers and covering the laying of the bridge at Pace's Ferry. It next day rejoined the corps near Buckhead. Palmer's corps crossed first at Pace's Ferry, and Hooker's followed. Palmer thus formed the right of the Army of the Cumberland, Hooker the centre, and Howard the left. Palmer was scarce more than a mile from Nancy's Creek when he crossed the river, and as that stream joins Peachtree only a little further to the right, it is evident that the extreme flank of the army must stand fast and be the pivot on which a wheeling movement was made.

On the 18th, Howard was at Buckhead, Palmer at the junction of Nancy Creek and Peachtree, with Hooker between. Schofield marched through Cross Keys south, to the north fork of Peachtree Creek. Sherman's headquarters were with Schofield that night. McPherson reached the Augusta Railroad early in the afternoon, at its north curve two miles from Stone Mountain, and seven from Decatur. There M. L. Smith's division of Logan's corps, with Garrard's cavalry, destroyed several miles of the railway. For the 19th, Sherman ordered Thomas to hold on with his right near Howell's Mill, let his left swing across Peachtree Creek about the South Fork, and connect with Schofield, who would approach Decatur from the north, while McPherson did the same from the east. Thomas kept his troops rather closer to the right than this order implied, for it would have taken

Hooker more nearly into Howard's position, and allowed the whole of the Fourth Corps to reach out toward Schofield; but as Sherman said a day or two later, the maps were all wrong, and the general officers were constantly misled in attempting to reckon distances or connections by them. There were in fact two "Howell's Mills," one on Nancy Creek, and the other on Peachtree, and the position of the right flank would be changed two miles, as one or the other of them were understood.

The 19th of July was spent by the Army of the Cumberland in its efforts to get a foothold on the south side of Peachtree Creek. Davis's division of Palmer's corps attempted to cross at Howell's Mill, but finding the resistance there very stubborn, made an effort somewhat lower down, and succeeded. One of his brigades (Dilworth's) was sharply assailed, but repulsed the enemy. A bridge was built, some hills covering the creek occupied, and the other divisions prepared to follow the movement next day. Geary's division of Hooker's corps got over in a bend of the stream, a little more than half a mile above Howell's Mill. Wood's division of Howard's corps, advancing on the principal road leading from Buckhead to Atlanta, found the bridge in its front burned, and the crossing commanded by an intrenched line of skirmishers on the high ground beyond. He, too, was obliged to resort to a flanking movement, and after a sharp contest established himself on the south bank. By night, therefore, Thomas had three heads of column over the stream, which, from its marshy banks and deep muddy channel, was no inconsiderable obstacle; and one or more bridges was built for each corps, besides repairing that at Howell's Mill, which the enemy was obliged to abandon after Davis's division had effected its crossing. At all these points the resistance had been made by infan-

try, and the stubbornness of it proved that the principal intrenched line was not far in front. From the road occupied
by Wood to that held by Geary was less than a mile in a
direct line with the valley of Shoal Creek between, and the
road from Howell's Mill, where the rest of the Fourteenth
Corps would follow Davis, ran into Geary's at the plantation
of one Embry, but a little way in front of Geary's position.
Newton's division of the Fourth Corps had marched on a
road nearly parallel to Wood's, but somewhat farther east.
He had found the bridge in his front destroyed, and reported the enemy's infantry in force on the other side, and
was therefore instructed by General Howard to move to the
right and support Wood, which he did. For practical purposes, therefore, nearly half of Sherman's army was showing
a front of only a mile on the right flank, while the other
half, though converging on Atlanta, reached all the way to
Decatur, some eight miles away. It was to remedy this
that Sherman's order was made directing Howard to connect
with Schofield.

Stanley's division had marched by the road from Buckhead toward Decatur, which crosses the north fork of
Peachtree about half a mile above its junction with the
south fork. The Confederate cavalry opposed him, and as
he approached the creek set the bridge on fire. Stanley
drove them off and got possession of the bridge before it
was much injured, quickly repaired it, and marched his division to the south side, where he encamped for the night.

The Confederate general, in executing the purpose of attacking already referred to, ordered Cheatham's corps and
the Georgia State troops to hold fast on his right, occupying the intrenched line from Jones's Mill on Clear Creek
eastward a mile, and then south to the Georgia Railroad.
This salient would interpose between the two wings of

Sherman's army as they were moving, and Stewart and Hardee were ordered to swing forward their right into the interval, to attack by division *en echelon* from the right, crushing Thomas's left flank if possible, and driving the Army of the Cumberland northward and westward toward the Chattahoochee, with the muddy and difficult bed of Peachtree Creek behind it.

But Schofield and McPherson were approaching Atlanta from the east faster than Hood was aware, in spite of very vigorous efforts of Wheeler's cavalry to retard them. On the night of the 19th Schofield was over the south fork of Peachtree, and at Pea Vine Creek on the Peyton plantations. The little stream before him is a branch of the south fork of Peachtree, and runs nearly due north, parallel to Cheatham's intrenchments, a mile and a half from them, with a high ridge and another deep hollow between. Dodge's (Sixteenth) corps of McPherson's army connected with Schofield's left, and on the morning of the 20th the whole of Sherman's left wing advanced, threatening to turn Hood's extreme right.

This necessitated the moving of Cheatham further in that direction, and the attack which Hood had planned for one o'clock was delayed till his whole command could take ground to the right for about the distance of a division front. His advance was thus delayed till the middle of the afternoon; but the movements of the Army of the Cumberland being continuous, the only effect of the delay was to shorten the distance he would have to traverse.

General Thomas was in some embarrassment to determine how best to carry out the orders to connect with Schofield on his left; for as his corps were advancing on parallel roads toward Atlanta, the character of the country was such that he could only move his troops to the left by considerable circuits to his rear. He concluded, therefore, to let Palmer and Hooker go forward by the roads they were on, to keep Newton's division of the Fourth Corps on the direct Buckhead and Atlanta road, and let Howard take Wood's division of his corps by a detour to the east, unite it with Stanley's, and with both divisions press forward till he should find himself within supporting distance of Schofield. Could Thomas have known the position of Hood's lines and that he was shifting his divisions eastward, he would no doubt have found a way of doing the same; for, as it turned out, Hood's attack fell upon Newton's division and Hooker's corps, leaving Palmer's corps almost wholly unemployed, while a gap of nearly two miles separated Newton from the rest of the Fourth Corps under Howard. But Thomas had no means of seeing through the impenetrable veil of the forest-covered hills in his front, and the accidental separation of his corps was in great part due to the misleading maps which deceived both him and Sherman as to the distance between the wings of the army.

On the morning of the 20th Palmer put Johnson's division over the creek at Howell's Mill, and it took position on the left of Baird, who had crossed during the night. Davis's division still retained its place as the extreme right of the army.

Hooker directed Williams's division to cross in rear of Geary, and move to his right. After getting over Geary's bridge, Williams took a country road leading to Embry's, where the direct road from Howell's Mill comes in, and thus extended Geary's line parallel to the general course of the creek. In similar manner Hooker directed Ward's division (formerly Butterfield's) to form on Geary's left. As the shortest way of doing this from his position on the north side of the creek, Ward marched to the bridge in rear of Newton's

division of the Fourth Corps, and after crossing took position behind some hills overlooking Shoal Creek, which lay
in a pretty deep valley between him and Geary.   In this
valley there was open country along the stream, especially
about Collier's Mill, which was a little in rear of his right
flank.

Newton had moved his division forward after relieving
Wood, and was about half a mile south of Peachtree Creek,
with his left flank toward Clear Creek, and his whole line
covering the cross road that leads to Collier's Mill.   All of
the divisions were deployed with two brigades in front and
one as a reserve.   Newton had a battery on the road in his
centre, and another in reserve, and had covered his front
hastily with a barricade of rails and timber.   Ward had not
been able to move his cannon across the ravines, and a battery of his division was left near the bridge and was used by
General Thomas with excellent effect later in the day.
Geary and Williams had their field batteries with them, and
so had the divisions of Palmer's corps.

About three o'clock Hood's lines appeared, and a violent
combat began at Newton's left, which by the *échelon* movement ordered by Hood, would be first reached in the attack.
The enemy passed Newton's flank near Clear Creek,[1] but was
there attacked by his reserve brigade (Bradley's) and a battery of artillery, and driven back.   The assault now reached
Newton's front, and Blake's brigade on the left of the road
with the battery easily held their ground.   On the right of
the road was Kimball's brigade, and the enemy's force far
outflanking it, it was forced to change front to the rear,
holding on by the left and refusing the right.   Ward's divi-

---

[1] It is called Pea Vine in Howard's report; but this is an error. See U. S. Engineers' maps.   Pea Vine Creek is a branch of the south fork of Peachtree, several miles higher up the stream.

sion was lying in a hollow below and farther to the right
rear, and to them it looked as if Newton was beaten. His
brigade commanders seized the initiative without waiting
for orders, and leading their brigades gallantly to the hill-
top before them, they struck the flank of the enemy which
was assailing Kimball. Coburn's and Wood's brigades came
up on the left, with Harrison's on the right, and their sudden
appearance at the crest of the hill threw the enemy before
them into confusion.

But the progressive attack had now reached beyond Shoal
Creek, and Geary's division was engaged. His left front was
covered by a ravine leading down to Shoal Creek and his
right was on high ground and thrown somewhat forward. In
front of his left was open ground, and here his artillery was
placed with Candy's brigade. Jones's brigade was on Candy's
right, with a heavily wooded country before it, and Ireland's
brigade was in rear of Jones. The shape of the ground
brought the collision first on Geary's right. He, too, had a
slight barricade and his centre and left held firm, but he was
obliged to change front of part of his right, and to deploy
Ireland's brigade so as to put it between Jones and Candy,
letting Jones continue curving rearward till he connected
with Williams. When the enemy advanced into the angle
between Ward's division and Geary's left, they were met with
canister from Geary's batteries and with the infantry fire in
front and flank. They lost their organization, and were
fearfully slaughtered. Few battlefields of the war have
been strewn so thickly with dead and wounded as they lay
that evening around Collier's Mill.

Williams was advancing his division when the heavy musketry firing on the left warned him to deploy. He was on
the right rear of Geary, and his left front was covered by a
ravine which ran into Shoal Creek in rear of Geary's line.

His right rested on a ravine also, which separated him from the Fourteenth Corps, and his centre was on the higher ground between. The direction of all these ridges and ravines from Newton to Williams was such as to throw forward the right of each command as it rested on them, and the division commanders, except Newton, all found their right flank receiving the brunt of the first attack. Williams deployed Robinson's brigade on his left, Knipe's on the right of it, and held Ruger's in reserve, distributing his batteries with special reference to sweeping the ravines on either flank and the wooded ridge in front of Knipe. The enemy pressing in between Geary's refused right flank and Robinson's brigade, suffered almost as severely as in the similar situation between Geary and Ward, though the woods and thickets here gave them some shelter. On Williams's right they tried to pass between him and Johnson's division of the Fourteenth Corps, but Williams, by deploying part of Ruger's brigade, defeated this. In front they were easily repulsed, though loth to withdraw.

The whole of the Confederate line of battle was now developed, and did not reach Palmer's corps. His left brigade (Colonel Anson McCook's) assisted in repulsing the attack upon Williams's right, but does not seem to have been itself assailed. A warm artillery fire was kept up from works in front of Palmer and was responded to by his batteries, but no advance was there made from either side.

Not content with this first repulse, Hood's division commanders rallied their men again and again to the attack. On Newton's left there was nothing to oppose them, and they tried again to turn his flank. General Thomas was there in person, and ordering up Ward's batteries, which, as we have seen, were left behind their division, he put them in a position to sweep the valley of Clear Creek, and drive

back the column that threatened to get in Newton's rear.
Along the whole line the attack had been repulsed, and its
only chance of success had been in the first surprise; yet
with sullen determination and unwillingness to accept defeat, the efforts to reform and advance again were continued
till sunset, when the enemy retired to his works.

The question of relative losses in this engagement is surrounded by the difficulties which have been discussed in
other places. Those of the Army of the Cumberland, except in Palmer's corps, are fully and officially reported, and
were 1,707 killed, wounded, and missing. Of these, Newton's division lost only 100, having succeeded apparently
in making better cover than the other divisions before the
attack was received; Ward lost 550, Geary 476, and Williams
580. Of these about one-fifth were killed. Geary alone reports any considerable number of missing, there being 165
in his division, and this no doubt indicates that there was,
in the early part of the battle, some confusion on his right,
which was "in the air" till he changed front and connected
with Williams.

As to the Confederate losses, Hood, though writing after
the publication of Sherman's "Memoirs," and quoting from
its account of this engagement, does not criticise its statement
of Hooker's estimate of 4,400 killed and wounded in front of
the Twentieth Corps. This is strong negative testimony,
and the other evidence more than sustains it. Geary's fatigue
parties buried 409 Confederates, and he reports these as
being in his front. It is probable, however, that they were
in both his front and Ward's, as the latter makes no report
on this point, and Collier's Mill, where the great loss was,
stood in a reëntrant angle between the divisions. Besides
these there were the losses in front and on the left of Newton, where it is admitted that the artillery posted by Gen-

eral Thomas made great havoc, and where 200 of the enemy's dead were buried. In front of Williams and between him and the Fourteenth Corps there was also severe fighting, and Williams reports the burying of dead, though without giving numbers. The losses in Williams's division were heavier than Geary's in killed and wounded, and the reputation of that division gives assurance that it gave quite as good an account of itself in the punishment of those who attacked it. In the absence of specific reports on this point from all the divisions, and even assuming that the burial parties from Geary's division acted for most of the Twentieth Corps, it would seem impossible to put the Confederate dead below 800. Hood's medical director's report makes the proportion of killed to wounded in the engagements around Atlanta, about one to six. This would make his casualties in all, including prisoners, about six thousand.

Hood and his subordinates agree in saying that this was intended for a decisive engagement, and that the order transmitted from the General-in-Chief down to regiments, was that the troops should attack desperately whatever they might find in their front, and strive to make there an end of the campaign. But the advance of Sherman's left wing on that day was more rapid than the Confederate general had reckoned on, and the urgent reports from Wheeler's cavalry and from Cheatham, that the National forces were outflanking them, disjointed his plans. First Cheatham was ordered to move a division's length to his right, as we have already seen; then the absolute necessity of covering the Decatur road was such that Cheatham ordered his right under General Brown to extend to the railroad. Even then he was obliged to put part of his troops in single line, and the movement to the right, instead of covering a division length of front, had been nearly two miles.

McPherson was advancing along the railroad, and Schofield upon a parallel road a mile and a half farther north.
Howard, with Stanley's and Wood's divisions was on Schofield's right, a mile distant.   He had found the bridge over
the south fork of Peachtree burned; but after some sharp
skirmishing Stanley succeeded in rebuilding it and getting
his column over and deployed.   Wood followed and deployed on Stanley's right.   The road on which Howard was
marching converged on that used by Schofield.   It was the
road known as the Cross Keys road, approaching Atlanta
from the northeast, by way of the Howard House and Lewis
Mill.   Schofield's advance division (Cox's) developed a
strong line of intrenchments crossing the road, but running
nearly parallel to it toward the north.   The leading brigade
was soon sharply engaged with intrenched skirmishers, and
the others formed forward on the left of it.   Hascall's division passed and formed in a similar way on the left of these,
Stanley's and Wood's divisions came into line on the right.
Dodge's (Sixteenth) corps had been abreast with Schofield
near Decatur, but the converging character of the roads had
brought Logan (Fifteenth Corps) on Schofield's left, Blair
(Seventeenth Corps) was on McPherson's left flank, and
Dodge was thus put in reserve.   Garrard's cavalry followed,
destroying the railroad.

At one o'clock, the hour set for the attack by Stewart
and Hardee on the Army of the Cumberland, Wheeler was
falling back so close to Atlanta that Hood ordered him to
hold on at all hazards, reminding him that General Smith
with all the reserve artillery was in the works behind him.
Gresham's division of Blair's corps (moving across the country over which Hardee, in a couple of days, was to march
upon the rear of the same division) pushed the Confederate
cavalry back upon a bald hill, which was to be the centre

and key of a desperate combat on the 22d. The energy of Gresham's movement was splendid, but in leading the advance of his column, he himself fell, terribly wounded. Yet the odds was still overwhelming, and about six o'clock it was so evident that Wheeler must be driven within the fortifications of the city and that Cheatham's line was stretched as much as it would bear, that Hood ordered Hardee to send a division at once to support the cavalry. Hardee directed Cleburne to march in obedience to the order, and this splendid division moved silently into the breastworks on the commanding ground, including the bald hill south of the railway, where the exhausted cavalry had made their last stand as night came on.

The order withdrawing troops from Hardee had been sent at a critical moment, and to understand its effect it is necessary to go back to the battle on Peachtree Creek and view the field from the Confederate side. The assault by Stewart's corps seems to have been west of Shoal Creek, his right entering the angle between Ward's and Geary's divisions, and his left extending somewhat beyond Williams. Hardee moved down the space between Shoal Creek and Clear Creek, and perhaps to the east of the latter stream. He had only Newton's division in his front, though Newton's right was supported by Ward. Hardee formed his troops with Bate's division on his right, Walker's in the centre, Maney's on the left, and Cleburne's in reserve. It will be remembered that Newton's right brigade changed front to the right rear as the enemy approached, and Walker's division first struck the breastworks. It was repulsed, but its persistent courage had been such that when it retired it was so shattered that it was unfit to be again put into action. Bate had found nothing in his front, but was seeking in the thicket a way to Newton's left flank.

Cleburne's division had been substituted for Walker's beaten men, and Hardee had given the orders for another attack when the command from Hood was received calling at once for a division to keep McPherson out of Atlanta, and Cleburne was sent. Hardee did not think it prudent to resume the aggressive with his diminished forces, and before Bate could be brought into line to supply Cleburne's place, night was upon him.

Hood did not make his official report till the next winter, when his campaign had closed in ruin at Franklin and Nashville; then he sought to hold Hardee responsible for this among other misfortunes around Atlanta. He was neither quite just nor generous. His defeat would have been only more costly if he had attacked at one o'clock, moving from the positions Stewart and Hardee then occupied; for they would have found the whole of Palmer's (Fourteenth) corps confronting them, as well as the troops which actually repulsed them. But the renewal of Hardee's effort toward evening was made impracticable by Hood's own order. This he issued simply because Sherman's combinations brought McPherson upon Cheatham's flank in abundant time to prevent the Confederate general from gaining any advantage by reason of the gap in the centre of the National line. If Hood had not moved his troops to the right, or if he had not taken Cleburne from Hardee to cover that flank, Cheatham would have been turned, and McPherson would have followed Wheeler's cavalry into the city.[1]

---

[1] The article in the Southern Historical Papers, before referred to (vol. viii., p. 337), puts this beyond reasonable controversy.

CHAPTER XIII.

THE 21st of July was spent by the Armies of the Cumberland and Ohio in advancing and intrenching skirmish lines as close as possible to the enemy's fortifications. General Wood was able to swing forward his division north of the great salient in his front, and formed a connection with Newton, thus bringing the whole of Howard's corps again into line together. McPherson made firm the connection with Schofield's left by Logan's (Fifteenth) corps, and directed Blair to carry the high, bald hill half a mile south of the railroad, forming the southern extremity of the line occupied by Cleburne's division the night before. The assault was made by Force's brigade of Leggett's division, supported on the right by Gresham's division, now commanded by General Giles A. Smith, General Gresham having been wounded, as we have seen, in the advance of the preceding day. Force advanced under cover of the hill itself, which, being steepest near the base, protected the attacking line from the enemy's fire at first. Soon, however, he came into the open, and dashed forward at the barricade before him. The intrenchment was a slight one, but Cleburne's men fought with their usual bravery, and were only driven out after a sharp combat, and with a loss on our side of 250 killed and wounded. The hill was at once intrenched, though subjected to an enfilading fire from the enemy's batteries north of the position, where their line was still intact. The intense heat was such that three staff officers in Force's brigade alone were prostrated by it, and sunstroke added considerably to the list of casualties. But the hill was strongly fortified by its captors, with traverses to protect the guns, and its value was tested next day. From its summit Atlanta lay in full view, with the large rolling mill just inside the city defences, and within range of Leggett's guns.

Both of Hood's flanks were now insecure, and he prepared to retire from the Peachtree line during the night. Colonel Prestman, his chief engineer, had reported that the works on the north side of the city were badly located, and selected a more advanced line on higher ground. The new line was staked off during the 21st, and intrenched during the night by portions of Cheatham's and Stewart's corps and the Georgia troops under Smith. It began at the former line, where the Cross Keys road entered the city, thence ran north about three-quarters of a mile, then west to the Chattanooga Railroad. A similar advanced line was run southward in front of McPherson's left flank.

Hood determined to withdraw into these works all of his army except Hardee's corps of four divisions, and to send this by a long detour to make an attack upon the extreme flank and rear of McPherson's Army of the Tennessee, expecting to follow up any success it might gain, by marching out with Cheatham's corps upon Schofield, and hoping thus to roll up Sherman's army from the south. His original orders contemplated a movement by the McDonough road, some four or five miles southeast, and then toward Decatur; but Blair's corps with its right at Leggett's hill had both its two divisions intrenched along the McDonough road, with the left refused so as to face the south. This made a change

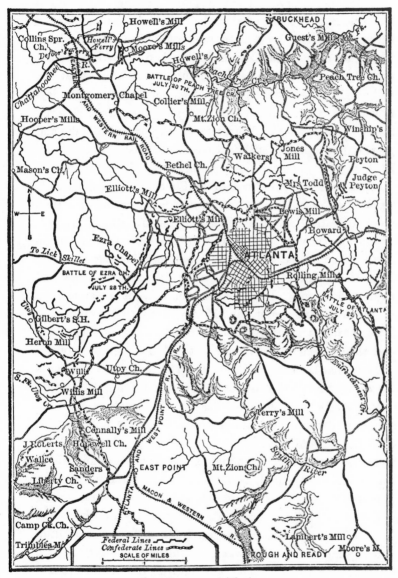

Operations around Atlanta.

of orders necessary, and Hardee, withdrawing in the night
from his line, two and a half miles north of Atlanta, marched
through the city by a road west of Entrenchment Creek
which he crossed at Cobb's Mills, then turned northeast
toward Decatur till his head of column was within about two
and a half miles of that place. It was now a little after daybreak, and he waited for his troops to close up and form,
facing the northwest. Wheeler's cavalry passed the line and
prepared to operate still further to the east. The column
had met with the usual delays of night marches. Cleburne's
division had left the front of McPherson's works, which it
was now to assault in rear, and had fallen in behind Hardee's other divisions in Atlanta about one o'clock. The cavalry moving through the column in the darkness had made
further annoyance and delay; but, considering that the
head of column had marched some fifteen miles, they had
made good speed. Beginning on the left, the divisions were
in the following order, viz., Maney, Cleburne, Walker, and
Bate. After a short rest, the order to advance was given,
and the Confederate divisions entered the densely wooded
country that lay between them and the National lines, moving at right angles to the road they were leaving.

Meanwhile, with the breaking day, Sherman's camps were
astir, and it was soon found that the intrenchments in front
of Schofield and Thomas were abandoned. A general advance was ordered. Schofield's head of column, which
Sherman accompanied, came in full view of the town at the
Howard House. The fortifications of Atlanta were on the
opposite hills, just across the deep valley in which was
Lewis's Mill, and the works were thick with men shovelling
and digging as if for life, their skirmishers holding the line
of Clear Creek which flows northward. Sherman rode forward to reconnoitre, till his escort drew the fire of the bat-

teries. There was some ostentation in the way the men on the fortifications worked, but no one suspected what ruse it might cover. A few batteries were soon in position and as they opened, the enemy vanished behind the works and the siege began. Our skirmishers pushed back the lines before them as far as possible, and trenches were begun on every commanding knoll, soon making a connected line from Thomas's right flank to the works held by McPherson since the day before. The extreme right of the army now rested near the railway, and the work of rebuilding the great bridge over the Chattahoochee was already progressing.

McPherson had also been ordered to close in on Atlanta when it was found that the enemy had withdrawn from the front; but Blair's corps was only separated from the city forts by a single valley with its creek (a branch of Entrench-ment Creek) flowing south. To make room for Logan he transferred G. A. Smith's division to his extreme left, leaving Leggett in position as before. Logan's corps was advanced till General Charles R. Woods's division connected with Schofield's corps, General Morgan L. Smith's division was in the centre, and General Harrow's division on the left, con-necting with Blair. Dodge's (Sixteenth) corps had been in reserve since July 20th, but had moved forward on the pre-ceding evening. Fuller's division bivouacked about a mile east of Leggett's division of the Seventeenth Corps, on the high ground between the branches of Sugar Creek, a tribu-tary of South River. Sweeny's division of this corps was near the line of the Augusta Railway, due north from Fuller's, and McPherson's headquarters were with it. The supply trains and field hospitals of the Army of the Tennessee were in the interval between the Sixteenth Corps and the front lines, except a part of the train which was at Decatur, guarded by Sprague's brigade of Fuller's division.

About noon on the 22d, both divisions of Dodge's corps were moving under orders toward Blair's left flank, when they were attacked by Walker's and Bate's divisions of Hardee's corps. Dodge's men were marching by the flank, right in front, and so, fortunately, had only to halt and face to be

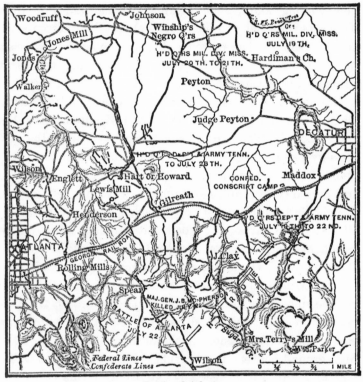

Battle of Atlanta.

in line of battle. McPherson, who had just left General Sherman at the Howard House, met Logan and Blair near the railroad, half way between their line and Dodge, and they were together when the continued musketry fire from the Sixteenth Corps, told that a heavy force of the en-

emy was in the rear. The corps commanders galloped to
their commands and McPherson hastened to Dodge, first
directing Blair to send two regiments to cover the trains and
hospitals. To reach the divisions of Fuller and Sweeny the
Confederates had to advance over some open fields, where the
well-sustained musketry fire upon them was terribly destructive. Fuller's division, which was on the right, sustained
the first brunt of the attack, and repulsed it; but it was
renewed with great determination. The Fourteenth Ohio
and Welker's batteries were put in position, and the unflag-
ging fire of the two divisions made it impossible for Walker
and Bate to force their way across the field. McPherson,
near Fuller's right, had ordered the trains out of the interval, and had received several messages from Blair informing
him that his flank was also engaged. He had also sent to
Logan for his reserve brigade (Wangelin's) to fill the gap
between the Sixteenth and Seventeenth Corps, when, satisfied that Dodge could hold his ground, he started at speed
to reach Blair's line by the road which till that moment had
been clear. He had hardly gone a hundred yards when he
ran full into the skirmish line of Cleburne advancing through
the gap. They called to him to surrender, but raising his
hat as if to a salute, he wheeled to gallop away, when a
volley was fired and he fell mortally wounded. His staff
had been scattered carrying orders, and he was alone with
an orderly, who was also shot and captured; but a wounded
soldier near by managed to get away and gave information
of the great loss the army had sustained. In a few moments the shifting tide of the battle had withdrawn the
enemy a little, and the general's body was recovered before
it was yet cold. Fuller, hearing the firing advancing beyond
his right, had sent the Sixty-fourth Illinois to cover that
flank. This regiment was armed with the Henry repeating

rifles and made so hot a fire that Cleburne's skirmishers were
checked with considerable loss, a flag and some forty men
being captured. Upon the prisoners were found McPher
son's equipments, together with a despatch to him from Sherman detailing the plans for the day, which there had not yet
been time to send to the Confederate commanders. Following this advance, Colonel Strong of McPherson's staff had
been able to secure and carry off the remains of his beloved
chief.

The advance of Hardee's left came out in full view of
Atlanta, and lapped a little over the front of Blair's refused
left wing. The form of the works enabled Smith's division
to repel the enemy there without trouble ; but as the rest of
Cleburne's and Maney's divisions moved forward into the
open rear, the courage of the troops became their destruction, for they were soon surrounded, and many were killed
and some captured. There was no time to change front except by facing about, and this the rest of Smith's division
did, leaping over their breastworks and fighting from the
other side. The enemy's advance pressed on till it reached
the foot of the bald hill and commenced the ascent to attack
Leggett over the very ground Force's brigade had assaulted
the day before. This division, too, was obliged to fight
from the reverse of its intrenchments, but determined to hold
the hill at all hazards. Force's adjutant, Captain Walker,
fell, shot through the thigh, and Force, leaning over to support his friend, received a ball through the head, though by
almost a miracle it passed below the brain and was not fatal.

All this was not the work of a moment, for the ground was
a thicket along most of the line of the enemy's advance, and
even the squads of men broken from their ranks, fought their
way slowly to the rear, making Hardee pay dearly for all the
ground he gained. Logan's reinforcement arrived, and push-

ing forward toward Dodge's right, assisted in covering a change of front for Blair's left, which was now able to pivot on the bald hill, and gradually, by stubborn fighting, to form a new line, which by the aid of Wangelin's brigade was almost continuous with Dodge's, and was on defensible ground.

On hearing of McPherson's death, Sherman ordered Logan, the senior corps commander, to assume command of the Army of the Tennessee, by an encouraging message full of confidence in that general and his troops. As he heard, however, that Sprague's brigade in Decatur was also attacked by Wheeler's cavalry, he ordered Schofield to send a brigade to cover the army trains behind Pea Vine Creek and to assist Sprague, and two others to cover the left flank of Dodge's corps on the railroad. Reilly's brigade of Cox's division was detailed for the former duty, and the division commander with Cameron's and Barter's brigades, and the Fifteenth Indiana Artillery, was sent on the direct Decatur road to report to Logan. As they passed out to the flank, Dodge asked for one of the brigades in his line, as another attack was imminent, and Barter's was sent him, while Cameron's was taken to commanding ground within a mile and a half of Decatur and intrenched. Sprague was soon hard pressed in Decatur, but Reilly going to his assistance, Wheeler was repulsed and the extreme flank in that direction was made secure. M. L. Smith succeeded Logan in command of the Fifteenth Corps, and Brigadier-General Lightburn took temporary command of Smith's division.

Hood himself was in a salient of the Atlanta fortifications from an early hour in the morning, and when the advance of Hardee's left reached the flank of Blair's corps, they came in full view, across an open valley. He watched their prog-

ress till, about three o'clock they had driven back Blair's
left so far that they were attacking the bald hill from the
south.   Then he ordered Cheatham to advance with his
corps against the hill and the line of the Fifteenth Corps
north of it, and Smith with the Georgia troops to attack the
lines of Schofield now held only by Hascall's division and
Byrd's brigade of Cox's.

In the advance of Logan's corps early in the morning,
Colonel Jones (Fifty-third Ohio) with two regiments of M.
L. Smith's division, had been pushed well forward and occupied the top of a hill half a mile in front of the rest of the
corps, having with them two guns from Battery A, First Illinois Artillery.   The advance of Cheatham's corps soon outflanked this force, but Colonel Jones withdrew it in good
order to the principal line.   At this point the railway passes
through a deep cut near which was a large house so situated as to mask the approach of the enemy and cover his
advance along the railway.   Jones asked leave to burn the
house, but failed to get it—a mistake which was, in part at
least, the cause of the break in the line which occurred
there a little later.

Leggett's division had just repelled the attack from its
rear, fighting from the front of their own breastworks, when
Cheatham's attack came, forcing the men to leap back to the
other side and again fight toward their proper front.   The
advantage of the ground enabled Blair to hold on to the hill
by desperate fighting, but part of Logan's (Fifteenth) corps
north of it, being on lower ground and taken in reverse
by the enemy's cannonade from the edge of the wood where
McPherson had been killed, broke, and were swept back to
the railroad, where they formed along it as a new line.   This
happened as follows.   Jones, temporarily commanding Lightburn's brigade, had for a time driven back the onslaught

upon his front, and the rest of the division in the second line had their attention directed to the rear where Hardee's fire was beginning to reach them. Cheatham pushed forward Manigault's brigade to the house in front of Jones, occupying it and firing from its windows, while the greater part of the same command, massing under cover of the house, rushed through the railway cut, turning the flank of Jones and forcing his men to fall back in disorder, though not till they had spiked the guns of the Illinois battery. The second line of the division gave way under this front and rear attack, and here it was that De Gres's battery of 20-pr. Parrotts was also taken.

Woods's division of the Fifteenth Corps hung on by its right to Schofield's position, but a great gap in the line was opened in the centre of the corps. Sherman himself, from near the Howard House, had this part of the field in full view, and immediately ordered Schofield to mass his artillery there and open upon the enemy's flank as they were crowding to the east. This was done, the smooth guns firing spherical case-shot rapidly, and Cockerell's battery of 3-inch ordnance rifles double-shotting with canister; those admirable little guns proving as useful in a close encounter of this sort as they were in longer range. The advance of Cheatham was checked with terrible carnage, and the Fifteenth Corps rallying and making a counter-charge, the enemy were driven back pell-mell, the lost guns, excepting two, were retaken and the intrenchments reoccupied. As Hardee and Cheatham were operating on the sides of a right angle, they were personally miles apart, and their attacks could not be made simultaneous. This had fortunately enabled Blair to repel the assaults in front and rear alternately, and in the lull of the strife when Cleburne and Maney were reforming for other efforts, his men suc-

ceeded in making a light line of breastworks,[1] connecting
the bald hill with Dodge, and the corps of the latter covered
its front in a similar way.

The crisis of the battle was now passed, and though the
Confederate generals led their men to the attack repeatedly,
they only increased their loss without seriously imperilling
the position of the Army of the Tennessee. Schofield's men
in single rank easily repulsed the efforts of Smith's Georgia
troops north of the Howard House, and though Thomas, in
obedience to Sherman's orders, felt of the works along the
front of the Army of the Cumberland, Stewart's corps, in the
elaborately prepared fortifications of the city, was able to
show a front which he did not think it wise to assault.

As night fell upon the field, Hardee withdrew his right
wing, making a half wheel to the rear, to the ridge between
Sugar Creek and Entrenchment Creek, by which he kept his
left in practical connection with the salient of the Atlanta
fortifications and intrenched in a tenable position. This
would no doubt have made the *point d'appui* from which
Hood would have extended his lines southward to cover the
Macon Railroad had Sherman continued to operate by our
left flank.

The pressing importance of increasing the gap broken in
the Augusta Railroad, in view of the warnings Sherman had
received from Washington to expect the enemy to be reinforced by that route, had made him send Garrard with the
cavalry eastward to Covington, to burn bridges and destroy
the railroad track. This Garrard did handsomely, but his
absence from the left flank of the army had enabled Hardee

---

[1] In Hood's Advance and Retreat, p. 189, by a typographical error in copying
a letter from General Blair, the "light line" is printed "tight line," and has
been copied in that way into Confederate accounts of the battle, as if it meant a
strong line, which in the circumstances was impossible.

to approach without warning, and gave the attack the momentary advantage which resulted from his sudden appearance in rear of the Seventeenth Corps. It was an attack of four divisions upon four, in the first instance, with the enormous odds of an attack in rear. In the midst of the *mêlée* resulting from this, Cheatham's assault came again in rear of part of Blair's troops, adding overwhelming odds in numbers to the disadvantage of position. To have repulsed the enemy from the key-points under such circumstances, and to have reformed on the interval between Blair and Dodge so as to present what proved an impregnable front there, must be held to have proven fighting qualities in the troops which have been rarely equalled, and a cool-headed readiness in commanding officers from the General-in-Chief downward, which combine to make an invincible army.

The results are in themselves a significant comment on Hood's new tactics of aggression. The total loss in the National army was 3,521 killed, wounded, and missing, with ten pieces of artillery. DeGres's battery, which was for a time in the enemy's hands, was retaken by the counter-charge of the Fifteenth Corps. The other guns lost were Murray's "regular" battery, which was captured while marching in the road in rear of Blair's corps at the first attack, and two guns of battery A, First Illinois, which had been with General Morgan L. Smith's division in the advanced line in front of Logan's corps, but were taken and dragged off when the line afterward broke.

Of the enemy, 1,000 dead were delivered to their flag of truce in front of one division of Blair's corps, 422 were buried in front of Dodge's corps, about 700 were buried in front of Logan's corps, and Blair estimated the number in front of his other division as many as those delivered under the flag, making a total of 3,200. Reducing by half the numbers that were estimated, and there would still be at least 2,500 killed. Two thousand Confederate prisoners were taken, of whom half were wounded. With these data, no ingenuity of figuring can reduce the enemy's total loss below the ten thousand at which Logan put it.

Hood afterward complained of Hardee's movement as made too slowly and not far enough to the east, and his attack as not vigorous enough. The facts do not justify the complaint. The route actually travelled was fifteen miles for the head of column, or more than seven hours ordinary marching. The night and the passing of cavalry made this slower and more difficult. After forming and moving through thickets and over broken country for two miles, where, as he said, it was often impossible to see ten paces in advance, upon dressing his lines for the attack, his extreme left just overlapped the left of Blair's corps, his alignment being at an angle of forty-five degrees to Blair's and in rear of it. The movement of blocks upon a map could hardly be more exact, and to those who were accustomed to march through that difficult country, the precision of it is marvellous. Hardee did not know of the presence of Dodge's corps till he struck it, but even so he outflanked it also on right and left, and could not have wished for a change in his line if he had known in advance exactly where it stood. The attack was to the full as vigorous and persistent as Hood's own in front of Marietta on the 22d of June, and it was made as early as could have been expected. The subordinate general's work, viewed as a piece of military manœuvring, will excite more admiration among students of the art the more it is examined. The causes of its defeat have been already stated.

CHAPTER XIV.

SIEGE OF ATLANTA—EZRA CHURCH.

SHERMAN'S purpose in moving the Army of the Tennessee upon Decatur and then to Atlanta on the east, had been to destroy the Augusta road for so great a distance as to prevent its being rebuilt and used during the rest of his operations about the city. Had Hood abandoned the town, this wing would have been ready to march to the Macon Railroad at Rough-and-Ready Station; but the question of supply and of easiest reaching the southern lines of railroad near the city decided Sherman to extend his lines by the right flank. He only waited for Garrard's return from the expedition to Covington and for resting and shoeing the horses of Rousseau, who had reached the army after cutting the Montgomery Railroad near Opelika.

Some delicate questions of organization also demanded his action. The lamented death of McPherson made it necessary to assign a commander to the Army of the Tennessee. Hooker was the senior officer available, if the whole army were considered, and Logan if the Army of the Tennessee should furnish the commandant. A doubt whether other corps commanders of the army would cheerfully serve under Logan, owing to some existing jealousies, was one of the reasons for making a selection outside of that organization. Logan and Blair had been very active and prominent in the political affairs of the country, and both ex-

pected to be so again; but Logan had won his military
promotion by brave and valuable service, and could show
honorable scars for each of his grades. The trait in him
most criticised by his companions in arms was his queru-
lousness and disposition to find fault with commands given
him. He could see fifty reasons why a different order should
have been issued; but when once in battle his conduct was
brilliant as well as judicious, and his personal gallantry was
proverbial. His conduct on July 22d had met Sherman's
warmest approval, and the despatches of the latter to the
Government earnestly disclaimed any implied derogation of
Logan's merits in appointing another to the command of the
army.

Hooker was the senior of both Sherman and Thomas, and
looked upon the appointment to the vacancy as his right.
Since the incident of June 22d, Sherman had found the dif-
ferences between them increasing, and honestly doubting
whether he could have the cordial co-operation from him
which was essential in his principal subordinates, he put
Hooker out of the list of those eligible for assignment. It
is possible that in his ultimate choice a predilection in favor
of officers bred in the so-called regular army might have had
some little influence, but Sherman repudiates any purpose
but that of securing the best organization, and he was too
broad a man not to know that the school of the war, for
men who had any military aptitude, had been a soldier's
education of such a sort that any question of the school they
had attended as boys would be ridiculous.

After consulting with Thomas, Sherman recommended
Howard for the position, and the President made the appointment. Howard and Slocum had respectively commanded the Eleventh and Twelfth Corps in the battle of
Chancellorsville under Hooker, and the latter had charged

Howard with much of the responsibility for the disaster. When the two corps were consolidated into the Twentieth, at the beginning of the present campaign, and Hooker was assigned to it, Howard had been given the Fourth Corps, and Slocum had been sent to the Mississippi River and put in command at Vicksburg. To Hooker, therefore, Howard's assignment seemed like a double affront, and he asked to be relieved. Major-General H. W. Slocum was then recalled from Vicksburg to take command of the Twentieth Corps, though it was near the end of August when he arrived.

In Howard, Sherman found most of the same traits which made his association with Thomas and Schofield a satisfactory one. Conscientiously true and loyal to their superior, all three of them asked only how they might most thoroughly carry out his views, without captiousness, hesitation, or complaint. Their abilities and experience made them at ease in the handling of large bodies of men, and it is rare that a large army has had its principal generals so cordial in co-operation, so free from jealousies or intrigues, and so able to relieve the General-in-Chief from the details of administration and of tactical handling of troops. For Thomas, Schofield and Howard both had a respect second only to that they felt for Sherman, and any accident which might have left Thomas in command, would have given him as able and faithful support in his subordinates as Sherman himself found.

In the command of the Fourth Corps, Howard was succeeded by Major-General D. S. Stanley, which completed for the present the more important changes in the organization. A lively correspondence, however, took place between Sherman and the War Department in relation to promotion given to two brigadiers who had asked to be relieved through discontent or on plea of ill-health, and had by

political influence at Washington got the promotion which
had not been accorded to any who had continued in the
field. A circumstance which had caused no little comment
in the army was the fact that with the general orders announcing these promotions, which were published to the
troops, were others in which officers of the line were sum-
marily dismissed the service for tendering their resignations
while their command was in the presence of the enemy.
Against the demoralizing influence of the "spoils system,"
which constantly tended to put influence at Washington in
lieu of faithful service, Sherman vigorously protested on
behalf of his army. The working of the system could not
be better illustrated than by the case of Colonel Poe, Sherman's chief engineer. This officer, a lieutenant of engineers
at the beginning of the war, after assisting the Governor of
Ohio to organize his State troops, was made colonel of a
Michigan volunteer regiment, and by distinguished ability
in the field, rose to the command of a brigade. For gallant
and meritorious service in the campaigns of 1861-62 in
Virginia, he was nominated brigadier-general, and resigned
the colonelcy to enable a good lieutenant-colonel to take
the rank. The President's list of appointments was in excess
of the number fixed by statute, and the Senate returned
them for reduction. Then came a general scramble among
the political "influences," and instead of a simple reduction,
a new list was sent in, containing some never before recommended, and dropping many of those who would not seek
such aid. In this way Poe lost his commission, and returned to his simple rank as a company officer in the staff
corps, after demonstrating his abilities as a general in the
field ; but his self-respect forbade his seeking afterward a
line command. His recognized talents were attested by his
being made the chief engineer of a great army with the lin-

eal rank of captain only: a thing unprecedented in army organizations. To understand what might seem almost insubordination in Sherman's correspondence above referred to, in which he said, "If the rear be the post of honor, then we had better all change front on Washington," it is necessary that such facts should be remembered.

In the Confederate army Hardee had sought to be relieved, owing to his dissatisfaction with Johnston's removal and the assignment of Hood to command; but he had withdrawn his request at the personal desire of the Confederate President. Lieutenant-General S. D. Lee was assigned to the command of Hood's old corps, and joined the army from the west, while Major-General Cheatham returned to his division in Hardee's corps. Major-General Walker had been killed in the battle of Atlanta, but Hardee's corps was so depleted by the terrible losses of that day, that that division was broken up and its regiments assigned to the others.

By July 25th the railway from Chattanooga was in running order to Thomas's camps, Colonel Wright having built the high bridge over the Chattahoochee in six days. Sherman was now ready for new movements of his infantry by the right flank, abandoning the Roswell road as a line for supplies. The Army of the Tennessee was ordered to send its trains and field hospitals to a point near the mouth of Peachtree Creek, and to move on the 27th by successive corps from the extreme left to the extreme right, leaving Schofield for the moment to hold the eastern end of the lines of circumvallation by drawing back part of his command into the intrenchments occupied by the enemy on the 20th.

Simultaneously with this, the cavalry on both flanks were organized for expeditions toward the Macon Railroad, for the purpose of cutting Hood's communications. Rousseau had returned to his district command, but Harrison's cavalry brigade, which had come with him from Opelika, reported to McCook, giving him a division about three thousand five hundred strong, on the right of the army. Stoneman united Garrard's troopers with his own on the left, and had about six thousand five hundred in all, near Decatur; but as Garrard's troops had recently been hard worked, these were to be used as a reserve, leaving less than three thousand for the more active duties of the expedition beyond Jonesboro. After carrying out his orders as to the railroad, Stoneman was authorized, at his own desire, to march on Macon and Andersonville, in an effort to rescue the National prisoners of war in the military prisons there.

On the morning of the 27th both cavalry and infantry were in motion. Dodge's corps (Sixteenth) first left its position, marching in rear of the army crossed Proctor's Creek before night, and passing Davis's division of Palmer's (Fourteenth) corps which had formed a recurved right flank, advanced till it was on a prolongation of the general line of the Cumberland Army, curving around the city. This brought it along the road leading south from Elliott's Mill to Mount Ezra Church, facing due east, and having before it a little valley in which ran one of the upper branches of Proctor's Creek. The other corps of the Army of the Tennessee followed during the night, Blair's (Seventeenth) getting into position on the right of Dodge early in the morning, and extending the line quite to the church, near which the north and south road is crossed by a more important one, leaving the southwest suburb of Atlanta near the racecourse, and running west to a village near the Chattahoochee, bearing the cacophonous name of Lickskillet.

The railways to the south and southwest leave the city at the south side of the race-course, and, as has already been noted, run together for five miles to East Point, where they separate. The railway line is the watershed, the head-waters of Proctor's Creek, Utoy Creek, and Camp Creek taking their rise in the ravines which break down by devious channels to the north and west toward the Chattahoochee, with smaller lateral branches often running between hilly ridges nearly parallel to the general line of the railway.

Near where the Lickskillet road leaves the city there was a strong salient and a bastion in the line of Confederate fortifications, which then turned a little east of south, cross-ing the railway in about a mile, but running pretty close to it for the last half of that distance. Blair's right was there-fore within a mile and a half of the railroad, and if the city defences continued to be Hood's line, a day or two would certainly enable Sherman to cut his communications. The Confederate commander already had his engineers at work with details of men staking out a new line for trenches, leaving the city fortifications at the bastion above described and running southwest some four miles, crossing the north fork of Utoy Creek, and resting on some very commanding hills with broken ground in front, near where runs the road from Atlanta to that same Sandtown on the Chattahoochee which gave the name to the oft-mentioned road north of the river. The course of this line diverged somewhat from the railway, so that at the Sandtown road it was nearly two miles away. Johnston's plans at Marietta were to be sub-stantially repeated, and the warfare of flanking lines was to be prolonged to East Point.

Hood had suffered so severely in the battles at Peachtree and on the east of Atlanta, that his troops were losing their stomach for assaulting intrenchments; but the implied con-ditions of his appointment to the command fettered him, and he could not adopt within a week the policy of his predecessor. While preparing for contingencies, therefore,

ho determined upon another effort to crush Sherman's
flank; and since the thing was to be again tried, it must bo
admitted that he was wise in determining to strike Howard's right while in motion, and before it could intrench.
He withdrew Loring's and Walthall's divisions of Stewart's
corps, to support General S. D. Lee, who with his corps
(lately commanded by Cheatham) was ordered to move out
on the Lickskillet road, attack Howard, and drive him
from that road and the one by Ezra Church. Stewart's
orders directed him to remain in support of Lee near the
fortifications till needed, and next morning (29th), reinforced by his other division (French's), to move beyond Lee
and turn completely the flank of Howard, attacking him in
rear. Hardee's corps and Smith's Georgians were ordered
to occupy the works in front of Thomas and Schofield.
This was the repetition of the tactics of the 22d, but with less
brilliancy; for the attack by Lee's corps on the 28th would
put Sherman on the *qui vive*, and the chances of Stewart's
following the movement up on the 29th would be small.

Meanwhile Logan was marching into position near Ezra
Church, and Davis's division of Palmer's (Fourteenth) corps
was ordered by Sherman, the evening before, to make a considerable detour from Elliot's Mill beyond where Logan was
expected to be, so as to strike in flank any force which
might attack him. Sherman himself, as well as Howard,
was with Logan's corps when the Confederates under Lee
deployed along the Lickskillet road and advanced to the
attack. Logan's men had made some cover for themselves
after the presence of the enemy was discovered, and the Fifteenth Corps line bent back from Ezra Church nearly at
a right angle to Blair's. The ground was high and the slope
in front partially open; and though the Confederates advanced with their usual bravery they were easily repulsed.

They were then reformed, and the order to advance again given and obeyed, but with no better result. Stewart moved forward his two divisions to Lee's assistance, and they also were soon hotly engaged. The general officers exposed themselves to encourage their troops, and Stewart, Loring, Brown, and Johnson were all wounded and disabled. In the intervals of the charges the National line was made stronger, and each attack was less vigorous and had less chance than the one before it. Blair and Dodge sent their reserves to support Logan, Howard massed his artillery to sweep the open ground on his flank, and before sunset the enemy acknowledged himself beaten, and drew out of musket range. In the last attacks portions of the command refused to advance, and line officers with their drawn swords were seen from our works to march to the front of troops that would not follow them.[1]

Sherman was hopeful that Davis's division would arrive in time to turn the repulse of the Confederates into a rout by a counter-attack upon their flank ; but the lack of accurate maps had caused it to get upon a wrong road, and it did not reach the field. The brunt of the attack fell upon the divisions of Harrow and Morgan L. Smith, which formed the centre and right of Logan's corps, but while warmly engaged, their line was never seriously in danger. Howard reported his losses under six hundred killed, wounded, and missing, which was less than the number of Confederate dead left upon the field and buried by Logan, for the total of these was almost seven hundred. Howard's estimate of the enemy's loss at five thousand in all forms, was therefore a reasonable one, and subsequent information led him to increase it.

---

[1] This was commonly told in camp at the time by officers of our skirmish lines, which were advanced as often as the enemy retired.

Hood, in his memoirs, passes lightly over this battle, as if it were a chance and unpremeditated engagement; but the reports of his subordinates show that it was the third of his serious and carefully planned efforts to defeat his adversary by a flank attack. For some reason not explained, he ordered Hardee to go to the front and assume command of both corps engaged, neither of which was Hardee's own; but the battle was over by the time that general could reach the field, and the condition of the troops was such as to forbid new efforts. The fact is, however, used with great force by Hardee, in repelling the subsequent assertions of Hood, that the latter had lacked confidence in either his energy or his ability. The argument which Hood also used, that Johnston's policy had made the troops timid, is not supported by the facts. If the offensive tactics which he had adopted was calculated to inspire his troops, this should have been the most confident and energetic of all his engagements; but it was, on the contrary, the least so, and the testimony of the prisoners who fell into our hands was uniform, that the slaughter which had occurred on the 20th, 22d, and 28th July in quick succession was looked upon as useless and hopeless by his army. In the chaffing between pickets which often occurred in the lulls of the long contest, a Confederate soldier, in answer to the question, "Well, Johnny, how many of you are left," replied, "Oh! about enough for another killing." This, at the end of July, was the camp judgment, and it came from an infantry never excelled in courage or tenacity. Hood's reasoning, if right, should have made these three contests the preparation for more efforts of the same kind; but the effect upon himself was such that he never repeated the method till his affairs had become desperate by the march of Sherman upon Jonesboro, more than a month later. By that time even Jefferson Davis was appalled at the results, and wrote him on the 5th of August, "The loss consequent upon attacking him in his intrenchments requires you to avoid that, if practicable." Johnston could hardly have dreamed of quicker or more complete vindication of his generalship.

CHAPTER XV.

THE cavalry expeditions had not been successful. Mc-Cook, on the right, had marched down the west bank of the Chattahoochee to Campbelltown, and crossing there had succeeded in reaching Lovejoy's Station on the Macon road, seven or eight miles below Jonesboro and about thirty from Atlanta. He hoped to make a junction with Stoneman there, but hearing nothing of him, he did much damage to the railway, burned army trains and some five hundred wagons, taking over four hundred prisoners. He undertook to return by the same route he had travelled, but was surrounded at Newnan's and lost his prisoners, though he fought his own way through with a total loss of six hundred men.

Stoneman had moved from the other flank, and leaving Garrard at Flatrock, east of Decatur, crossed the Ocmulgee River near Covington and made for the railroad running from Macon to Augusta, on which he destroyed a large number of engines and cars at Griswold. He went eastward far enough to burn the bridge over the Oconee, then reunited his detachments before Macon; but the river was between him and the city, and after shelling the town he moved back toward Clinton. Being intercepted and surrounded by what he supposed was a greatly superior force, he authorized his brigade commanders to cut their way out, while he, with about seven hundred of his men, held the enemy in check till the others got through and then surrendered. His sacrificing himself to enable his subordinates to make good a retreat was personally honorable to him, but the facts as afterward discovered showed that he had been deceived as to the enemy's force, and that his position was by no means desperate. Sherman was dissatisfied with the lack of enterprise shown by Garrard during Stoneman's absence, and rated the usefulness of his cavalry rather low.

The movement of the Army of the Tennessee to the right was followed by that of the Army of the Ohio, which moved from its position on the left flank in the night of the 1st of August. General Thomas had been ordered to take a division from the Twentieth Corps, which General Williams temporarily commanded, and with it and Davis's division already beyond the flank of the Army of the Tennessee, swing forward that wing toward Atlanta. He took Ward's division and placed both it and Davis's upon the Lickskillet road a mile west of the Alms House, and Howard wheeled his right forward to connect with them. On the 2d, Schofield moved up the Twenty-third Corps, intrenching on the banks of the north fork of Utoy Creek, and the Army of the Tennessee again brought the right shoulder forward and gained nearly a mile of new ground on that flank. Ward's division was now sent back to the Twentieth Corps, which extended its lines so as to relieve Palmer, who with the rest of the Fourteenth Corps joined Davis's division on the right.

Sherman was now of the opinion that his right wing must be near the railroad, and for the purpose of giving unity to movements on that flank, directed Palmer to report to Schofield and act under his orders temporarily. This raised a question of rank, as Palmer's commission ante-dated Schofield's, though both were made to take effect on the same day, and Schofield was senior in previous grade. Sherman decided in favor of Schofield's claim, but Palmer protested, and asked to be relieved of the command of his corps. After vainly endeavoring to persuade Palmer to withdraw his request, and suffering for two days a game of cross purposes which greatly obstructed and delayed movements on that flank, Palmer was relieved, and soon after General Jefferson C. Davis was assigned by the President to the corps command, with rank of Brevet Major-General, by recommendation of both Sherman and Thomas. This, however, anticipates the order of events.

On the morning of August 3d, Palmer's corps was ordered forward to co-operate with the Twenty-third, both under command of Schofield, who determined to force a crossing of the north fork of Utoy Creek where it makes a considerable bend to the north. Hascall's division of the Twenty-third Corps, and Baird's of the Fourteenth were assigned this duty. Hascall promptly crossed with but little opposition and occupied a high ridge on the south, above and east of Heron's Mill, taking ground to the left in accordance with his orders, till that flank rested near the creek at its southward curve. Baird was to follow Hascall and extend on his right, but did not do so (owing to the disputes about the general command of the movement) till five o'clock in the afternoon, when General Sherman in person peremptorily ordered the division over, and it took the position assigned with its right resting on the other south curve of the creek. On the following morning Cox's division of the Twenty-third Corps crossed the creek and formed in rear of Baird, with orders to support the advance of the latter. Palmer was ordered to move Baird's division strongly against the enemy in front, putting over Davis's and Johnson's

divisions of the corps (the former temporarily in command
of General Morgan), and, as ground should be gained, swinging the whole out to the south and east. Again delays occurred, which Sherman characterized as unpardonable, till
toward evening, when a reconnoissance was made by Gleason's brigade of Baird's division, capturing 25 prisoners,
and sustaining a loss of 26 in killed and wounded; but no
general movement of the division was made. Morgan and
Johnson crossed the creek somewhat farther to the right
and within easy supporting distance. Orders for the 5th
were issued directing Palmer to move Baird's division forward and endeavor to carry the position before him or drive
the enemy into their principal works; to move Morgan's
division in *échelon* on Baird's left flank, taking advantage of
any success he might have to continue his line to the right;
and to march Johnson's division to the right beyond Morgan and advance him in *échelon* also to the front. Hascall's
division of the Twenty-third Corps being in a bend of the
creek where most of the division could not advance, was
ordered to support Baird's left. Cox's division was ordered
to march to the right to support Johnson's division. The
whole movement was to begin at six o'clock. Duplicates of
the orders to Palmer were sent to his division commanders
by General Schofield, to make sure they were known. Before the time of moving in the morning Baird notified Schofield that he did not recognize his authority, had received
no orders from his corps commander, and no notice that the
Fourteenth Corps was under Schofield's command. His report states that when finally he received orders from the
corps commander he had no information of the position of
Morgan's division on his right, and moved forward about
eight o'clock. The advance was courageously made when it
began, and the enemy's intrenched skirmish line, which had

been greatly strengthened since the day before, was carried
with a loss of 83 killed and wounded. One hundred and
forty prisoners were captured from the enemy. Morgan's
division moved up and connected with Baird's right, but
with the line retiring along the road which runs from the
Sandtown road to the village of Lickskillet. Johnson's
division formed on the right of Morgan's, and afterward, in
pursuance of orders, marched to a wooded ridge overlooking
a small stream, tributary to the principal Utoy Creek and
flowing southwest into it, Cox's division being in close
support. The narrow valley was open, and to the east the
hills on the other side were wooded. No effort was made
to cross the creek, Johnson resting on the western side
during the afternoon. That evening Schofield reported to
Sherman : " I am compelled to acknowledge that I have
totally failed to make any aggressive movement with the
Fourteenth Corps." Cox's division of the Twenty-third
Corps was ordered to relieve Johnson's, which in turn was
ordered to relieve Hascall's. The latter was then marched
to right and rear of Cox's. This was early in the morning
of the 6th, and during the night the constant chopping and
falling of trees along the hillside east of the creek had given
evidence that the enemy's infantry had moved in force upon
it. Encouraged by the delays of the past forty-eight hours,
Hood had determined to intrench the line of the Sandtown
road and had put part of Hardee's corps upon it, making a
line from the rough and high ground in front of Baird across
the ridge dividing the branches of Utoy Creek, and then
down the east side of the tributary above mentioned to the
principal stream ; thence it recurved sharply along its north
bank. The distance across the forks of Utoy on this line is
about two miles. Cox was ordered to make a reconnoissance
in force by one brigade, supporting it so that if the enemy's

line were carried the advantage could be followed up.
Reilly's brigade was detailed for the purpose, supported by
Casement's (formerly Cameron's). The advanced brigade
was formed in line, and the farther margin of the open
ground being held by our skirmishers, it marched rapidly
over the brook and up the slope beyond. It soon found
itself in the entanglement of felled trees, and of undergrowth half cut off, then bent down and interlaced, but it
pushed on to the intrenchments. They were found to be
strongly held, and though some of the assailants reached the
parapet, the advance of the brigade was arrested. It held
its position at the entanglement, a hundred yards from the
parapet, until the reconnoissance developed the solid line of
breastworks extending far to right and left, occupied, as was
learned from prisoners, by Bate's division. Casement's brigade in line was advanced to the east side of the valley, and
under its cover, Reilly was withdrawn, with a loss of a little
over three hundred men. A well supported skirmish line
was intrenched close to the abatis and held there, preventing the enemy from coming outside his works.

Hascall marched to the main stream of Utoy Creek and
succeeded in crossing with two brigades, driving away the
enemy's cavalry after a sharp combat. The position thus
acquired enfiladed Bate's line, and in the night it was
abandoned. The Confederate troops retired into a strong
line of fortifications extending from the high hills near the
north fork of Utoy Creek southward across the Sandtown
road about a mile and a half, thence bending a little toward the east it followed the hilly ridges behind the south-
ernmost branches of Utoy Creek till it reached the railway a
mile beyond East Point.

While matters had been thus progressing on the extreme
right, active demonstrations had been made on other parts

of the line. Stanley had advanced strongly supported skirmish lines in front of the Fourth Corps, and had taken the
enemy's intrenched pickets along most of his front. The
same had been done by Williams with the Twentieth Corps,
and the front of the Army of the Tennessee had been advanced with similar results. The Fourteenth and Twenty-
third Corps advanced on the 7th, crowding their skirmish
lines close to the Confederate fortifications, meeting with
opposition which General Sherman described in his despatches to Washington as a "noisy, but not a bloody battle." Schofield's advanced division (Cox's) occupied the
hills immediately in rear of Willis's mill pond, its right
resting on the principal south fork of Utoy Creek, Hascall's
division being in reserve on that flank. The Fourteenth
Corps (Brigadier-General R. W. Johnson in temporary command) swung its right forward till it formed a connected
line with Schofield's.

Sherman felt that he had now stretched his line about as far
as could be safely done, and determined to try the effect of
cannonade with heavier ordnance, while parallels should be
worked up closer to the enemy's fortifications. Hood had
the Georgia troops with heavy artillery in the works in front
of Thomas, with reserves of his regular troops ready to
move quickly to any point which might be threatened.
Hardee held his extreme left in front of Schofield, and the
rest of his army was in the space between, confronting
the Army of the Tennessee. Some 4½-inch Parrott rifled
cannon were ordered up and put in battery on Thomas's
front, and with these and the other artillery of the army,
Sherman cannonaded the town and the enemy's forts for
several days. He directed Schofield, however, to continue
extending his flank as far as he could, and on the 8th a brigade of Hascall's division was put over Utoy Creek on the

south, and intrenched on a hill south of that stream. It was followed by the rest of that division in a day or two, and on the 12th, Cox's division of the same corps made a reconnoissance in force to the junction of the Campbelltown road with the road to East Point, and half a mile eastward along the latter. This demonstrated the fact that the Confederate lines were farther in front of the West Point Railway than either Sherman or Schofield had thought. The division, however, was not brought back to its place in line, but encamped on Hascall's right rear, the Fourteenth Corps extending its front so as to fill the gap and reach Utoy Creek. On the 15th Schofield advanced his right again, putting Cox's division at the crossing of the Campbelltown and East Point roads, its flanks covering them both, and on the 18th it was pushed out three-quarters of a mile southeast and intrenched in a nearly semicircular position with the left covering the upper valley of Utoy Creek and the right that of Camp Creek. This was the extreme point reached in the advancing of Sherman's lines, and this became the pivot on which the movement to the south of Atlanta was made. The successive advances had been made in the face of stubborn resistance of cavalry supported by infantry skirmish lines, but Hood did not repeat his former attacks upon the flank in force.

On the same day that this last advance was made, Kilpatrick was sent with a large division of cavalry to make a lasting break, if possible, in the Macon road. Starting from the right rear, he crossed the railroad to West Point at Fairburn, and that to Macon about Jonesboro, doing both some damage. Hood had sufficient notice, however, to send Jackson to meet him, and although Kilpatrick made the entire circuit of Atlanta, and had done some brilliant fighting, no permanent interruption of the railway was made, and the cars were running into Atlanta as usual in a day or two. During Kilpatrick's absence constant demonstrations along the line were made, and reconnoissances in force from the right flank on the 19th, 20th, and 21st, were pushed as far as Camp Creek Church, and half a mile on the road to Liberty Church, close to the forts in front of East Point. These were continued with varying strength, down to the time of the general movement to be narrated.

Sherman was now convinced that he could expect no permanent results from cutting the enemy's communications, unless it were done in force, and he seriously resumed the plan which he had communicated to his principal subordinates in orders a week before, viz., to intrench the Twentieth Corps (Slocum's), at the Chattahoochee bridge, and swing all the rest of his army to the south of Atlanta. He ordered half of all baggage sent to the rear, and each army to provide itself with ten days' full rations, which should be issued so as to last fifteen days.

Since the 14th, the greater part of the enemy's cavalry under Wheeler had been operating against the railroad north of the Chattahoochee. He attacked Dalton, where the garrison under Colonel Laiboldt was able to hold him in check, till General Steedman from Chattanooga could come to its assistance, when Wheeler was repulsed. The railroad and telegraph were cut in several places, but the damage was trifling, and yielding to the common temptation of cavalry to make too much of the distance they may go behind the hostile lines, Wheeler marched into East Tennessee, where he could by no possibility do anything to affect the campaign.

Satisfied that no serious mischief was occurring in his rear, Sherman began his movement on Thursday, August 25th. Stanley's (Fourth) corps, now the left flank on the north of Atlanta, marched to the rear of Williams's (Twentieth), and Garrard's cavalry, dismounted, held the Fourth Corps lines. Next day Stanley was at Utoy Creek, massed in rear of Davis's (Fourteenth) corps, which also abandoned its lines to its skirmishers, and was massed near Stanley. During the night Williams's corps marched to the works prepared at the railway crossing of the Chattahoochee, where General Slocum arrived and assumed command. At the same time the Army of the Tennessee marched by roads west of Thomas, to the vicinity of the village of Utoy, and was also massed, facing southward and now forming the right of the army. Dodge's corps (Sixteenth), in consequence of his having been disabled by a wound, was temporarily placed under command of General Ransom. Garrard's cavalry covered the movement at the rear, Schofield's corps (Twenty-third) holding fast in its positions in front of East Point, and demonstrating in front and flanks.

By the evening of the 27th, it will be seen, all of Sherman's army except the Twentieth Corps was between Atlanta and Sandtown, échelloned along that road. Hood had not interfered with the movement, and had only followed it with light cavalry reconnoissances. But his horsemen, skirmishing with Garrard on the north and with Kilpatrick on the south, were able to locate the National forces with sufficient accuracy, and he jumped at the conclusion that Wheeler's expedition had been successful to the full extent of his hopes, and that Sherman was retreating across the Chattahoochee by the Sandtown road, short of supplies. His illusion was confirmed by an incident which occurred the same evening. An old woman of the neighborhood had applied to some of Hardee's troops for food, and stated that she had been within the lines of Schofield's division which lay nearest, and had been refused food with the assertion that the troops had not enough for themselves. She had managed to pass the lines and carried her budget of news to the enemy. She was sent to Hardee, and the latter thinking her knowledge of positions of some importance, carried her to Hood's headquarters, where she repeated her story. Hood, seizing upon her statement that the National forces were short of rations, exclaimed that it fully corroborated his belief that Sherman was crossing the Chattahoochee at Sandtown.[1] To this conviction he stubbornly adhered for forty-eight hours longer, when it was quite too late to make new combinations to keep his adversary from the railroad. Had he suspected the truth, as some at least of his subordinates did, Lee's and Stewart's corps would have been in line in front of Red Oak and Fairburn when Sherman approached the West Point Railway; his right would have covered East Point, and another long flanking operation, probably this time by the left, would have been imposed upon the National army. Atlanta would have been abandoned, but Atlanta was only a name—the thing it stood for was the junction of the western and southern railways, which Hood would still have held.

The trains of Sherman's whole army marched between the two corps of the Army of the Cumberland, and Schofield was kept in position till they were well on their way from Mount Gilead Church, which is four miles southeast of East Point, to Red Oak, a station on the West Point Railway, seven miles from the former place, and near which Thomas encamped on the night of the 28th. Howard, with the Army of the Tennessee, reached Fairburn the same evening, five miles farther southwest on the same road. A day was now given to thorough destruction of some miles

---

[1] The story was narrated to the writer by General Hardee, at the time of Johnston's surrender in North Carolina the following spring.

of the railway, burning the ties and twisting the heated rails. Schofield withdrew a little from his isolated position on the 28th, putting his corps in line a mile northeast of Mount Gilead, and next day moved into connection with the left flank of Stanley's corps. The 30th the movement was resumed, and the whole army was between the two rail-roads, except Schofield's corps, which moved from Red Oak Station a mile and a half toward East Point, and took position there, covering the movement of the army trains. The Twenty-third Corps was thus separated fully three miles from supports, and fully expected a blow from Hood. He contented himself, however, with a brisk cavalry recon-noissance, and during the skirmish Schofield's troops threw up a light intrenchment in preparation for more serious contingencies. His dream of a flying enemy was dispelled, however, and in its place he substituted that of a movement of two corps of Sherman's army to his line of communica-tions. He now ordered Hardee with his own and Lee's corps to Jonesboro, and directed an attack next morning on that flank of the National forces.

The Macon Railway runs along the ridge separating the waters of the Flint on the west from those of the Ocmulgee on the east, and Hardee was expected to drive Sherman's corps over the former stream if they had crossed it. Gen-eral Cleburne was in command of Hardee's own corps, and no officer of the Confederate army had a better established reputation for courage and energy. He was delayed in get-ting into position by finding that Howard was already upon the road he expected to take, and in order to reach the right flank of the National forces he had to open a new road. It was nine in the morning of the 31st before Cleburne's corps was in position, and Lee's corps did not get up on his right for two hours more. Finding that this was giving Howard time to intrench, Hardee, by telegraph, urged Hood himself to come to the front, but the latter deemed it unwise to leave Atlanta.

Howard had been advancing on the 30th along the road from Fairburn to Jonesboro, impeded all day by cavalry of the enemy, who made a stubborn skirmishing resistance in order to give Hardee time to reach Jonesboro and to form at Flint River.

Sherman had indicated the Renfro place as the position where his right wing should rest at the close of the 30th, but he had authorized Howard to move on to the railroad at Jonesboro if the opportunity offered. There was no water at Renfro's, and although he got reports of a force intrenched at Jonesboro, sometimes called a division and sometimes a corps, Howard decided to advance at least to the Flint River, which was the nearest point before him where water enough for the troops could be had. After a brief halt, therefore, the Army of the Tennessee marched again, in two columns, Logan's (Fifteenth) corps on the left, and Ransom's (Sixteenth) on the right, both preceded by portions of Kilpatrick's cavalry. The advance was so rapid that the Confederate cavalry was unable to make any considerable stand. At the Flint River the bridge was found still uninjured, and the cavalry covered it by a rapid fire from the river bank, while Hazen's (formerly M. L. Smith's) division carried it and the barricades defending it, by a brilliant dash. The head of Logan's column was now over, and giving the enemy no time to rally, though night was coming on, he advanced to the highest ground between the river and the railroad, where, by Howard's directions, he intrenched, putting Hazen's division on the left, Harrow's on the right, and Osterhaus's in second line.

As Ransom came up with the Sixteenth Corps, he was

placed in position west of the river facing to the south, his left being nearly opposite Logan's right. Blair's (Seventeenth) corps did not get up till morning, when it was placed also on the west of the Flint, but in rear of Logan's left, and facing northeast.

At daylight of the 31st, Logan rectified his lines on the right and Ransom built a bridge in front of his left, so that he connected with Logan. Bridges were also built by Blair and Logan, so that the three corps were in mutual support and were prepared for a new advance. Howard knew by the noise of the trains on the railway that a concentration was making during the night. His position was somewhat perilous till he knew the rest of the grand army to be within supporting distance, and he spent most of the day in making his position strong, meanwhile communicating with Sherman. The General-in-Chief was with Thomas's columns, which were in motion, and it was not till late in the day that the orderlies sent with despatches from Howard found him and he became aware of Hood's new movement.

About three o'clock in the afternoon Hardee advanced against the Army of the Tennessee, his attack extending along the whole front of Logan's corps and one division of Ransom's. Howard sent C. R. Woods's division from Blair's corps across the river to support Logan's left, fearing the enemy might get between that flank and the stream. The attack was fierce, but neither in weight nor persistency did it seem to equal former efforts of the Confederate infantry. The most determined part of the assault fell on Hazen's division ; but here as elsewhere it was repulsed, and the enemy retired, leaving over four hundred dead upon the field. The Confederates engaged were mostly of Lee's corps, and their reports would indicate that that officer, supposing he heard the signal agreed upon between him and Cleburne, had ordered the attack before the latter was ready. It appears certain that there was some failure in the coöperation intended, and Cleburne's corps took little part in the affair beyond preventing Kilpatrick with his cavalry from crossing the river farther to the right, as he was trying to do under Howard's orders. Cleburne followed Kilpatrick across the river, and Howard, to meet this movement and protect his trains, directed Blair to send a division from his corps to the right of Ransom's, and Giles A. Smith's was detached for that purpose.

But a little farther to the north other events were occurring. Schofield moving in the morning past Morrow's Mill, the position of Stanley's corps, took a road leading to the Macon Railway, about a mile south of Rough-and-Ready Station. Stanley took one a little farther to the south, and both advanced as rapidly as a strong opposition from cavalry would permit. Schofield's leading division (Cox's) reached the railway at three o'clock in the afternoon, and found there an intrenched line covering it and occupied by dismounted cavalry. This was carried by a charge and a considerable number of prisoners taken. A railway train was within sight but stopped at the noise of the combat and steamed back to Atlanta. The division marched north to Rough-and-Ready and encamped, and Hascall's division, reaching the road at the same place as the other, was employed in destroying the railway south to the point reached by Stanley's corps at four o'clock. Stanley also began the work of destruction. At six in the evening Carleton's brigade of Baird's division (Fourteenth Corps) reached the same road about four miles north of Jonesboro, but the rest of the division did not get up that night.

The retreating railway train which carried the news to Atlanta that Sherman's infantry were moving northward on

Rough-and-Ready Station, carried consternation with it. Hood himself seems to have been bewildered, and to have seized at once upon the idea that this was the beginning of a general attack upon Atlanta, and that Sherman had only moved by his right flank across the railways, facing northward. He had not heard of Hardee's combat of the afternoon, and without awaiting reports from him, sent at six o'clock peremptory orders for the return of Lee's corps to the city, directing it to move by two o'clock in the morning. Hardee was ordered to cover the railway and the provision and ordnance trains behind him as well as he could. Hood's despatches informed Hardee that there were indications of an attack on Atlanta, as the National forces were in considerable force at Rough-and-Ready, and it was thought they would strike East Point the next day. As the railway and telegraph were cut, these despatches were sent by courier, and Lee's movement was timed accordingly. Lee's corps marched as ordered, but was not destined to reach Atlanta. Other orders met it on the way. Hardee, putting a bold face on his losing game, stretched his corps as well as he could to hold the lines intrenched in the afternoon, resorting to the old device of heavy skirmish lines in front, with reserves ready to move at double-quick step to a threatened point. Meanwhile he reported to Hood the actual situation, and was greatly helped in his defence of Jonesboro by the fact that Howard knew he had two corps of the Confederate army before him at nightfall, and no one could suspect that one of them would be recalled to Atlanta during the night. Hood's misjudgment of the state of affairs was one of those inexplicable things which could enter into nobody's calculation.

On the night of the 31st, Sherman knew that he held the railway from Rough-and-Ready to near Jonesboro, and that

Hardee and Lee were in position at the latter place. It was possible that a garrison might be left in the *enceinte* of Atlanta, but it was probable that the whole Confederate Army would be before him next day. He therefore sent orders by courier to Slocum, directing him to be active in discovering the condition of things at Atlanta, and to enter the place if possible. Thomas was ordered to march Davis's (Fourteenth) corps to Howard's left, destroying such portions of the railway as it could reach in passing. Stanley with the Fourth Corps was directed to march down the railway, destroying it thoroughly and then joining Davis's corps. Schofield's orders were to perform a similar work of destruction from Rough-and-Ready southward. All these orders looked to the termination of the campaign when Hood should be driven south of Jonesboro, for otherwise the railway would have been carefully preserved instead of destroying it. Sherman was only anxious to press the enemy enough to make sure of the evacuation and the complete possession of the railway connections at Atlanta; for this carried with it every material advantage which would follow from holding any point north of Macon, the next important intersection of railroads. For this reason, he did not hasten the movement to Howard's support beyond the speed which might be consistent with thorough work in burning the ties, twisting the rails and blowing up the masonry of the road. But in the afternoon he joined Howard in person, accompanying the march of Davis's corps, and learned that Lee's corps had disappeared, and only Hardee's was before him. This put a new face on affairs, and he despatched orders to concentrate the Army of the Cumberland in haste, so that Hardee might be surrounded and, if possible, captured while isolated from the rest of Hood's army. Thomas ordered Stanley to suspend other work and hurry forward to Jonesboro. Davis was ordered to put his corps on Howard's left, and swinging his own left boldly forward, endeavor to envelop Hardee's right. Howard was directed to send two divisions of Blair's corps by a detour to his right and put them, if possible, upon the railroad south of Jonesboro. Schofield turned his head of column south, moving close behind the Fourth Corps.

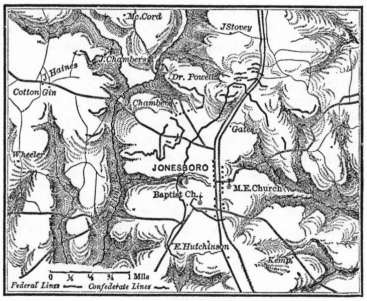

Jonesboro.

Hardee's lines had been formed to meet Howard's advance from the west, and their direction was nearly north and south. His extreme right was sharply refused, and where it reached the railroad, ran toward the southeast, behind a small stream and valley. Cleburne's own division was on that flank, Govan's brigade holding the angle, with Granberry on his left, and Lewis still farther to the right and

rear. As Davis's corps approached, Morgan's division connected with the Army of the Tennessee, having Carlin's
(formerly Johnson's) division on the left, and Baird's in reserve. Staff officers were despatched to hasten the movement of Stanley's corps, and Sherman's impatience at the
delay became so great that Thomas galloped away in person
on the same errand. Davis sent forward Edie's brigade of
Carlin's division to reconnoitre the ground toward the railroad, and after a brisk skirmish it occupied a hill or ridge
extending beyond the salient angle of the enemy's lines.
The rest of Carlin's division was now formed on the left of
Edie, and Morgan's division moving by the main road leading by Chambers's Mill, there turned to the left and formed
on Carlin's right. Baird's division was held in reserve in
rear of Carlin. Prescott's battery was put in position on
the hill held by Edie, and its fire, enfilading part of the
enemy's line near the angle, disabled a number of his guns
there and did much execution. Davis's formation was in
two lines, the divisions as near each other as was practicable. Being ordered forward they advanced toward the
angle of Hardee's works, but were much impeded by the
tangled and broken character of the ground. Edie's brigade
struck the salient in the enemy's line and carried it, suffering considerably in the attack. The Confederates rallied
and repulsed the assailants, Edie's supports not arriving in
time to enable him to hold the works he had gained. The
line was reformed near the foot of the slope on which the
enemy's breastworks were, and the alignment was rectified.
Este's brigade of Baird's division was deployed in close support of Carlin's right and put under his orders. The advance was again ordered, just before five o'clock, and this
time Este's brigade found itself in front of the salient, and
carried it with a dash, losing, however, nearly one-third of

its numbers in the few minutes it was under the enemy's fire. The rest of Carlin's men, sweeping in from the left, with Morgan's on the right, surrounded the Confederates in that angle of their line, and General Govan with nearly his whole brigade and two batteries of artillery were captured, the gun-carriages being a good deal injured by the previous fire of Prescott's battery. Lewis's brigade on Hardee's extreme right, and Granberry's, which was next on the left of Govan, now fell back, making a new line and showing a bold front, while Hardee's centre and left still held to their intrenchments. Stanley's head of column had come up before Davis's attack was made; but before the corps was deployed and ready to advance on Davis's left, darkness covered the field and put an end to the day's operations.

The losses in Carlin's division were 371; in Baird's (Este's brigade) 330, and in Morgan's division about the same number. Over three hundred of the enemy's dead were left on the field. Eight hundred and sixty-five were surrendered with General Govan, and on the following day nearly a thousand, including wounded left in hospitals by Hardee, were added to the list of captured.

Before Lee's corps, which had left Hardee in the night, had made more than half the distance back to Atlanta, Hood discovered his mistake, and countermanding its orders, directed it to take position to cover the movement of Stewart's and Smith's corps from Atlanta. It was too late to save anything which had not been removed, and large trains of ordnance and other stores, numbering over eighty cars and six locomotive engines, were left to be destroyed by the cavalry rear-guard. During the night Hardee also evacuated his lines, and on September 2d, Hood once more assembled his army at Lovejoy Station. About midnight of the 1st, the noise of explosions was heard in the direction of

Atlanta, and it hardly needed the courier whom Slocum
sent forward next day to tell that the city was abandoned
and the stores burnt and destroyed. Slocum had been met
on his advance in the morning by the mayor of the city, who
formally surrendered the place, and he lost no time in for-
warding the confirmation of the welcome news to Sherman,
who had already followed the retreating Confederates to
Lovejoy Station and was developing Hood's lines there by
the sharp skirmishing which had been the everyday work of
the campaign.

It was now definitely known that Atlanta was ours, and
" fairly won," as Sherman said in his despatches to Washington, and he issued his orders for the withdrawal of the army
to the vicinity of that place, for a brief period of rest and
preparation for a new campaign. The Army of the Cumberland occupied the city, the Army of the Tennessee was encamped at East Point, and the Army of the Ohio at Decatur.
The cavalry covered the flanks and rear, from Sandtown to
Roswell along the Chattahoochee.

Hood affects to wonder that Sherman did not attack
Stewart's corps on the march from Atlanta on September 1st.
The reasons are twofold. The presumption was that Lee's
corps was still within supporting distance of Hardee. In
the absence of positive evidence, his eccentric march back
toward Atlanta, in obedience to Hood's order, could not have
been imagined by any military man. To get up the Fourth
Corps on the left and envelop Hardee or force him back
upon any new position Lee might be supposed to be taking
in rear, was the plain dictate of wisdom. This was what
Sherman was doing, and he was exasperated at not being
able to complete the work before night came on. The cavalry brought no information of the movements of either Lee's
corps or the rest of Hood's army ; and judging by probabili-

ties alone, every maxim of sound strategy dictated the plan of interposing as much as possible of the army between Hardee and the remainder of Hood's forces, which must unite with him by some road coming in from the east.

Hood also intimates that in calling Lee to him it was his purpose to attack the exposed flank of Sherman's army. This was what Sherman expected and what Schofield also was looking for; but Hood's despatches to Hardee prove that he was not thinking of aggression; he talked only of defence, and was seeking in vain to settle in his own mind any satisfactory theory of his adversary's plan. Had he meant to attack the flank, surely never was a better opportunity than that of September 1st, when Hardee was fighting against odds to hold his position, and Schofield had turned his back on Atlanta to march into position at Jonesboro. The Confederate General must be held to have misconceived utterly Sherman's movements from August 25th, and to have been made inconsistent and feeble in action by his uncertainty as to the situation. Of all the theories as to his purposes at that critical time, the one which would make him take the bold initiative, as he had done in the first week of his command, is the one most entirely unsupported by evidence. The order to Hardee to march to Jonesboro was neutralized by the recall of Lee, and loses its appearance of energy, while everything else combines to show that he was groping in the dark. Sherman's movement, on the other hand, was boldly conceived and systematically executed. His corps was so écheloned that had the enemy marched out of Atlanta to attack the nearest flank, Schofield would have been able to hold him in check till the Army of the Cumberland could have come to his assistance. The other contingency was the one which was tested. Howard was attacked by Hardee's and Lee's corps, and easily repulsed the assault till the arrival of Davis's corps enabled Sherman again to assume the aggressive.

The campaign as a whole will remain a most instructive example of the methods of warfare which may be said to be the natural outcome of modern improvements in weapons, and in means of transportation and communication when used in a sparsely settled and very difficult if not impracticable country. At the time, the successful termination of the long hand-to-hand struggle was hailed as the assurance that the war approached its close ; and the thanks which Congress and the President bestowed upon Sherman and his army were only the faint expression of the enthusiasm of the nation toward the General and his troops.

CHAPTER XVI.

RESULTS.

THE investigation of the comparative losses of the con-tending armies is, like that of their comparative strength, one of no little difficulty. The system of returns of the armies of the United States is one in which every man en-listed must be accounted for, and the figures, like the debits and credits of mercantile account-books, are expected to balance. For various reasons, no such fulness of accounts is found in the printed reports of the Confederate armies. The publication of the archives collected at Washington will at some future day do much to clear up the question, but we are forced for the present to rely upon approximate esti-mates. First, however, it must never be forgotten that the exact system of the National army was not enforced by the Confederates. It is unnecessary to inquire whether this was a purposed omission, made through the unwillingness of the Richmond Government to let the Southern people know the terrible cost of the struggle they were making, or whether it resulted from the embarrassments of poverty and the lack of the means for keeping up elaborate systems of field statistics. The fact is enough, and of it there can be no doubt. At the surrender of General Joseph E. Johnston, in the spring of 1865, that officer responded to an inquiry by General Schofield as to the number of his forces, that his report of effectives was about sixteen thousand men, yet double that number appeared at the Provost Marshal's office at Greensboro, and received their certificates of parole. At that time General Johnston, who was perfectly familiar with both systems of returns, added the remark that they had not pretended to keep up the accurate forms of report in·sisted upon by the Adjutant-General's Office at Washington.

It may be that this statement should apply chiefly to the field returns, which were those made use of by the com·manding officers in active operations, and that more sys·tematic tables were made by the Adjutant-General's office. If so, it is evident that the Confederate writers have not had access to them, and that their assertions are based upon the imperfect returns to which reference has been made.

In the controversies between Confederate officers them·selves we get the most valuable light on this subject. All the testimony supports the conclusion that they rely upon estimates only, and that from a very early period of the war a systematic habit was formed of underestimating their own numbers and their own losses, by way of exaggerating the odds at which they were fighting, and of keeping up the popu·lar illusion that the preponderance of strength in the North was made up by superior military qualities in the South. The declarations of Hood and of Jefferson Davis in reference to the strength of Johnston's army in May have already been mentioned, and their significance shown. Those of Johnston and other Confederate authorities in regard to Hood's army in the next campaign are equally instructive. Taken to·gether they make satisfactory proof that during the summer of 1864, the proportion of seven to ten is a fair statement of the relative strength of the Confederate and National armies in Georgia, and the numerical superiority on the one side was more than counterbalanced by the defensive tactics on the other, so long as assaults upon intrenched lines were avoided. The palpable fact that the odds would be not only reversed, but made still greater against him, if he adopted the policy of carrying the enemy's lines by main force, was what constituted the difficulty of Sherman's position; and the movements by which he made his advance to Atlanta and Lovejoy Station without sacrificing his advantages, are what constitute the most solid foundation for the highest military reputation.

As to the losses in the campaign, the table given by General Sherman in his "Memoirs" is based on the returns in the Adjutant-General's office, and must be admitted by all to be thoroughly reliable in regard to the infantry and artillery. Sherman tells us that the cavalry were irregular in their returns, and he therefore treats the imperfection of statistics in that arm of the service as a fair offset to the acknowledged omission of any report from the Confederate cavalry by Johnston and others.

The first and most noticeable omission in Confederate reports is of the list of "missing." This does not include those absent at home without leave, and who are technically classed as deserters, but those who have disappeared during an engagement, and are presumed to be in the enemy's hands, either dead or as prisoners. Of prisoners alone Sherman's army captured twelve thousand nine hundred and eighty-three (12,983), which were officially reported and made subjects for exchange. These nowhere appear in the Confederate reports of losses, and are as completely ignored as if no such class existed.

Both Johnston and Hood refer to the returns of Surgeon-General Foard for their account of losses, and the appearance of official formality in these statistics is well calculated to impose upon the investigator. The essential question is what Surgeon Foard really reports upon. He certifies that the reports quoted are from returns made to his office; but what was required to be returned or in fact reported is left entirely to conjecture. The natural assumption would be that it would be a return of all casualties which occurred , but it is now demonstrably evident that this is not true. A statement of General Hardee on this subject has already been quoted, but a more explicit reference to it will be useful. Owing to the vicissitudes of the campaign and of the war, Hardee's report was never fully made, but on April 5, 1865, he made a partial report to the Adjutant-General of the Confederate Army, in which he reviews some of the statements of Hood's reports which had then been published. It is in this official report that he makes the assertion before referred to, that while Hood sums up the total losses of his entire army, "from the date of his assuming command on the 18th July to the Jonesboro fight inclusive, at five thousand two hundred and forty-seven (5,247), the casualties in my corps alone during that time considerably exceeded seven thousand (7,000) in killed, wounded, and captured."[1]

In the battle of Peachtree Creek the greater part of the losses fell upon Stewart's corps. In that of Ezra Church they were wholly in the corps of Lee and Stewart. At Jonesboro the heaviest loss was in Lee's corps, which attacked Howard's intrenchments. At the battle of Atlanta the losses were almost equally divided between Hardee's and Cheatham's (afterward Lee's) corps, as is shown by Logan's report, which gives the parts of the field on which they fell. Surgeon Foard's report appears to make no return of the losses of the Georgia State troops under General G. W. Smith, which had been active in the campaign from the time

---

[1] Southern Historical Society Papers, viii., 344.

of the engagements around Marietta in the latter part of
June. If under these circumstances the casualties in Hardee's corps "considerably exceeded seven thousand," it is
asking too much of our credulity to put the whole of Hood's
losses in the same period at less than three times that number.

If we draw our conclusions from the number of dead left
upon the field in the sanguinary engagements of the last six
weeks of the campaign, a very similar result will be reached.
In these battles over four thousand of the Confederate dead
were buried by Sherman's troops or delivered under flags of
truce. At the common estimate of five wounded for one
killed, which accords well with the statistics on our own
side, the wounded of Hood's army must have exceeded
twenty thousand in the period in question, and his total
losses from all causes, including prisoners, must have closely
approached thirty thousand, which was the number commonly accepted by the National officers who made the most
careful investigation at the time.

Hood has constructed an ingenious argument, for the purpose of reducing his losses, out of the comparative effective
strength of the army at different dates. Nothing could be
more fallacious, as a single consideration will show. On the
31st July his tables show an aggregate of absentees belong-
ing to his army of nearly one hundred and thirty-seven thousand.[1] These are supposed to be men organized into the
regiments constituting the army, but who were away from
the colors, with or without leave. The sweeping conscription of the South put the whole able-bodied population into
the army, those who were absolutely necessary to the continued organization of the home communities being fur-

---

[1] Advance and Retreat, p. 218.

loughed or excused from active military service. These, however, remained as a body from which men could still be drawn, and the number of those only temporarily excused or absent without leave was very large. We must know how many were returned to the regiments from this source before any comparison of the reported effective force at two dates can have even an approach to value. The same tables show on September 20th an aggregate of these absentees of one hundred and twenty-three thousand, or fourteen thousand less than at the close of July. If this represents, as it would seem to do, the number which the extraordinary efforts of the Confederate Government brought back to the colors during that period, it of course increased Hood's effective force by so much, and shows the addition which must be made to his acknowledged losses in order to make an approximate total. The result thus reached is significantly close to that which is arrived at by the other and independent methods of inquiry. In whatever way the subject is examined, we are forced to the conclusion that the guesses and estimates of the Confederate officers are not in any sense complete official reports, and are scarcely half of their casualties in the campaign.

At the lowest computation the destruction of life and the sufferings of the many thousands of wounded and sick who filled the hospitals, made a terrible expenditure of all that is most dearly prized by a civilized people. The generous mind glows with the excitement of courageous strife and sets no bounds to its admiration for military heroism, whether it be shown by the general who commands or the soldier who pushes his way through the *abatis* to his enemy's works. But when the struggle is over, and the fearful spectacle of suffering and bereavement is forced upon us, when we must reckon the cost by the unnumbered graves and the almost incalculable destruction of wealth, the only comfort or consolation which can be found must be the conviction that the cause was so holy a one as to be worth the sacrifice.

The men never doubted of this who fought under Sherman over every rood of ground from Dalton to Atlanta; and their intelligence being equal to their faith they made an army which has perhaps never been excelled. Their opponents, too, were worthy of them; for they also had persuaded themselves that they fought for independence and liberty. Brothers of a common stock, of equal courage and tenacity, animated by convictions which they passionately held, they did on both sides all that it was possible for soldiers to do, fighting their way to a mutual respect which is the solid foundation for a renewal of more than the old regard and affection.

This union of courage, intelligence, and zeal was also the source of new expedients in warfare. The methods used at the close of the campaign were such as had been developed by the wonderful experience of that summer's work. From general-in-chief to the men in the ranks, all were conscious of having learned much of the art and practice of warfare; and he would be a rash critic who would confidently affirm that he could find better means to attain desired ends than those which were employed in attack or defence over a hundred miles of mountains and forests in Northern Georgia.

CHAPTER XVII.

THE MOVEMENTS IN OCTOBER—HOOD UPON SHERMAN'S LINES OF COMMUNICATION.

THE capture of Atlanta was followed by a few weeks of repose which was welcome to both officers and men. For Sherman himself it was a period of mental activity, scarce less intense than the conduct of the active campaign. The success of the past was the pledge of even greater labors for the future. The very fact that the President, Congress, and the country echoed in general acclaim the flattering judgment of Grant that Sherman had " accomplished the most gigantic undertaking given to any general in the war," foretold that he and his army must prepare themselves for new campaigns and new struggles.

It was no easy matter to settle a satisfactory plan of operations for the fall and winter. The line of communications, which had seemed much too long for safety when the army was at Chattanooga in the spring, was now 140 miles longer. Wheeler, with the Confederate cavalry, was still far in the rear, and though his raid had stripped Hood of his mounted troops and had thus greatly helped Sherman's plans in the movement south of Atlanta, the National general knew very well that there was still much risk that some serious interruption of his railway might at any time make short rations in his camps. It had been his hope that by the time he should reach Atlanta, Mobile would have been taken, and a shorter line for his supplies opened by the

way of Montgomery, or still better by the lower Chattahoochee to Columbus. If the troops under General Canby
in the Department of the Gulf could occupy Southern Alabama, coming into direct coöperation with him upon his
right flank, another great section of the Gulf States would
be lost to the Confederacy, and Sherman could face to the
East with the assurance that every day's march was diminish-
ing the territory from which the Richmond Government
could draw its supplies of men and subsistence.

But Canby had not been able to get on as fast as was
hoped. The naval squadron under Admiral Farragut had
forced the entrance of Mobile Bay, and Fort Morgan was in
our hands ; but just at this time a new outbreak occurred in
Missouri, where General Price had succeeded in organizing
a considerable force of Confederates, and A. J. Smith with
two divisions of the Sixteenth Corps had been ordered into
that State. Canby's power to advance was thus lost, and
Sherman was in no little doubt whether any plan of campaign would be free from very serious embarrassments. He
thought that no good could come of merely penetrating
deeper into the State of Georgia till some definite objective
point could be aimed at. It seemed wise, therefore, for him
to look to occupying Hood pretty closely till the capture of
Wilmington and Savannah should give assurance of a new
base for his columns if he marched across the State, and a
solid footing upon the lower Chattahoochee should guarantee
the safe possession of the country behind him. This done,
he was ready to pledge himself to occupy Macon and a point
on the Savannah River below Augusta by any day which
Grant would name as one on which Savannah should be in
the possession of the National forces.[1]

---

[1] See his letter to Grant of September 20th. Sherman's Memoirs, ii., 115.

Whatever the plan might be, nobody dreamed of abandoning any ground already gained. Atlanta must be held and
the railway to Nashville protected till some new and decisive
advantage should move the theatre of operations much
farther to the east. The captured city must be made a fortified depôt of supplies in which reserve stores for a great
campaign might be accumulated. Its military importance
had been fully recognized by the Confederates in making it
a great intrenched camp covering the radiating railway lines
which ran from it to all points of the compass; but its present trenches required an army to fill them, and Sherman
could not spare an army for that purpose. He determined,
therefore, to contract its *enceinte* to a size which a moderate
garrison could defend, and to occupy the buildings within
this limit for military purposes only. It would thus be
ready to stand a siege, if need be, whilst he was operating
toward Columbus or Augusta. This necessarily involved
the removal of the non-combatant population, and he notified
Hood of his purpose and of his desire to make the measure
as little distressing in its details as possible. His right to
do so and the necessity of it from a military point of view
are beyond dispute, though the aggressive course which
Hood subsequently took gave an opportunity for a much
more brilliant stroke than was then hoped for, and allowed
Sherman to cut quite loose from his base of supplies.

Hood and the Confederate authorities seized upon Sherman's order as a means of exciting the zeal and animosity of
their people. The correspondence between the two generals
was spicy, but Hood's part of it is so manifestly meant for
popular effect that it may be doubted whether Sherman
might not as well have contented himself with the mere
reiteration of the order, and of the terms on which the removal must be made. His directions to furnish transporta-

tion for families and household stuff were so ample, and his intention was so generously carried out by Colonel Willard Warner of his staff, that nothing was left which the citizens desired to carry away, and at the close of the business, Colonel Clare, who had been appointed by Hood as his representative under the flag of truce, volunteered a written testimonial to his associate that the execution of the order had been the most considerate and courteous possible.

The Confederate leaders must have been dull indeed if they had failed to understand the meaning of the notice. Davis hastened in person to Macon to consult with Hood, and the result of their conference was a decision to try the fortunes of war by a bold initiative. Hood was authorized to place himself by a rapid march upon Sherman's lines of communication before the latter could complete his provisioning and fortifying of Atlanta. In a speech at Macon on September 22d, Davis endeavored to rally deserters to their standards by foreshadowing an attempt to transfer the war again to Tennessee. Sherman understood the warning and published the speech in the North to hasten the recruiting which might save him the necessity of sending back part of his army to Nashville.

The number of regiments whose term of service was expiring was so great as to reduce our forces by nearly one-third during the month of September, and except for the veterans who had re-enlisted during the last winter, Sherman could hardly have kept the field. Recruits were collecting rapidly in the depôts and camps of instruction in the North, but the policy (wretchedly false from a military point of view) of organizing them into new regiments, was not only causing delay, but was wasting the prestige and the experience of the old organizations at the front. These were dwindling to a tithe of their original numbers and dying of inanition, when new and doubly vigorous life would have been given them by adding the new material to their skeletons. The recruits, under flags which were already blazoned with the names of Donelson and Vicksburg, of Stone River and Mission Ridge, of Knoxville and Atlanta, would have become soldiers of double value with double speed; but political reasons were powerful and the efficiency of the army was sacrificed to them.

For the time, therefore, the account showed only losses in Sherman's numbers, and the apparent necessity of waiting till the new regiments could reach the front made officers of all grades anxious for leaves of absence, and the men in the ranks for furloughs. Schofield had taken advantage of the quiet to visit Louisville and Knoxville and look after the business of his department; Logan and Blair went North to take part in the Presidential canvass. Division and brigade commanders and subordinate officers of all ranks pressed so eagerly for an opportunity to visit their families and homes that it was thought politic to allow considerable numbers to do so. When, then, toward the end of September rumors began to thicken that Hood was moving, Sherman would have been quite willing that the opening of the fall campaign might be a little longer delayed.

Whilst Wheeler was trying to break the railroad in Northern Georgia, General Forrest had already started upon a similar movement in Middle Tennessee. Crossing the Tennessee River on September 20th, and following the line of the Nashville and Decatur Railway, he frightened the commandant at Athens into an unnecessary surrender and marched north as far as Pulaski, but declined an engagement there with General Rousseau, who was awaiting him. A portion of his command moving eastward found itself in danger of being caught between the columns of Steedman, who was marching from Chattanooga, and Rousseau who was closely following from Pulaski. General Buford, who commanded it, made attempts to capture small garrisons at Huntsville and Athens, but was repulsed and driven south of the Tennessee on October 3d. Forrest remained north of the river a few days longer, destroying a few miles of railway, but accomplishing nothing whatever of importance, and retreated across the river on the 6th, to avoid the forces Thomas was concentrating upon him. Like nearly all the cavalry raids, it was a mere diversion with no perceptible influence on the campaign, and the damage done to communications was repaired almost by the time the troopers were out of sight.

The threatening character of the rumors which had preceded this raid showed that it had a good deal of importance in the eyes of the Confederates, and by the end of September Sherman had thought it wise to send Thomas back to Chattanooga, where he also placed Wagner's division (formerly Newton's) of the Fourth Corps, and Morgan's of the Fourteenth, whilst he sent Corse's division of the Sixteenth Corps to Rome, where it covered the railway north of the Etowah. The cavalry movement alone would have been treated with contempt, but all indications pointed to activity on the part of Hood himself, and on the 29th Sherman had definite information that the Confederate Army had taken the initiative, and two-thirds of it had crossed the Chattahoochee some twenty-four miles south of Atlanta. This had been easy for Hood, for the river there runs due south near the confines of Georgia and Alabama, and after a short flank movement to the west he had been able to pass it in safety. It was now the important question to Sherman to decide what his adversary would do, for he did not mean to be led off upon a wild-goose chase if he could avoid it, nor had he any thought of transferring the principal theatre of operations to Tennessee. He notified Cox, temporarily in command of the Army of the Ohio, to be ready for a counter movement to the south and east, and directed Thomas to make such combinations north of the Tennessee as should quickly dispose of Forrest and his cavalry. On October 1st, in issuing preparatory instructions to his subordinates, he informed them that if Hood should march into Alabama with a purpose of reaching Tennessee, he should order northward to General Thomas the garrisons and detachments as far as Kingston, and with the rest move upon Savannah and Charleston, believing that this would force Hood to follow him. If, however, the latter should try to strike the railroad south of the Etowah, he would turn upon him. In this purpose he ordered General Corse at Rome to hold fast unless the Confederates should strike south of Alatoona, but in that case to join his forces to those of General Raum, who commanded between the Etowah and Oostanaula, and act against the enemy from Alatoona.

For a day or two strong detachments were pushed out on different roads, a division being sent from the Army of the Ohio southeast to Flatrock, to create the impression of a formidable movement in that direction. On the 2d, however, it became clear that Hood was marching in the direction of Marietta, and Sherman determined to wait till he was fully committed to the movement, then cross the Chattahoochee and interpose between him and his pontoon bridge. Next day the order of march was issued. The Twentieth (Slocum's) Corps was to hold Atlanta and the Chattahoochee bridge, and the rest of the army to go at once to Smyrna Camp Ground, south of Marietta.[1] General

---

[1] The "Camp Grounds" of the South are places where religious camp meetings were held from time to time, giving a name to the locality.

Howard was in command of the Army of the Tennessee, General Stanley of that of the Cumberland, and General Cox of the Army of the Ohio. In the absence of Logan and Blair, the Fifteenth and Seventeenth Corps were commanded by Generals Osterhaus and Ransom, the Sixteenth being broken up and its two divisions put into these corps.

Hood's general plan was, as he himself tells us, to cut our line of communications, and if followed by Sherman, retire westward till he should reach the Blue Mountain Railroad, which runs from Selma in Central Alabama northeast through Talladega, reaching at that time a point about sixty miles southwest of Rome and near Gadsden. He hoped thus to lead Sherman away from Atlanta and transfer the seat of war again to the valley of the Tennessee River. On October 3d, the main body of his forces were near Lost Mountain, whilst Stewart's corps was sent to the railroad north of Marietta, to destroy it and to attempt the capture of Alatoona and the destruction of the bridge over the Etowah if he should find it feebly guarded.[1] Stewart captured the small posts at Ackworth and Big Shanty, and rejoined Hood on the morning of the 5th, sending French's division of that corps with twelve pieces of artillery against the rocky gorges of Alatoona.

But during the 3d and 4th Sherman's army was in motion. The Army of the Cumberland passed the Chattahoochee at the railway bridge on the 3d, and concentrated at Smyrna Camp Ground. The cavalry was weak, consisting of only

---

[1] In an important paper of General French, published in the Louisville Courier Journal of June 11, 1881, he gives a copy of Hood's official orders on this point, which are the basis of the statement of the text, and shows that Hood was in error in saying in his Advance and Retreat (p. 257) that the destruction of the supplies at Alatoona was contemplated. It is hardly conceivable that they should not be mentioned in such a case. French's official report is to be found in Annals of the Army of Tennessee, vol. i., p. 316.

two small divisions under General Elliott (Kilpatrick's and Garrard's), and these found the enemy in force already astride of the railroad, near Big Shanty. On this report Sherman naturally concluded that the whole of Hood's army was there, and pushed the head of his column straight through Marietta to Kenesaw Mountain, whilst he signalled to Corse, over the heads of the Confederates, to go at once to the relief of Alatoona. It will be remembered that the Etowah River runs due west, and that Alatoona is a pass in the high ridge on its southern bank. It looked as if Hood might be caught between Sherman's army and the river if Alatoona were held.

Stanley reached Marietta in the afternoon of the 4th, and the Army of the Cumberland bivouacked at the base of Kenesaw, from whose crest could be seen the destruction of the railway. Howard with the Army of the Tennessee crossed the Chattahoochee and reached Smyrna Camp Ground. The Army of the Ohio, moving from Decatur, had to make a detour to find a crossing of Peachtree Creek where a bridge was carried away, the water being swimming deep, and after getting over the Chattahoochee, about two o'clock, were ordered to march up the river to the Pace's Ferry and Marietta road, as the other was filled by troops and trains. To do this another deep stream filled by back water from the Chattahoochee was bridged, and that command rested at Pace's Ferry for the night. Sherman went forward to Marietta early in the morning of the 5th, and there learned that the enemy had moved northward toward Alatoona. From Kenesaw he could see the smoke marking the mischief done along the railroad, and get a distant view of the combat raging at Alatoona, eighteen miles away. But he could also see the smoke of great camps in the direction of Dallas, where Hood's principal force was lying, that officer being in this instance too wary to venture his whole army in a *cul-de-sac* between Sherman and the Etowah. He had placed them where it was impossible for the National forces to envelop him, and where French could join him toward Rome by a shorter road than his opponent must travel. The reports got from prisoners and the country people were conflicting, and Sherman's first orders were for the Army of the Ohio to come forward to Marietta, while that of the Tennessee covered the line to the Chattahoochee facing toward the part of the Confederate army which was between Lost Mountain and Dallas. Meanwhile reconnoissances were pushed from Kenesaw forward, to get more reliable news, and the signal corps with flags and telescopes endeavored to open communication with Alatoona.

The garrison at Alatoona was a small brigade of three regiments under Lieutenant-Colonel Tourtellotte of the Fourth Minnesota, insufficient to man all the works which had been constructed for the defence of the post ; but General Corse arrived with reinforcements in the very nick of time and assumed command. He brought with him Rowett's brigade of three regiments, which increased the garrison to almost two thousand men. The train which was sent back to Rome for the remainder of his force was a good deal delayed, and did not get back till the battle was over. The Confederate advance was in the night, and at daybreak of the 5th, French pressed in quickly upon the place, and after a vigorous cannonade for some two hours demanded a surrender, which was refused.[1] He then assaulted the works, sending Sears's brigade to the north side or rear of

---

[1] General French says no answer to his summons was returned, and his adjutant, Major Sanders, came back without one, after waiting seventeen minutes, which were given for a reply. General Corse, in his official report gives a copy of French's letter, which only granted five minutes for consideration, and of his own tart response ; but it is not improbable that Major Sanders had gone back when the messenger reached the outpost.

the place to begin the attack, while Cockrell's brigade, supported by Young's, should assault from the west. The defensive works consisted of two field redoubts, one on each side of the railway and covering the storehouses near the track. Some temporary lines of trench had been formerly made outside of these, and were held with some tenacity, but they were no part of the permanent fortifications of the post. The redoubts were so placed that they each swept the front of the other with its fire, the cut in which the railway ran being sixty-five feet deep. The redoubts crowned the crests of hills which formed part of the general ridge running east and west, and from which spurs ran off on both sides. French placed his artillery on commanding ground across a hollow on the south of the place, with two regiments supporting it. His batteries not only enfiladed the trenches facing westward, but commanded the railway cut itself and made communication between the little forts almost impossible. Tourtellotte had himself occupied the eastern fort and had a section of the Twelfth Wisconsin battery there. Corse occupied the fort on the west when he came on the ground, and the other section of Tourtellotte's battery was also kept there, as he had not been able to bring any artillery with him. Most of Rowett's brigade, however, was put in the advanced line across the ridge facing west, supported by the Ninety-third Illinois from Tourtellotte's, and light lines of skirmishers, with such supports as could be given, were placed both north and south of the forts.

Sears's brigade reached the position assigned to it by French, his line extending on both sides of the railway. He marched swiftly up the hill, drove off two companies that supported the skirmishers on a spur in that direction, and charged down in flank and rear of Rowett's men, who at the same moment were attacked in front by Cockrell's Missourians supported by Young. The Thirty-ninth Iowa, which was on Rowett's right, changed front in part to the right, and resisted like veterans as they were, and the Seventh and Ninety-third Illinois, facing still to the west, bore the brunt of Cockrell's attack from that direction. Tourtellotte had repulsed the assault on his fort across the railway, and his guns making havoc in Sears's flank enabled Rowett to make a long and effective resistance, inflicting great loss on his assailants. The odds were too great, however, and after two hours of stubborn fighting, Corse was obliged to draw back his line to the trenches immediately around the redoubt. In doing this, the Thirty-ninth Iowa hung on to cover the retreat of their comrades and to keep it from becoming a rout. Colonel Redfield fell, shot in four places, and a hundred and seventy casualties out of two hundred and eighty men who went into the engagement, attested the devotion of the regiment to its duty. The Seventh Illinois suffered almost as much.

The attack being now chiefly concentrated on the west redoubt, Tourtellotte sent from his side strong reinforcements, which crossed the railroad and the defile which was swept by the Confederate guns. For a time the Fourth Minnesota held the east redoubt alone, but it was joined by part of the Eighteenth Wisconsin, and maintained a steady fire upon the assailants of their comrades across the ravine, as well as upon those who made weaker demonstrations on the east. The guns in the west redoubt were out of ammunition, and a brave fellow volunteered to cross to the other side and bring back an armful of canister cartridges, which he did in safety. Corse himself received a rifle ball in the face about one o'clock, and was insensible for half an hour or more, but rallied in a critical juncture to encourage his men to "hold the fort." Rowett was severely wounded, so was Tourtellotte, and the trenches without and the ramparts within were encumbered with dead and wounded, for the enemy's fire swept every line in flank, and but for the cross fire which the guns of the east redoubt had upon the faces of the other, the western one must have become untenable.

The charges of French's troops, which had been repeated at intervals for more than four hours, grew sensibly weaker after one o'clock, and his nearly disorganized brigades contented themselves with keeping up a desultory fire, picking off every one who showed himself above the works. Before two o'clock Sears and Cockrell were recalled, and partially reforming them behind what was left of Young's brigade, French marched away, about three o'clock, in the direction of New Hope Church. Whilst the sharpshooters still made the signal platform a place of extreme peril, Lieutenant Mc-Kensie of that corps himself signalled to Sherman the message which he would not order any of his squad to transmit, and which announced that the attack had failed.

French had sent a detachment to take the block-house at the Etowah River and burn the bridge there during his engagement at the post, but this also failed. Another block-house on the south of Alatoona, where the railway crosses the creek of the same name, was, however, made untenable by a cannonade, and its garrison surrendered. The bridge there was burned, but it was of inferior importance.[1]

Hood's orders had declared the destruction of the Etowah bridge to be of the greatest importance, and French had made a desperate effort to accomplish it. He acknowledges

---

[1] In his description of the place, General French speaks of "three redoubts on the west of the railroad cut and a star fort on the east." In this he is wrong. The authority of Colonel Poe, the Chief Engineer who laid out the works, is explicit in support of the assertion that there were only two redoubts in all, and no star fort. French is also mistaken in saying that he carried the principal redoubt on the west. Corse remained there in person till the combat closed.

a loss of 800, of which 120 were killed ; but as General Corse buried 230 of the Confederate dead and had over 400 prisoners (among whom was Brigadier-General Young), the enemy's loss was plainly greater than French reported. Even after Corse had returned to Rome, numerous dead bodies of Confederates were found in the woods, where the wounded had evidently crawled away from the fire and had died after French's retreat.

In Corse's command the casualties were 705 in killed and wounded, and French claims to have taken 205 prisoners, including the block-house garrison.

Looking to the numbers engaged, this was no doubt one of the most desperately contested actions of the war. The character of the ground gave great opportunity for the enemy to use his artillery, and the partial successes at the beginning encouraged French's brigades to renewed assaults, which cost them dear. The garrison, with Corse's reinforcement, was not large enough to hold all the detached works : they tried, perhaps, to hold more than was prudent, and in the forced abandonment of some of these under fire, they suffered losses which could not have occurred in the ordinary and successful defence of intrenchments.

During the engagement a cavalry reconnoissance on Stanley's front gave French some uneasiness, and he learned that our infantry were at Kenesaw; but while this information may have hastened his retreat, all the circumstances make it plain that he was fairly beaten in his efforts against the forts.[1] He claimed to have had in his possession the ware-

---

[1] By a singular error, Sherman's and Howard's reports, and nearly all subsequent accounts, including General French's paper above referred to, speak of a movement of the Twenty-third Corps as hastening French's retreat. Historical candor compels the writer to disclaim for his command this honor. On October 5th, the Twenty-third Corps was marching from Pace's Ferry to Marietta, and its movement on the 6th is correctly described in its place. See Appendix D.

houses which contained nearly three million rations of bread ;
but this must have been a momentary thing, for it is incredi-
ble that they should not have been destroyed before the retreat, when every soldier's cartridge-box contained all that
was needed to make port-fires. At all events, the stores
were saved, and Corse was able to signal his commander
that, despite his losses and his own wound, there was no
need of anxiety about the post.

Meanwhile Sherman was concentrating his army and endeavoring to learn what part of the opposing forces were
toward Dallas.   He had left Slocum's (Twentieth) Corps to
hold Atlanta and the bridge-head at the Chattahoochee
crossing, but a flood in the river had partly destroyed the
bridge and all the roads were heavy, so that all movements
were laborious.   During the 5th, the Army of the Tennessee
moved into the old lines of the Confederates near Culp's
Farm, covering the approaches to the railroad between Marietta and the river.   The Army of the Ohio marched from
Pace's Ferry to Brushy Mountain, about three miles north of
Marietta, where they relieved the Army of the Cumberland,
which moved to the left.   The cavalry was not strong enough
to act with much confidence, and had not succeeded in opening communication with Alatoona by the morning of the
6th, bringing in only rumors obtained from the country, and
Sherman was uncertain whether Stewart's corps had rejoined
Hood.   Impatient that the cavalry had not accomplished
more, on that morning he ordered General Elliott to open
the line of communication with Corse by roads east of the
railroad and bring something " official " as to the situation
there.   Stanley was ordered to connect with Howard, covering the roads toward Dallas, with his right at Pine Mountain, while Cox with the Twenty-third Corps was directed
to make a reconnoissance in force westward on the Burnt

Hickory road, sending detachments by lateral roads and endeavoring to get definite knowledge of the enemy's position, and especially of the whereabouts of French. At nine o'clock the corps left the position on Stanley's right, which it had moved into that morning, and marched westward by Pine Mountain, on whose top Sherman stationed himself, directing that fires should be lighted from time to time, so that by the smoke of these he could mark the extent of the reconnoissance. The roads through the country, which had been so thoroughly cut up in June, were almost impassable, but by two o'clock definite information was sent back that French had rejoined Hood the previous evening. The advance was pushed to Alatoona Church, which had been the left of our lines before New Hope Church, while the road from Mount Olivet Church north to Ackworth was explored by one detachment, and another pushed southward nearly to Lost Mountain, driving back Hood's cavalry and getting satisfactory evidence of his presence in force in that direction, though probably moving toward Kingston or Rome. The pillars of smoke mapped out the country to Sherman's eye as he looked down from the place where Polk had been killed in June, while with Johnston and Hardee he was watching, in a similar way, the movements of the National Army. Toward evening the corps was recalled to the junction of the roads near Mount Olivet Church, where its detachments concentrated, and the General-in-Chief felt that he was master of the situation.

He contented himself with observing his adversary for a few days, putting a large force upon the repairs of the Chattahoochee bridge and getting out ties for the railway. On the 7th, Casement's brigade of the Twenty-third Corps was sent to Alatoona, the cavalry were watching the movements of Hood, skirmishing with those of the enemy near New

Hope Church. Clearly divining his adversary's purpose of drawing him back from his position in the heart of Georgia, Sherman refused to be toled away, but sent Corse back to Rome with his division, where, in the forks of the Etowah and the Oostanaula, he covered the railway between Resaca and Cartersville. Notwithstanding his very painful wound, Corse kept the field, sent detachments to destroy all the bridges over the Etowah, and watched the crossing of the Coosa below the junction of its tributaries. Sherman now formally repeated his proposal to Grant to break up the railroad to Chattanooga and turn his back on Hood, marching directly for Savannah by Milledgeville and Millen. On the 10th, however, he received news from Rome that Hood was crossing the Coosa about twelve miles below, threatening to turn upon Corse's command and operate still further to the north and rear. As this promised active work close at hand, Sherman immediately ordered a concentration of his own army at Rome, directing Thomas at the same time to collect his forces toward Stevenson so as to resist any effort of the enemy to cross the Tennessee. At Kingston, on the 11th, he learned that Hood had not approached Rome, but moved in some other direction, his whereabouts being again a mystery. Again he urged upon Grant the plan of moving upon Savannah. Hood says that it had been his purpose to attack Rome and then march to the railroad at Kingston, but he formed a more prudent plan, and crossing the Coosa about fifteen miles below Rome he followed the line of the long valleys, protected by high rocky ridges, to Resaca. In this movement, as all the rivers were high, the Oostanaula covered his right flank, and he hoped to take Resaca by a *coup-de-main*. If this were done and the railway bridge destroyed, Sherman would necessarily be much delayed in following him, and he would have his choice, to march upon Chattanooga or to follow down the left bank of the Tennessee westward. He sent his trains and reserve artillery to Jacksonville and Gadsden, and moved without incumbrances.

Sherman's whole army was assembled about Rome on the 12th, and on the 13th he pushed strong reconnoissances down both banks of the Coosa, Corse's division on the left, and Garrard's cavalry on the right. A little later in the morning, his impatience increasing, he ordered Cox with the Twenty-third Corps to follow Garrard, and reach, if possible, the site of Hood's bridges, to learn if they were taken up and the enemy thus committed to a definite movement north of the river. The infantry overtook the cavalry, and giving them confidence by strong and close support, Garrard ran over the Confederate horsemen and captured two guns and about a hundred prisoners. The combined movement was pressed vigorously. The place where the bridge was laid was reached, and a part of the cavalry went two miles beyond. The bridge was up, and it was learned that Hood had taken the pontoons north with him, giving out that he was going to Tennessee. The news was passed by signal to Sherman, and the infantry returned to Rome the same night.[1]

Hood reached Resaca on the 12th, approaching the place by the north bank of the Oostanaula, and summoned it to surrender, saying he would take no prisoners if he carried it by assault. Colonel Wever, commanding the garrison, returned a defiant answer.[2] Hood took position about the fortifications, his flanks resting on the Oostanaula and the

---

[1] See Appendix E.

[2] Hood says that General S. D. Lee was in front of Resaca with his corps and made the demand ; but the summons was signed by Hood himself. Sherman's Memoirs, vol. ii., 155.

Connasauga, but he did not assault. A reinforcement of 350 infantry under General Raum reached the garrison from Calhoun, and General McCook with his cavalry covered the movement of railway trains and stores to Kingston, and then himself marched to Resaca.

Sherman got the news about noon of the 13th, and put Howard and Stanley at once in movement for Resaca, signalling Cox to follow as soon as the work on which he had been sent was accomplished. Leaving Lee's corps before Resaca, Hood marched Stewart's to Tilton and to Dalton, capturing the garrison at the latter place (Forty-fourth United States colored troops) without resistance. But at Tilton the block-house and little intrenchment was held by the Seventeenth Iowa under Lieutenant-Colonel Archer, and his answer to Stewart's summons was like Wever's. The little garrison of less than two hundred men resisted an overwhelming force for several hours, and only showed the white flag when a concentration of artillery fire had knocked the block-house to pieces about their ears. A block-house in Millcreek Gap, near Buzzard's Roost, also made a stout resistance, but was captured.[1] General Schofield had reached Dalton the same morning, hastening from Knoxville to resume the command of the Army of the Ohio, and finding that Hood's whole army was near the place, had sent back to Cleveland all trains along the road. Reporting thence by orders from Washington to General Thomas, who was at Nashville, the latter directed him to assume command at Chattanooga, to concentrate all trains there, and hold that place. All the available troops in Kentucky were ordered forward to Nashville, General Steedman with his command

---

[1] General Howard's report says the garrison at Dalton surrendered without a blow. For the defence of Tilton, see Iowa Colonels and Regiments, by A. A. Stuart, p. 338.

was sent back to his post at Chattanooga, and Schofield prepared to move out with Wagner's and Morgan's divisions, which had been sent back from Atlanta two weeks before.

Meanwhile Sherman reached Resaca on the 14th,[1] and Hood, having failed even to damage the railroad seriously, made haste to retreat westward to Villanow, having gained nothing by the rapid movement except to give Wheeler the opportunity to join him with the cavalry which had been operating in that region. True, he had drawn Sherman a hundred miles from Atlanta, but the Twentieth Corps occupied that place, and the whole line of railway from there to Chattanooga was solidly held, except for the momentary break at Dalton. Sherman yielded nothing of the territory he had conquered, and still had in hand an army with which he was anxious to meet Hood in the open field, while Schofield was ready to join him with the two veteran divisions at Chattanooga. The Confederate general was only making a "raid," a brilliant one in its way, but the care with which he avoided battle, or even an attack with his whole army upon a post like Resaca, garrisoned by a single brigade, proved conclusively that he had no serious purpose of staying long away from his base of supplies in Alabama. In the retreat, part of his command went by way of Snake Creek Gap, blockading that gorge by felling the timber, so as to delay Sherman's pursuit. The latter sent Stanley over the ridges north of the blockade, whilst Howard, followed by Cox, cleared out the road through the gap. The evening of the 15th found Howard's head of column near Villanow and Stanley coming in on his right, the opposition of Hood's rear guard being but trifling. On the 16th, C. R.

---

[1] Sherman's Memoirs say 13th, but it would seem to be a misprint. His official report says "evening of the 14th," and this agrees with the reports of his subordinates.

Woods's division of the Army of the Tennessee carried Ship's Gap in Taylor's Ridge, capturing part of the small rear guard which held it. The ridge is a high and almost un-broken mountain chain, running nearly north and south, on the west of which is the pleasant and fertile valley of the Chattooga, down which Hood had retreated, doubling his track upon the line of his march northward a few days before.

Sherman hoped his adversary would continue on to Ten-nessee, feeling absolutely sure of forcing a surrender of the whole army in that event. In his despatches to Schofield, this feeling found vent in strong expressions. "Invite him in," he said; "send him a free pass." He halted the army, and spent a day in active reconnoissances, whilst his com-munications with Chattanooga were reopened, and the work of repairing the railway was begun. He sent to the rear his disabled animals and his field hospitals, and by evening of the 17th, was assured that Hood had gone south by way of Summerville toward Gadsden, giving up the attempt to cross the Tennessee anywhere above Muscle Shoals. Hood was not unwise in this, for the upper river was patrolled by light-draught gunboats, and with Thomas's detachments actively watching the northern bank he could hardly have crossed without Sherman's overtaking him, unless the "pass," jocu-larly spoken of, had been indeed given.

On the 18th the National Army was again in motion. Howard and Stanley marched down the Chattooga Valley on parallel roads, whilst Cox took the road on the east side of Taylor's Ridge to Subligna, and thence over the mountain by Gover's Gap to Summerville. The heads of columns skirmished with a rear guard of cavalry as they advanced, but there was no serious fighting. At Gover's Gap the road was scarped in the side of a precipitous mountain, and this shelf had been dug away. A stubborn defence had been prepared here, but the columns on both sides the ridge were so nearly abreast of each other that the pass was abandoned and the Twenty-third Corps occupied it before evening. The day's march by this route had been twenty-two miles. Next day Summerville was passed, Howard's head of column was at Alpine and Cox's at Melville, and on the 20th the whole army was concentrated at Gaylesville in Alabama.

Hood reached Gadsden that day, where he met General Beauregard, and a plan of future operations was discussed. That subject belongs more properly to the next volume. Sherman remained at Gaylesville seven days, watching the movements of his adversary, proposing to follow him if he attempted to cross the Tennessee near Guntersville, but determined to carry out his plan of a march to the sea if Hood should go to Decatur or Florence. Detachments were stationed on the Coosa at Cedar Bluffs, the Twenty-third Corps bridged the Chattooga at that place, and preparations were made for a new campaign.

The month had been a busy one. Hood's activity and generalship had been worthy of high praise, but he had been everywhere foiled, doing very little damage in comparison with the means used. Sherman had refused to give up his hold on Georgia, had driven the enemy from his line of communications, and now stood upon the edge of Alabama, fully in possession of all the valuable results of the campaign, arranging the details of a movement that was not to be a brilliant and barren march, but one that was attractive to him because it promised to be decisive of the whole war.

APPENDIX A.

STRENGTH OF THE CONFEDERATE ARMY.

THE limit necessarily placed to the size of this volume forbids the detailed examination, in the text, of the evidence on which the estimate of the Confederate forces is based. The official reports and returns now in the military archives at Washington must be the basis of every reliable calculation, and are unquestionably trustworthy as far as they go. These demonstrate the fact that the Confederate statements of "effectives" exclude officers, who make about ten per cent. of a command, as well as all private soldiers either temporarily sick or not bearing arms with the colors.

The separate histories of State troops and memoirs of regiments furnish very valuable aids in checking the returns of strength and especially the statements of losses in action. As an example of results thus obtained, the following summary of evidence in regard to the strength of General Johnston's army, at the opening of the campaign and subsequently, will be found interesting. It is based upon careful researches made by Major E. C. Dawes, late of the Fifty-third Ohio, independent of those upon which the statements in the text were made, but which the author has verified in all essential particulars.

The Confederate official returns above referred to and on file in the War Department, show that on April 30, 1864, the force of General Johnston "present for duty," not including men on "extra or daily duty," but only officers and men available for action, was as follows, viz. :

	Officers.	Privates.	Total.
General Johnston's staff	14	——	14
Hardee's corps	2,000	18,634	20,634
Hood's corps	1,575	18,614	20,189
Wheeler's cavalry	757	7,679	8,436
Artillery	164	3,113	3,277
Engineer battalion	17	425	442
	4,527	48,465	52,992

This force was increased before the opening of the campaign. General Hood ("Advance and Retreat," p. 79) says that General Hardee and himself, in comparing notes about May 7th or 8th, found they had about 42,500 "effectives," infantry and artillery, in their corps besides the reserve artillery. The "effective" enlisted men in those corps on April 30th was shown to be 38,104, infantry and artillery. The increase, therefore, in one week was about 4,500 privates, or 5,000 officers and men. This is confirmed by Hardee's memorandum of operations during the campaign, in which he states the force of his corps at the beginning of the campaign at "about 20,000 muskets and four battalions of artillery." (Johnston's narrative, p. 578.)

Mercer's brigade joined Johnston May 2d. It consisted of four Georgia regiments (First, Fifty-fourth, Fifty-seventh and Sixty-third), which had been on garrison duty at Savannah. The last of these alone had an "effective" total of 814. It is safe to estimate the four regiments at 2,800, officers and men. About August 1st, after passing through the terrible battles about Atlanta, the division (Walker's) to which Mercer's brigade belonged was broken up because of its heavy losses. A note to the return of that date gives the "present and absent" total of the brigade, 3,583.

Loring's division joined the army at Resaca, May 12th. General S. D. Lee's return of May 10th shows that it numbered "for duty" 429 officers and 4,716 men.

Canty's division also joined Johnston at Resaca about May 7th or 8th. This division was composed of Canty's brigade and Reynolds's, formerly McNair's. Canty's old brigade was made up of the First, Seventeenth, Twenty-sixth and Twenty-ninth Alabama and the Thirty-seventh Mississippi. Reynolds's contained the First, Second, Fourth and Fifth Arkansas and Thirty-ninth North Carolina. The division had also two batteries of field artillery (fourteen guns) and two organizations of cavalry commanded by colonels. The return of General D. H. Maury for the "Army in the District of the Gulf," April 22, 1864, gives the effective strength of this division at 5,564 privates, with 421 officers. It contained a brigade of heavy artillery which had been in the forts about Mobile. The sketch of the Seventeenth Alabama in "Brewer's History of Alabama" says that, while at Mobile, it was drilled as heavy artillery and had charge of eight batteries on the shore of the bay. The Twenty-ninth Alabama had also been on garrison duty at Mobile from July, 1863, till about the date of this return.

French's division joined at Cassville. It was composed of Cockrell's, Ector's and Sears's brigades. By General S. D. Lee's return of May 10th, it numbered for duty 385 officers and 4,028 men.

Quarles's brigade, as Johnston himself tells us, joined him near New Hope Church, with 2,200 "effectives," to which must be added 200 for officers.

Jackson's cavalry division joined at Adairsville, with a strength in l:ne of battle, as given by Lee's return of May 10th, of 405 officers and 4,072 men.

A division of Georgia militia also joined before the battle of Kenesaw Mountain. It consisted of two brigades and one battalion of artillery, the whole commanded by General G. W. Smith, who reported them ("Advance and Retreat," p. 352) as "a little over 3,000." It is safe to call this force 3,300, officers and men, and it was increased to over 5,000 subsequently. Avery's "History of Georgia" says there were ten thousand in the trenches of Atlanta.

SUMMARY.

General Johnston's force at Dalton, May 1, 1864, being officers and men then present for duty	52,990
Increase in Hood's and Hardee's corps	5,000
Mercer's brigade, May 2d	2,800
Loring's division, May 12th	5.145
Canty's division (except First Alabama), May 8th	5,300
Total at Resaca	71,235
Jackson's cavalry, Adairsville, May 17th	4,477
French's division, Cassville, May 18th	4,413
First Alabama (Canty's division), May 24th	650
Quarles's brigade, New Hope, May 24th	2,400
Georgia militia, Kenesaw, June 20th	3,300
Total before crossing the Chattahoochee	86,475

There must still be added the constant and large increase in all the corps of the army from recruits, conscripts, convalescents, and return of men from detached service. As the life of the Confederacy was at stake, it is unreasonable to suppose that any effort was spared to increase Johnston's strength to the utmost. At the end of April, there were troops under General S. Jones in the Department of South Carolina, Georgia, and Florida, numbering 25,498 "effectives." In the Department of Alabama, Mississippi, and East Louisiana, there were under S. D. Lee, on June 1st, present for duty, 16,562 officers and men, as shown by his official return.

The last return of General Johnston in this campaign, dated July 10, 1864, shows the number of troops to have been as follows, viz., aggregate present and absent, 135,092, present 73,849, effectives 50,932.

The first return of General Hood, dated July 31, 1864, shows aggregate present and absent, 136,684, present 65,601, effectives 44,495.

Here is an apparent diminution of the number present, while there is an increase of the aggregate. This is accounted for as follows. Three battalions of reserves joined, numbering 1,348, and 193 recruits, making an increase of 1,541 in aggregates. But the number of "absent without leave" (prisoners) increased by 5,047, "with leave" 300, sick 3,752, detached 700; total decrease in the "present" 9,799. The sudden increase in sick (wounded), and absent without leave (prisoners), tells part of the story of the battles of Peachtree Creek and Atlanta.

An analysis of the reports in the Government archives will ultimately throw great light on the question of the losses of the Confederate Army under General Johnston during this campaign. The example of a single division will illustrate this. French's division joined Johnston about May 20th and down to the end of June it was engaged only in the affairs about New Hope Church, Pine Mountain, and Kenesaw. It made no assaults, fought defensively behind breastworks, and was not seriously assaulted except at Kenesaw, where its loss was light.

Yet, on July 15th, in response to a circular from the army headquarters, General French submitted a report in which the casualties in that division foot up 1,178, viz. : killed 154, wounded 675, prisoners 349. Of the ten infantry divisions of that army, French's certainly must have suffered the least, and probably not more than half as much as either Loring's, Stevenson's, Hindman's, Stewart's, or Bate's; for all of them had met with disastrous repulses in assaults upon our intrenched lines. Stevenson's losses in May alone were, killed 121, wounded 565, prisoners 531, total 1,217, as appears from his report found in the third volume of the Southern Historical Society's papers.

French's report above mentioned shows also the increase of the army, by additions of conscripts, return of absentees, etc., there being an addition of 1,046 to his list of " effectives " during the two months referred to.

APPENDIX B.

Organization of the Army in the Field, Military Division of the Mississippi.

Major-General WILLIAM T. SHERMAN Commanding.

ARMY OF THE CUMBERLAND.

Major-General GEORGE H. THOMAS Commanding.

FOURTH ARMY CORPS.

1. Major-General OLIVER O. HOWARD Commanding.
2. Major-General DAVID S. STANLEY Commanding.

FIRST DIVISION.

1. Major-General D. S. STANLEY Commanding.
2. Brigadier-General NATHAN KIMBALL Commanding.

First Brigade.—(1) Brigadier-General Charles Cruft; (2) Colonel Isaac M. Kirby. *Second Brigade.*—(1) Brigadier-General Walter C. Whittaker; (2) Colonel Jacob E. Taylor. *Third Brigade.*—Colonel William Grose. *Artillery.*—Battery "B," Independent Pennsylvania, and the 5th Indiana Battery.

SECOND DIVISION.

1. Major-General JOHN NEWTON Commanding.
2. Brigadier-General GEORGE D. WAGNER Commanding.

First Brigade.—Brigadier-General Nathan Kimball. *Second Brigade.*—(1) Brigadier-General G. D. Wagner; (2) Colonel Emerson Opdycke. *Third Brigade.*—(1) Brigadier-General C. G. Harker; (2) Colonel Luther P. Bradley. *Artillery.*—Batteries "G," 1st Missouri, and "M," 1st Illinois.

THIRD DIVISION.

Brigadier-General THOMAS J. WOOD Commanding.

First Brigade.—Colonel William H. Gibson. *Second Brigade.*—(1) Brigadier-General William B. Hazen; (2) Colonel P. Sidney Post. *Third Brigade.*—(1) Brigadier-General Samuel Beatty; (2) Colonel Frederick Knefler. *Artillery.*—6th Ohio, and Bridges' Illinois batteries.

FOURTEENTH ARMY CORPS.

1. Major-General JOHN M. PALMER Commanding.
2. Brevet Major-General JEFFERSON C. DAVIS Commanding.

FIRST DIVISION.

1. BRIGADIER-GENERAL RICHARD W. JOHNSON COMMANDING.
2. BRIGADIER-GENERAL JOHN H. KING COMMANDING.

First Brigade.—Brigadier-General WILLIAM P. CARLIN. *Second Brigade.*—
(1) Brigadier-General JOHN H. KING; (2) Colonel WILLIAM L. STOUGHTON.
Third Brigade.—(1) Colonel JAMES M. NIEBLING; (2) Colonel BENJAMIN F.
SCRIBNER. *Artillery.*—Batteries "A," 1st Michigan; and "C," 1st Illinois.

SECOND DIVISION.

1. BRIGADIER-GENERAL JEFFERSON C. DAVIS COMMANDING.
2. BRIGADIER-GENERAL JAMES D. MORGAN COMMANDING.

First Brigade.—Brigadier-General J. D. MORGAN. *Second Brigade.*—Colonel JOHN G. MITCHELL. *Third Brigade.*—(1) Colonel DANIEL MCCOOK; (2)
Colonel CALEB J. DILWORTH. *Artillery.*—2d Minnesota, "I" 2d Illinois, and
5th Wisconsin batteries.

THIRD DIVISION.

BRIGADIER-GENERAL ABSALOM BAIRD COMMANDING.

First Brigade —(1) Brigadier-General JOHN B. TURCHIN; (2) Colonel MORTON
C. HUNTER. *Second Brigade.*—(1) Colonel F. VANDERVEER; (2) Colonel NEW-
ELL GLEASON. *Third Brigade.*—Colonel GEORGE P. ESTE. *Artillery.*—7th In-
diana and 19th Indiana batteries.

TWENTIETH ARMY CORPS.

1. MAJOR-GENERAL JOSEPH HOOKER COMMANDING.
2. MAJOR-GENERAL HENRY W. SLOCUM COMMANDING.

FIRST DIVISION.

BRIGADIER-GENERAL ALPHEUS S. WILLIAMS COMMANDING.

First Brigade.—Brigadier-General JOSEPH F. KNIPE. *Second Brigade.*—
Brigadier-General THOMAS H. RUGER. *Third Brigade.*—(1) Brigadier-General
H. TYNDALE : (2) Colonel JAMES S. ROBINSON. *Artillery.*—Batteries "M" and
"I," 1st New York.

SECOND DIVISION.

BRIGADIER-GENERAL JOHN W. GEARY COMMANDING.

First Brigade.—Colonel CHARLES CANDY. *Second Brigade.*—(1) Colonel A.
BUSCHBECK; (2) Colonel PATRICK H. JONES. *Third Brigade.*—Colonel DAVID
IRELAND. *Artillery.*—Battery "E" Independent Pennsylvania, and 13th New
York.

THIRD DIVISION.

1. MAJOR-GENERAL DANIEL BUTTERFIELD COMMANDING.
2. BRIGADIER-GENERAL WILLIAM T. WARD COMMANDING.

First Brigade.—(1) Brigadier-General W. T. WARD; (2) Colonel BENJAMIN
HARRISON. *Second Brigade.*—Colonel JOHN COBURN. *Third Brigade.*—Colonel
JAMES WOOD, Jr. *Artillery.*—Batteries "C," 1st Ohio, and "I," 1st Michigan.

CAVALRY.

BRIGADIER-GENERAL W. L. ELLIOTT, CHIEF OF CAVALRY.

FIRST DIVISION.

COLONEL EDWARD M. MCCOOK COMMANDING.

First Brigade.—Colonel A. P. CAMPBELL. *Second Brigade.*—Colonel O. H. LA
GRANGE. *Third Brigade.*—Colonel L. D. WATKINS. *Artillery.*—18th Indiana.

SECOND DIVISION.

BRIGADIER-GENERAL KENNER GARRARD COMMANDING.

First Brigade.—Colonel WILLIAM B. SIPES. *Second Brigade.*—Colonel R. H. G. MINTY. *Third Brigade.*—Colonel A. O. MILLER. *Artillery.*—Chicago Board of Trade Battery.

ARMY OF THE TENNESSEE.

1. MAJOR-GENERAL JAMES B. McPHERSON COMMAND-ING.

2. MAJOR-GENERAL OLIVER O. HOWARD COMMANDING.

FIFTEENTH ARMY CORPS.

MAJOR-GENERAL JOHN A. LOGAN COMMANDING.

FIRST DIVISION.

1. BRIGADIER-GENERAL PETER J. OSTERHAUS COMMANDING.
2. BRIGADIER-GENERAL CHARLES R. WOODS COMMANDING.

First Brigade.—(1) Brigadier-General CHARLES R. WOODS; (2) Colonel WILLIAM B. WOODS. *Second Brigade.*—Colonel JAMES A. WILLIAMSON. *Third Brigade.*—Colonel HUGO WANGELIN. *Artillery.*—Battery " F " 2d Missouri and 4th Ohio Independent.

SECOND DIVISION.

(1) BRIGADIER-GENERAL MORGAN L. SMITH COMMANDING.
(2) BRIGADIER-GENERAL J. A. J. LIGHTBURN COMMANDING.
(3) BRIGADIER-GENERAL WILLIAM B. HAZEN COMMANDING.

First Brigade.—(1)Brigadier-General GILES A. SMITH ; (2) Colonel J. S. MARTIN ; (3) Colonel THEODORE JONES. *Second Brigade.*—(1) Brigadier-General J. A. J. LIGHTBURN ; (2) Colonel WELLS S. JONES. *Artillery.*—Battery " H," 1st Illinois, and " A," 1st Illinois.

THIRD DIVISION.[1]

BRIGADIER-GENERAL JOHN E. SMITH COMMANDING.

First Brigade.—Colonel JESSE I. ALEXANDER. *Second Brigade.*—Colonel GREEN B. RAUM. *Third Brigade.*—Colonel JABEZ BANBURY.

FOURTH DIVISION.

BRIGADIER-GENERAL WILLIAM HARROW COMMANDING.

First Brigade.—Colonel REUBEN WILLIAMS. *Second Brigade.*—Colonel CHARLES C. WALCUTT. *Third Brigade.*—Colonel JOHN M. OLIVER. *Artillery.*—1st Iowa Battery.

SIXTEENTH ARMY CORPS.[2]

MAJOR-GENERAL GRENVILLE M. DODGE COMMANDING.

SECOND DIVISION.

(1) BRIGADIER-GENERAL THOMAS W. SWEENY COMMANDING.
(2) BRIGADIER-GENERAL JOHN M. CORSE COMMANDING.

First Brigade.—Colonel ELLIOTT W. RICE. *Second Brigade.*—(1) Colonel P. E. BURKE ; (2) Colonel AUGUST MERSY ; (3) Lieutenant-Colonel PHILLIPS ; (4)

---

[1] This division garrisoned Alatoona and other posts, and was not with the moving column.

[2] The First and Third Divisions of this corps were left in the Mississippi Valley. After the fall of Atlanta the Second Division was transferred to the Fifteenth Corps, and the Fourth to the Seventeenth.

Colonel R. N. ADAMS. *Third Brigade.*—(1) Colonel M. M. BANE; (2) Brigadier. General WILLIAM VANDERVEER. *Artillery.*—Battery "H," 1st Missouri Light Artillery.

FOURTH DIVISION.

(1) BRIGADIER-GENERAL JAMES C. VEATCH COMMANDING.
(2) BRIGADIER-GENERAL JOHN W. FULLER COMMANDING.

First Brigade.—Brigadier-General JOHN W. FULLER. *Second Brigade.*—Colonel JOHN W. SPRAGUE. *Third Brigade.*—(1) Colonel JOHN TILLSON; Colonel JAMES H. HOWE. *Artillery.*—14th Ohio Battery.

SEVENTEENTH ARMY CORPS.

MAJOR-GENERAL FRANK P. BLAIR, JR., COMMANDING.[1]

THIRD DIVISION.

BRIGADIER-GENERAL MORTIMER D. LEGGETT COMMANDING.

First Brigade.—(1) Brigadier-General MANNING F. FORCE; (2) Colonel GEORGE E. BRYANT. *Second Brigade.*—(1) Colonel ROBERT K. SCOTT; (2) Lieutenant-Colonel G. F. WILES. *Third Brigade.*—Colonel ADAM G. MALLOY. *Artillery.* —3d Ohio, Battery " D " 1st Illinois, 8th Michigan Battery.

FOURTH DIVISION.

(1) BRIGADIER-GENERAL WALTER Q. GRESHAM COMMANDING.
(2) BRIGADIER-GENERAL GILES A. SMITH COMMANDING.

First Brigade.—(1) Colonel WILLIAM L. SANDERSON; (2) Colonel B. F. POTTS. *Second Brigade.*—Colonel GEORGE C. ROGERS. *Third Brigade.*—Colonel WILLIAM HALL. *Artillery.*—Company "F," 2d Illinois.

Besides the artillery above mentioned, the following batteries were in the Army of the Tennessee, viz.: Illinois, batteries " E," " F," and " G " of 1st Light Artillery; batteries " F " and " G " of 2d Light Artillery, and Cogswell's Battery. Indiana, 3d, 9th, and 14th. Michigan, 2d Battery. Minnesota, 1st Battery. Ohio, 7th, 8th, 10th, 15th, and 26th batteries. Wisconsin, 6th, 7th, and 12th. Only part of them were at any one time with the moving column. They were under the direction of Colonel Andrew Hickenlooper, Chief of Artillery.

ARMY OF THE OHIO.

TWENTY-THIRD ARMY CORPS.

MAJOR-GENERAL JOHN M. SCHOFIELD COMMANDING.

FIRST DIVISION.[2]

BRIGADIER-GENERAL ALVIN P. HOVEY COMMANDING.

First Brigade.—Colonel RICHARD F. BARTER. *Second Brigade.*—(1) Colonel JOHN C. MCQUISTON; (2) Colonel PETER T. SWAINE.

---

[1] The First and Second Divisions of this corps were left in the Mississippi Valley.
[2] At the beginning of June this division was distributed, the 1st Brigade to the 3d Division, and the 2d Brigade to the 2d Division of the corps.

SECOND DIVISION.

(1) Brigadier-General HENRY M. JUDAH Commanding.
(2) Brigadier-General MILO S. HASCALL Commanding.

First Brigade.—(1) Brigadier-General NATHANIEL C. McLEAN; (2) Colonel JOSEPH A. COOPER. *Second Brigade.*—(1) Colonel JOHN R. BOND; (2) Colonel WILLIAM E. HOBSON. *Third Brigade.*—Colonel SILAS A. STRICKLAND. *Artillery.*—Shields' 19th Ohio and Paddock's 6th Michigan batteries.

THIRD DIVISION.

BRIGADIER-GENERAL JACOB D. COX Commanding.

First Brigade.—Colonel JAMES W. REILLY. *Second Brigade.*—(1) Brigadier-General M. D. MANSON; (2) Colonel DANIEL CAMERON; (3) Colonel JOHN S. CASEMENT. *Third Brigade.*—(1) Brigadier-General N. C. McLEAN; (2) Colonel ROBERT K. BYRD; (3) Colonel THOMAS J. HENDERSON. *Artillery.*—Harvey's 15th Indiana; Wilber's 23d Indiana, and "D" 1st Ohio (Cockerill's).

CAVALRY, ARMY OF THE OHIO.

MAJOR-GENERAL GEORGE STONEMAN Commanding.

FIRST DIVISION.

COLONEL ISRAEL T. GARRARD Commanding.

The cavalry of the army, though nominally connected with the three subordinate armies, was, during the active campaign organized into four commands, which were assigned to duty by General Sherman as circumstances required, and as will be seen by the narrative of the campaign. One division was usually upon each flank and one covering the communications at the rear, whilst the fourth was ready for expeditions in front which might be ordered. The nearest subordinate army commander usually exercised authority over the cavalry coöperating with him.

In the War Department records for June, they are stated as follows:

PRINCIPAL CAVALRY COMMANDERS.

MAJOR-GENERAL GEORGE STONEMAN.
BRIGADIER-GENERAL JUDSON KILPATRICK.
BRIGADIER-GENERAL KENNER GARRARD.
BRIGADIER-GENERAL EDWARD M. McCOOK.

APPENDIX C.

CONFEDERATE ARMY.[1]

Organization of the Army of Tennessee, commanded by GEN-ERAL JOSEPH E. JOHNSTON for period ending June 30, 1864.

HARDEE'S ARMY CORPS.
LIEUTENANT-GENERAL WM. J. HARDEE COMMANDING.

MAJOR-GENERAL B. F. CHEATHAM'S DIVISION.
Brigades.—Maney's, Wright's, Strahl's, Vaughn's.

MAJOR-GENERAL W. H. T. WALKER'S DIVISION.
Brigades.—Mercer's, Jackson's, Gist's, Stevens'.

MAJOR-GENERAL PAT. R. CLEBURNE'S DIVISION.
Brigades.—Polk's, Loring's, Govan's, Smith's.

MAJOR-GENERAL W. B. BATE'S DIVISION.
Brigades.—Tyler's, Lewis's, Finley's.

HOOD'S ARMY CORPS.
LIEUTENANT-GENERAL J. B. HOOD COMMANDING.

MAJOR-GENERAL T. C. HINDMAN'S DIVISION.
Brigades.—Deas', Colonel J. G. COLTART Commanding; Manigault's; Tucker's, Colonel J. H. SHARP Commanding; Walthall's, Colonel SAM. BENTON Commanding.

MAJOR-GENERAL C. L. STEVENSON'S DIVISION.
Brigades.—Brown's, Cumming's, Reynolds', Pettus'.

---

[1] The Confederate Army did not have its corps, divisions, etc., numbered; they were known by the names of the commanders, and in the case of the brigades, seem to have continued to bear the name of the brigadier commanding at the beginning of the campaign, even when changes in command occurred.

MAJOR-GENERAL A. P. STEWART'S DIVISION.

Brigades.—Stovall's, Clayton's, Gibson's, Baker's.

WHEELER'S CAVALRY CORPS.

MAJOR-GENERAL JOS. WHEELER COMMANDING.

MAJOR-GENERAL WM. T. MARTIN'S DIVISION.

Brigades.—Allen's, Iverson's.

BRIGADIER-GENERAL J. H. KELLEY'S DIVISION.

Brigades.—Anderson's, Dibbrell's, Hannon's.

BRIGADIER-GENERAL W. T. C. HUME'S DIVISION.

Brigades.—Ashby's, Harrison's, Williams'.

ARTILLERY.

BRIGADIER-GENERAL F. A. SHOUP COMMANDING.

BATTALIONS [1] ATTACHED TO HARDEE'S CORPS.

COLONEL M. SMITH COMMANDING.

Battalions.—Haxton's, Hotchkiss', Martin's, Cobb's.

BATTALIONS ATTACHED TO HOOD'S CORPS

COLONEL B. F. BECKHAM COMMANDING.

Battalions.—Courtney's, Eldridge's, Johnston's.

WHEELER'S CORPS.

LIEUTENANT-COLONEL F. W. ROBERTSON COMMANDING.

Five Batteries.

RESERVE BATTALIONS.

Eight Batteries.—Williams', Palmer's, and Waddell's battalions.

DETACHMENTS.

ESCORTS (CAVALRY).

General Johnston's Headquarters, Company "A" and Company "B."
Headquarters—Cheatham's, Cleburne's, Walker's, Bate's, Hardee's, Hindman's, Stevenson's, Stewart's. One company each.

ENGINEER TROOPS.

MAJOR J. W. GREEN COMMANDING.

Divisions.—Cheatham's, Cleburne's, Stewart's, Hindman's, Buckner's, Detachment of Sappers and Miners. One company each.

---

[1] Three batteries in each battalion.

Organization of the Army of Mississippi, commanded by Major-General W. W. Loring for period ending June 30, 1864.

MAJOR-GENERAL S. G. FRENCH'S DIVISION.

Brigades.—Ector's, Cockrell's, Sears's.

MAJOR-GENERAL W. W. LORING'S DIVISION.

BRIGADIER-GENERAL W. S. FEATHERSTONE COMMANDING.

Brigades.—Adams's, Featherstone's, Scott's.

MAJOR-GENERAL ED. C. WALTHALL'S DIVISION.

Brigades.—Quarles's, Canty's, Reynolds'.

CAVALRY.

BRIGADIER-GENERAL W. H. JACKSON COMMANDING.

BRIGADIER-GENERAL W. H. JACKSON'S DIVISION.

Brigades.—Armstrong's, Ross's, Ferguson's.

ESCORTS (CAVALRY).

Three companies.

ARTILLERY.

Brigades.[1]—Storrs's, Meyrick's, Preston's, Waitie's.

---

[1] Three batteries each.

APPENDIX D.

BATTLE OF ALATOONA.

THE numerous authorities which have perpetuated the error referred to in the foot-note on p. 231, make it proper to refer a little more fully to the evidence. The writer's field despatches for October contain the following:

No. 169.

PACE'S FERRY ROAD, October 5, 1864, 5.45 A.M.

MAJOR-GENERAL SHERMAN, Smyrna Camp Ground:

By working late last evening, we got over our train, the head of my column resting on the Pace's Ferry and Marietta road. We had to bridge a creek forty feet broad, which was filled by back-water from the Chattahoochee, swimming deep. The road along the Chattahoochee is not good, but we shall get along. The column is now starting. I can get no definite information of roads on right of railroad, but from my remembrance of what we learned when we were at Smyrna Station in July, I hope to get through.

(Signed) _____ J. D. COX, B. G.

No. 170.

SMYRNA CAMP GROUND, October 5, 1864.

BRIGADIER-GENERAL COOPER, Commanding Second Division:

Sir—The third division is marching along the railroad to Marietta, and I am very anxious that the trains should reach there also at an early hour. If you have not crossed the railroad when this reaches you, you may put your whole command on the railroad, except one regiment for a rear guard for the train, to follow the wagon-road. A corps has been stationed at Ruff's Mills (between here and the Sand-town road) to cover this road, which makes it safe. I will either meet you at Marietta, or leave orders for you. Try to prevent all straggling, and do not hurry your men too much.

(Signed) _____ J. D. COX, B. G.

No. 171.

NEAR MARIETTA, October 6, 1864.

BRIGADIER-GENERAL REILLY, Commanding Third Division:

General Vanderveer had two regiments and a section of artillery on Brushy Mountain, the high ground a little further to the right than your right now rests. I think you will have to put your left brigade over there, and let General Cooper take the place vacated on your left. Please look at the ground, and do so unless you can detach a regiment or so with a section, and so hold the right by a detachment.

(Signed) J. D. COX, B. G. Commanding.

No. 172. ————

NEAR MARIETTA, October 6, 1864.

BRIGADIER-GENERAL COOPER, Commanding Second Division:

You may put in your command on Reilly's left this morning—putting them in two lines for the present.

(Signed) J. D. COX, B. G. Commanding.

————

Special field-orders, No. 85.

HEADQUARTERS MILITARY DIVISION OF THE MISSISSIPPI,
In the field, KENESAW MOUNTAIN, October 6, 1864.

I. Major-General Stanley, Army of the Cumberland, will occupy a strong defensive position across the Marietta and Burnt Hickory, and Marietta and Dallas roads, his right near Pine Hill, and left behind Noses Creek.

II. Major-General Howard, Army of the Tennessee, will join on the left of General Stanley, and make a line covering the Powder Spring road; and the cavalry on that flank, General Kilpatrick, will prevent any enemy from reaching the railroad below Marietta.

III. Brigadier-General Cox, Army of the Ohio, will move out on the Burnt Hickory road, *via* Pine Hill, and Mount Olivet Church, west, until he strikes the road by which the enemy have moved on Alatoona. He will have his columns ready for a fight, but not deployed. He will park his wagons near Kenesaw.

IV. General Elliott will send cavalry to-day to Big Shanty, Ackworth, and Alatoona, and bring back official reports.

V. The utmost attention must be given to the grazing of animals, parking wagons, and economizing rations.

By order of MAJOR-GENERAL W. T. SHERMAN,
(Signed) L. M. DAYTON, Aide-de-Camp.

————

My pocket-diary contains the following entry:

"Thursday, October 6th.—March at nine o'clock *via* Pine Mountain to Sandtown road, and make reconnoissances in all directions. On the right, nearly to Ackworth; in front, to Alatoona church; on left, nearly to Lost Mountain and to Hardshell church. The enemy have retreated south beyond Lost Mountain."

In making reports after a considerable interval of time, General Sherman evidently made by accident a mistake of a day in the dates, and the error has perpetuated itself in numerous ways.

APPENDIX E.

MOVEMENTS OF OCTOBER 13, 1864.

In his Memoirs, General Sherman, misled, apparently, by his formal orders for the day which he subsequently modified, has inadvertently spoken of the movement of Corse's division on the left bank of the Coosa as that which resulted in the capture of the guns and the accomplishment of his wish for definite information. His official report has it correctly. It says: "I therefore on the 11th moved to Rome and pushed Garrard's cavalry and the Twenty-third Corps, under General Cox, across the Oostanaula, to threaten the flanks of the enemy passing north. Garrard's cavalry drove a cavalry brigade of the enemy to and beyond the narrows leading into the valley of the Chattooga, capturing two field pieces and taking some prisoners."

The following are from the field despatches of the writer.

No. 179.

HEADQUARTERS, ARMY OF THE OHIO,
October 13, 1864, 8 A.M.

MAJOR-GENERAL SHERMAN, Commanding, etc. :

Your despatch received. Garrard fills the road ahead of me and is pushing on. My infantry is close on his heels. He finds some cavalry in his front, but no serious resistance as yet. He has not reached the position where the enemy had their battery yesterday. As soon as he is seriously checked, I will have him give way and let the infantry through. Very respectfully, etc.,

(Signed) J. D. COX, B. G. Commanding.

No. 180.

HEADQUARTERS, ARMY OF THE OHIO,
5½ miles from Rome, October 13, 1864.

MAJOR-GENERAL SHERMAN, Commanding M. D. M. :

Garrard is pushing on finely, my infantry in close support. He has driven Armstrong's cavalry the last two miles, captured two pieces of artillery and a number of prisoners. Citizens report a larger force of cavalry (Harrison's division) ahead. I leave one division of infantry to cover the roads coming in from Summerville by Texas Valley, and push the other forward.

Very respectfully, etc.,

(Signed) J. D. COX, B. G. Commanding.

No. 183.

HEADQUARTERS, ARMY OF THE OHIO,
October 13, 1864, 1.45 P.M.

MAJOR-GENERAL SHERMAN:

We have found the place where the bridge was. The information is positive that Hood took it north with him. A brigade of cavalry went two miles beyond. I am returning with the infantry.

(Signed) J. D. COX, B. G.

INDEX.

Note.—*Regiments, batteries, etc., are indexed under the names of their States, excepting batteries called by their captain's or by some other special name. These are indexed under* Batteries.